ORANGE PARADES
The Politics of Ritual, Tradition and Control

Dᴏᴍɪɴɪᴄ Bʀʏᴀɴ

Pluto  Press

LONDON • STERLING, VIRGINIA

First published 2000
by PLUTO PRESS
345 Archway Road, London N6 5AA
and 22883 Quicksilver Drive,
Sterling, VA 20166–2012, USA

www.plutobooks.com

British Library Cataloguing in Publication Data
A catalogue record for this book is available from
the British Library

ISBN 0 7453 1418 X hardback
ISBN 0 7453 1413 9 paperback

Library of Congress Cataloging in Publication Data
Bryan, Dominic.
Orange parades : the politics of ritual, tradition, and control /
Dominic Bryan.
    p. cm. —(Anthropology, culture, and society)
ISBN 0–7453–1418–X (hardback)
1. Parades—Northern Ireland—History. 2. Orange Order—History. 3.
Social control—Northern Ireland. 4. Social classes—Northern Ireland.
5. Nationalism—Northern Ireland. 6. Political customs and rites—
Northern Ireland. 7. Northern Ireland—Politics and government.
I. Title. II. Series.
GT4046.A2 B78 2000
394'.5—dc21
                                                              00–008816

        09 08 07 06 05 04 03 02 01 00
        10 9   8   7   6   5   4   3   2   1

Designed and produced for Pluto Press by
Chase Production Services, Chadlington, OX7 3LN
Typeset from disk by Stanford DTP Services, Northampton
Printed in the European Union by TJ International, Padstow

For Elizabeth and Peter

CONTENTS

ACKNOWLEDGEMENTS

The research for this book was made easier thanks to the assistance, encouragement and financial help of a number of departments and individuals. I have received a lot of time and patience from members of the Orange Institution and other individuals, and political groups in Northern Ireland, the Republic of Ireland, England and Scotland for their time and patience. To all of these people I am grateful. I have not quoted directly from the interviews I conducted but I hope the views and understandings people have given me are reflected in what I have written.

Funding, whilst conducting this research, was difficult. I am particularly grateful to the Cultural Traditions Group (now the Cultural Diversity Group), part of the Community Relations Council, to the University of Ulster for providing me with a studentship in 1995 and 1996, and to the Central Community Relations Unit for providing funding for work on related issues. Staff at the former Department of Sociology and Social Anthropology, now the School of Social and Community Sciences, at the University of Ulster have been supportive over many years. I am also grateful to the School of Anthropological Studies at the Queen's University, Belfast, to the Centre for the Study of Conflict at the University of Ulster and Democratic Dialogue, Belfast, for their encouragement and help in facilitating research needs.

A lot of people have helped me over the past few years. My thanks, in particular, go to Gerard Bryan, Paul and Jake Campbell, Maurna Crozier, Julita Clancy, Hastings Donnan, Ciro De Rosa, Seamus Dunn, Tom Fraser, Gordon Gillespie, Colin Harper, Simon Harrison, Arthur McCullough, David Officer, Sophie Richmond, Andrew Sanders, Elizabeth Tonkin, Robin Wilson and Tom Wilson. Most of all I have been lucky enough to have enjoyed a productive working relationship with my friend Neil Jarman. Many of the ideas in this book derive from collaborating with Neil over seven years.

Body and soul have been held together by Deidre, Nessie, Harry, Elizabeth and Peter.

In the end, of course, the responsibility for this work is my own.

ABBREVIATIONS

AOH	Ancient Order of Hibernians
MSU	Mobile Support Unit
DUP	Democratic Unionist Party
INF	Irish National Foresters
IOO	Independent Orange Order
IRA	Irish Republican Army
LOCC	Lower Ormeau Concerned Community
LOL	Loyal Orange Lodge
LVF	Loyalist Volunteer Force
NICRA	Northern Ireland Civil Rights Association
NILP	Northern Ireland Labour Party
PUP	Progressive Unionist Party
RUC	Royal Ulster Constabulary
SDA	Shankill Defence Association
SDLP	Social Democratic and Labour Party
UDA	Ulster Defence Association
UDP	Ulster Democratic Party
UDR	Ulster Defence Regiment
UFF	Ulster Freedom Fighters
UPV	Ulster Protestant Volunteers
UUP	Ulster Unionist Party
UVF	Ulster Volunteer Force
YCV	Young Citizens Volunteers

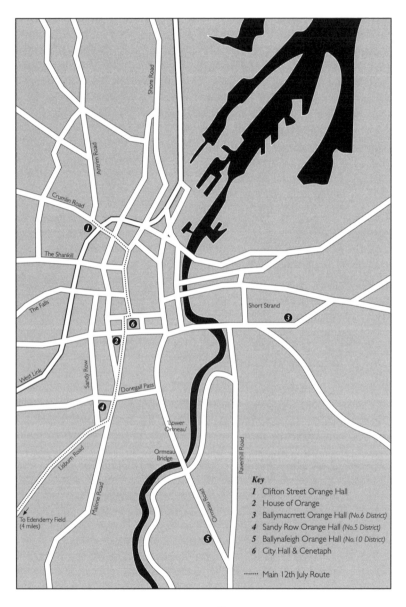

Key

1   Clifton Street Orange Hall
2   House of Orange
3   Ballymacrrett Orange Hall *(No.6 District)*
4   Sandy Row Orange Hall *(No.5 District)*
5   Ballynafeigh Orange Hall *(No.10 District)*
6   City Hall & Cenetaph

······ Main 12th July Route

Map 1 Belfast

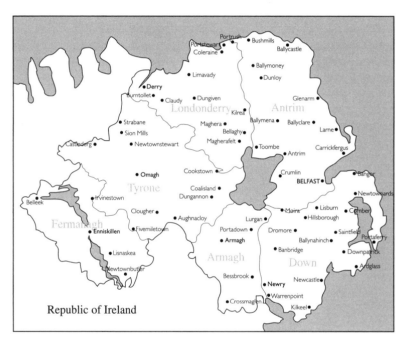

Map 2 Northern Ireland

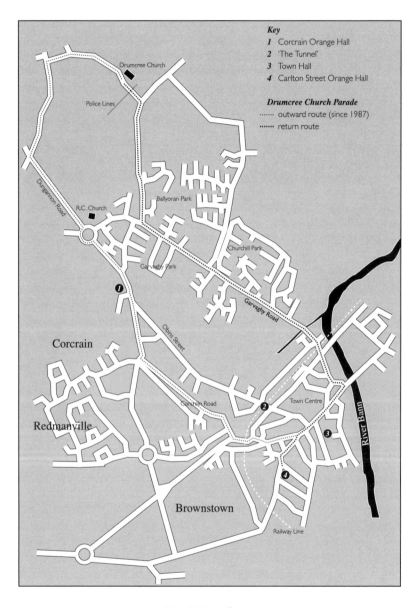

Map 3 Portadown

1 DRUMCREE: AN INTRODUCTION TO PARADE DISPUTES

On the evening of Monday 10 July 1995 I stood on a hill by the stone wall of a church graveyard, and watched two men walk down the hill to talk to some policemen. One was wearing an orange collarette, or sash, the other a crimson one. By Friday 8 September, one of those men, David Trimble MP, had become leader of the Ulster Unionist Party, the largest political party in Northern Ireland. After being elected to that post Mr Trimble was asked if his success in becoming leader was due to the events of July along the road from that church. He answered that it was not. However, in my view, whilst it is true to say that those events alone did not make David Trimble leader, had they not taken place he may well have had to wait a few more years.

What took place that July evening? The graveyard is situated around Drumcree church about a mile outside Portadown in County Armagh. Standing on the hill were thousands of Ulster Protestants, most of them members of an institution known as the Orange Order. Along with us were cameras from major television companies as well as journalists from around the world. Consequently, a global audience saw those two men walk down the hill to talk to the policemen. Many watching would have recognised the man walking with David Trimble as the Reverend Ian Paisley, a man whose reputation as orator, defender of Protestantism and scourge of 'Popery', is second to none. Paisley had just climbed down from a platform where, in characteristic style, he had told the gathered crowd that the future of Ulster might be decided that night. He is not a member of the Orange Order. Rather the crimson collarette he wears represents a separate yet similar organisation known as the Apprentice Boys of Derry.

Along with us all at Drumcree were the policemen of the Royal Ulster Constabulary (RUC). Dressed in riot gear, hundreds of them stood along the narrow country lane beside dozens of the armoured Land Rovers that have been such a distinctive part of policing in Northern Ireland. The previous afternoon, a number of policemen had accompanied lines of Orangemen on a parade up to the church for a religious service in commemoration of the Battle of the Boyne (a battle fought in Ireland over 300 years ago). However, senior policemen, aware of a counter-demonstration, had decided under legislation specific to Northern Ireland that the Orangemen could not parade

1

back to Portadown via the route the Orangemen had annually walked. The route they wanted to take was the Garvaghy Road a few hundred yards up from the church, which runs through a predominantly Catholic housing estate. The large majority of the residents of that estate did not want the Orangemen to march through their estate and some had been campaigning for the previous ten years to have them stopped.

The Portadown Orangemen stood facing the police determined that they would be allowed to parade down the Garvaghy Road. The police introduced reinforcements when, despite attempts to stop the word spreading, more Orangemen started to arrive from other parts of Northern Ireland to support their brethren. Meanwhile the residents of the Garvaghy Road waited apprehensively, keen to demonstrate their opposition to the parade and well aware of the possible results of a confrontation. There was a stand-off.

On that Monday evening Trimble and Paisley made speeches from a platform in an adjacent field. Paisley received the biggest applause.

We are here tonight because we have to establish the right of the Protestant People to march down the Garvaghy Road and our brethren of the Orange Institution to exercise their right to attend their place of worship and leave that place of worship and return to their homes. That is the issue we are dealing with tonight and it is a very serious issue because it lies at the very heart and foundation of our heritage. It lies at the very heart and foundation of our spiritual life and it lies at the very foundation of the future of our families and of this Province that we love. If we cannot go to our place of worship and we cannot walk back from our place of worship then all that the Reformation brought to us and all that the martyrs died for and all that our forefathers gave their lives for is lost to us forever. So there can be no turning back. (Ian Paisley, 10 July 1995)

Even as Paisley spoke, a hundred yards down the lane there were clashes between the crowd and the lines of police. A running battle developed across the fields as Orangemen and their supporters tried to reach the Garvaghy Road. A school and other buildings on the edge of the estate were attacked. Police fired baton rounds into the groups of men. Although ostensibly used as a crowd control measure the baton rounds are potentially lethal. Paisley attempted to calm the crowd with the news that he and Mr Trimble would negotiate with the police.

Behind the scenes, other negotiations had already begun. Members of the Mediation Network for Northern Ireland had been brought in to aid negotiations between the residents' group and the police since great distrust of the police exists in Catholic communities. At the same time the police talked to Orangemen and unionist politicians who refused to talk to the representative of the residents' group. Much was at stake. A peace process had developed the previous year and had apparently brought an end to the military conflict that had been ongoing in Northern Ireland since 1969. Both the Irish Republican Army (IRA), seeking a united Ireland, and loyalist paramilitary groups, aiming to keep Northern Ireland within the United Kingdom, had announced cease-fires; but, as in the late 1960s, it was beginning to look as if parades and street demonstrations would lead to civil disturbances serious enough to bring about renewed armed conflict.

Finally, on the morning of Tuesday 11 July, a deal was negotiated. The Orangemen from the District of Portadown would walk down the Garvaghy Road without the band they had originally brought with them, who had gone home anyway, and the residents would stand by the side of the road and make their protest. Two lines of about 600 Orangemen walked in a dignified way past silent protesters; but when the parade reached Portadown, Trimble, Paisley and a crowd of supporters were waiting. The two politicians joined the parade and received the adulation of the crowd in triumph. To the dismay of mediators and police, and to the anger of residents of the Garvaghy Road and the wider Catholic community, the Orangemen claimed victory. Drumcree was seen by many loyalists as the Protestant people fighting back. Within months medals were struck commemorating the 'Seige [sic] of Drumcree', a video was produced depicting the events, and Trimble was, to the surprise of many, elected leader of the Ulster Unionist Party.

On 12 July 1995, all over Northern Ireland, members of the Orange Institution, their families, friends and supporters, prepared to celebrate the 305th anniversary of the Battle of the Boyne. This is the battle, in 1690, at which the Protestant King William III, the Dutch Prince of Orange, won a victory against King James II, an English Catholic, and is thus perceived by Protestants in Northern Ireland to have secured the civil rights and religious liberties of Protestants within predominantly Catholic Ireland.

The largest of the parades is held in Belfast. From early morning Orangemen, usually dressed in suits and wearing Orange collarettes around their necks, meet at Orange Halls to prepare for the day with fellow members of their Orange lodge. The lodge banners depicting places, people, and events of significance to the lodge, as well as its name and number, are unfurled and attached to poles ready to be carried through the streets. Members line up in military-style files behind their lodge banner and are led by a band hired for the occasion. The bands wear distinctive, brightly coloured, pseudo-military uniforms, some carry flags, and many have the name of their band and other loyalist insignia on the big bass drum which forms the centre-piece of the band. Most of the bands are flute bands, with some side drummers, and are almost exclusively male. There are some accordion bands and a few play bagpipes. Many of the larger bands have a group of teenagers, mainly girls, who follow them on the parade.

The officials of the Orange Institution accompanied by a colour party carrying flags lead the parade. The crowd cheers as the bands start playing, with the bass drummer, thumping his drum as hard as possible, almost jigging down the road. Along most of the route spectators are three or four deep but in the Catholic areas passed by this parade the only spectators are policemen, soldiers and a few children. The parade route is well over 6 miles long and there are a number of stops for participants to take on refreshment, a soft drink or perhaps a swig from a bottle of beer, and relieve themselves behind a house or in an alleyway.

By midday the first of the marchers reach 'the Field'. Some participants rush off to meals prepared in church halls and hotels, others buy from the food stalls, whilst still others concentrate on consuming the beer transported to the Field. At the bottom of the Field is a platform where a few spectators, journalists and social researchers gather to hear a religious service and some resolutions proposed by senior Orangemen and politicians. Many of the bandsmen are more interested in the teenage girls who have accompanied them.

At around four o'clock the parade re-forms with a little less discipline and decorum. Some Orangemen and bandsmen are just returning from their hotel meal and look to find their places in the parade. Some members of the parade are as sober and dignified as at the start. Others, particularly members of some of the bands, have entered into a little carnival spirit. Face masks, funny hats, wigs and false beards all appear. The performances are even more boisterous and the music is a little less disciplined. One song is played and sung above all others as they return to the centre of Belfast – 'The Sash'.

> It is old but it is beautiful, and its colours they are fine;
> It was worn at Derry, Aughrim, Enniskillen and the Boyne;
> My father wore it when a youth in the bygone days of yore;
> So on the 12th I always wear the Sash my father wore.

As lodges parade to the area of the city in which they are based they get a rousing reception. Bands finish by playing the national anthem, but some go on to play and drink back in their club until well into the evening. The streets of Belfast are almost deserted by mid-evening. Another Twelfth has come and gone.

On the afternoon of Sunday 7 July 1996, I was back at Drumcree watching another stand-off. The RUC Chief Constable, Sir Hugh Annesley, had announced that the Boyne Church Parade would not be allowed down the Garvaghy Road. There had been a few attempts to set up negotiations during the year but Orangemen had refused to meet the chairperson of the residents' group on the grounds that he had a terrorist conviction. When the parade left the church and reached the bottom of the hill they were confronted by more than just a line of police officers. The forces of the state had prepared more thoroughly than the previous year. Rows of barbed wire had been erected across a number of fields on either side of the road and in the distance a line of army trucks could be seen parked within the perimeter of a school playing field.

The mood amongst Orangemen and their supporters was relaxed. Some Orangemen were organising the parking of cars as the narrow country lanes started to clog up with families, journalists and at least two anthropologists. Many people were in their Sunday best and mothers were negotiating pushchairs down towards the church. At the church a Tannoy system was being set up to relay information to the crowd. Down by the Land Rovers a number of unionist politicians milled around making statements to the press. A few conversations quickly revealed what many people had suspected, that the Orangemen had also been preparing. This year the tactic was not to bring as many Orangemen as possible to Portadown but for the Institution, and others, to make their presence felt all over the countryside. The previous week, Orangemen in other parts of Northern Ireland had put in applications for parades to be held on the 8th, 9th, and 10th, taking routes that were deliberately close to Catholic areas, to put pressure on the police. They had decided that if the police wanted a battle of strength, that was what they were going to get. By the time we left Drumcree on the Sunday evening the roads into Portadown were already blocked by men wearing masks, men more than likely belonging to the mid-Ulster unit of the Ulster Volunteer Force (UVF) an outlawed paramilitary group. Back in Belfast youths were gathering on street corners preparing to build bonfires on roads. Could the forces of the state cope or would loyalists be able to face down the police in demanding their right to march?

Later on the evening of 7 July, a Catholic taxi driver was shot dead outside Lurgan, a town 10 miles from Portadown. The mid-Ulster UVF were widely believed to be the perpetrators although no one claimed responsibility. Mainstream unionist politicians made thinly veiled threats about the further consequences if the situation was not resolved. Despite this murder, the loyalist paramilitary cease-fire was still deemed to be in place.

The news the following morning reported a few incidents from the front line at Drumcree, but, more importantly, road blocks had been set up by Orangemen and their supporters in Protestant areas all over Northern Ireland. The police were either unwilling or unable to clear the roads quickly. On Monday evening Belfast emptied quickly and pubs closed their doors. Orangemen in the city prepared to go on parade. As the police tried desperately to place officers near to likely flash-points, of which there are many in Belfast alone, youngsters took control in particular areas. In Protestant areas of the city bonfires were lit across roads and bottles and stones were thrown at the police with relative impunity. Soon, not only bonfires, but cars, vans, buses and business premises were burning. Some car showrooms had had the foresight to remove all their cars. Protestant-run businesses in Protestant areas were being attacked by Protestant youths. I heard of one Orangeman out on parade in east Belfast who returned to find his car gone as well. In north Belfast there were serious clashes between youths in both communities. And most worrying of all, some Catholics were apparently intimidated out of their houses.

The violence became worse on the 9th and 10th, and 1,000 extra British troops were sent to Northern Ireland. By the end of Wednesday the RUC announced that over the previous four days there had been 156 arrests, over 100 incidents of intimidation, 90 civilian and 50 RUC injuries, 758 attacks on police and 662 plastic baton rounds fired.[1] At Drumcree there had been intermittent violence, a bulldozer had been brought up by the local para-militaries and the army had placed concrete blocks on the road. Secret negotiations were taking place between the Northern Ireland Office and members of the Garvaghy Road Residents' Group, and the heads of the main Churches also tried to broker a deal. By Wednesday evening rumours were rife that the Chief Constable would change his mind and allow the parade down the road. On the morning of 11 July it became clear that, with the threat of thousands of Orangemen arriving in Portadown for the Twelfth, the parade was to be given access to the Garvaghy Road.

Residents tried to conduct a protest but were forcibly removed from the road. The parade took place to the sound of a single drum and with hundreds of Orangemen, not all from Portadown, taking part. This time Trimble and Paisley steered clear of the overt triumphalism they had displayed the previous year, but Orangemen all over Northern Ireland were jubilant. Rioting now started in nationalist areas. Police fired thousands of plastic bullets and nationalist protesters threw thousands of petrol bombs. One nationalist protester in Derry was killed when an armoured car hit him.

As the events of Drumcree in 1996 proceeded one particular comment was repeated by journalists time and again: 'All this just to walk down one bit of road?' When outsiders watched the events at Drumcree in 1995 and 1996, or saw reports of the Twelfth parades, they were inevitably left somewhat bewildered by the apparent importance attached to these parades by people in Northern Ireland. The right to perform a particular ritual does not usually become a central political issue in a modern industrial European state. Yet in 1995 Drumcree was only one, albeit the most serious, of forty-one such disputes in eighteen different areas of Northern Ireland (Jarman and Bryan 1996: 85–93); and over four days during that July week in 1996 the forces of the British state in Northern Ireland were brought to breaking point over the right to parade. Thousands of policemen and soldiers were deployed, and millions of pounds spent, to try to stop around 600 Orangemen from walking down a particular length of road, that is, from performing a brief and simple ritual. This book will explain why Orange parades are such a prominent issue in the politics of Northern Ireland and how the rituals have been, and continue to be, utilised as a political resource. I will argue that by under-standing the nature of ritual action we can better comprehend the dynamics of political divisions in the north of Ireland.

In tracing the role of ritual in the field of politics I will utilise historical and anthropological approaches. Abner Cohen argues that 'the challenge to social anthropology today is the analysis of this dynamic involvement of symbols, or of custom, in the changing relationships of power between individuals and groups' (1974: 29). This book takes up that challenge. Since the 1790s the rituals and symbols of Orangeism have played a significant part in the political development of Ireland. Orangeism is popularly viewed as reflecting centuries of an unchanging political opposition: the opposition of Protestants to a predominantly Catholic Ireland. The annual parades therefore, perhaps more than any other aspect of politics in Ireland, appear to symbolise stasis. Orangemen claim an uninterrupted 'tradition' of parades reaching back into the eighteenth century. Many of their opponents and observers argue that Orangeism is unchanging and that Orangemen are 'trapped in their history'. Yet Ireland has quite evidently undergone enormous changes since the end of the seventeenth century when William of Orange – or King Billy as he is affectionately termed by Orangemen – fought King James at the Boyne. The north of Ireland has developed from a largely rural economy into a complex industrial society. Has the apparent continuity of Orange parades really been maintained throughout this period? I will argue that to accept the apparent continuity of ritual and symbol at face value is to misunderstand the roles of these rituals in politics. The ritual commemorations and symbols of Orangeism have played a far more complex and dynamic role in Irish politics than is generally understood. In explaining the way the functions of symbolic forms might change Abner Cohen provides the same warning.

To the casual observer this [continuity in symbolic forms] seems to be a manifestation of social conservatism and reaction, but a careful analysis shows that the old symbols are rearranged to serve new purposes under new political conditions. In ethnicity, old symbols and ideologies become strategies for the articulation of new interest groups that struggle for employment, housing, funds and other benefits. In Northern Ireland old religious symbols are used in a violent struggle over economic and political issues within the contemporary situation. (Abner Cohen 1974: 39)

This book examines the political control of Orange parades. It contrasts the appearance of continuity in an annual commemorative occasion, the Twelfth, with the clear evidence of political changes both within and outside the event. I will show how various class interests have attempted to control the rituals. I will argue that the political functions of the ritual vary historically depending upon those class interests, the interests and power of ethnic and denominational communities, and particularly the position of the British state in Ireland.

Part of the process of the political control of rituals is the attempt to control the meaning of symbols. Through both ethnographic and historical material I will show that the confrontation between social groups in Northern Ireland often takes the form of a competition over the meaning of particular symbols. There is a continuous attempt by those in power to impose an understanding of the parades that reinforces their political position. Yet the parades are large, complex events, drawing together diverse Protestant groups with diverse political and economic interests. These groups have significantly different relationships both with the Catholic community and with the

British state. Under such circumstances particular ritual meanings that might sustain those in power are not so easily imposed. I will argue that the ability to utilise ritual events by providing them with a dominant meaning rarely goes unopposed and that even within the parades there is resistance to these processes. Most obviously this resistance reflects opposed class interests within Protestantism. The parades may act as a symbolic reference for the Protestant community but they also form part of the confrontation between the powerful and the relatively powerless. More than one interpretation of the events exists and the dominant meanings come from a negotiation between interests.

This confrontation within ritual is the site of the formation of group identity, of 'the labour of representation', which Bourdieu regards as the very essence of the political process (Bourdieu 1991). It is part of an effort by an elite to represent a unified community in contrast to other possible representations, such as those of class, denomination or perhaps generation, and in doing so sustain its own political position. It is through this process that the ethnic identities in the north of Ireland developed, and that the nature of a Protestant identity as opposed to a Catholic identity is formulated. The formation of these identities is not simply a matter of examining the boundary between Protestant and Catholic but also involves the complex class relationships that exist within the communities and the relationship that those communities have with the state.

To examine the dynamic struggle over the meaning of parades, and the confrontations that are part of identity-formation, I will explore some historical moments, tracing the history of commemorations of William's campaign in Ireland from their origins in the eighteenth century to their appropriation and use by the Orange Institution in the nineteenth and twentieth centuries. I argue that there is a generalised discourse, emanating from the landed class attempting to control the Orange Institution, around what I call 'respectable' Orangeism. The generalisation of 'respectable' Orangeism has been mentioned by others (Smyth 1995: 52; Jarman 1997a: 67) and whilst I will use it as a term for particular types of discourse emanating from particular class interests it is also a term used by Orangemen themselves. By 'respectability' I mean the quality of perceived decency and the esteem gained from social correctness. And of course what is deemed 'respectable' is defined by the powerful. This notion of 'respectability' is similar to the idea of the civilising process as applied to parades in Ireland by Jarman (1995: 47–50, 1997a: 28). It implies a form of control on the 'rougher' elements of society likely to disturb the status quo. 'Respectable' Orangemen highlight the religious and 'traditional' meanings of Orangeism and make claims that the Institution is non-sectarian. This view of Orangeism has found its clearest and most recent expression in Ruth Dudley-Edwards' book *The Faithful Tribe* (1999) in which she argues that the Orange Order has been misunderstood and misrepresented.

From 1795 until the 1870s Orange parades were widely viewed, even by many Protestants, as 'rough' events that simply served to foster disturbances and demanded heavy policing. In the period after the 1870s Orangeism became patronised by many more Ulster landowners, the bourgeoisie and petit-bourgeoisie in Belfast, parades came to be seen as more 'respectable' and there was a consistent attempt to marginalise the rougher elements. 'Respectable' Orangeism reached its zenith with the formation of the state of Northern Ireland in 1920 and the parades effectively became rituals of state. I am not arguing that what is deemed 'respectable' has remained constant over 200 years and I am certainly not suggesting by using the word 'respectable' that middle-class Orangeism is somehow non-sectarian or 'better' than that of the working classes. The argument is that discourses of respectability were bound to develop amongst those whose class interests were to maintain their position of power with regard to both working-class Protestants and the Catholic community, but that these political relationships also relied upon the stability of the state. When Orange parades caused major civil disturbances which required massive policing, then the utility of Orangeism to those class interests was reduced. It is my contention that, in attempting to buttress their power, middle-class and capital-owning Protestants have continually found Orangeism, and particularly the parades, a useful and yet awkward, unwieldy, even dangerous, resource in the maintenance of that power.

In the second half of this book I will undertake an ethnographic analysis of the parades I witnessed in the 1990s in an attempt to reveal the complex relationships of power, and resistance to power, within the ritual and between the Protestant community, the forces of the state and the Catholic community. I will look in more detail at the structure of the Orange Order and the two other large 'loyal orders' the Black Institution and the Apprentice Boys of Derry, the annual cycle of parades commonly referred to as the marching season, the preparations that are made for the Twelfth and the events that take place on 12 July. In doing so I will point out not only some of the tensions within unionism, but also the nature of authority within the Orange Institution and the way in which this authority structure affects the control of parades. Specifically, I examine the crucial role played in the parades by marching bands, and suggest that, as broadly independent from the Orange Institution, they have their own particular interests and input into the rituals. The political nuances, the contradictions, and the lines of cleavage that exist within the parades reveal the Twelfth to be a dynamic political ritual quite in contradiction to the discourse of 'tradition' which suggests that the rituals have remained unchanged for centuries. That the discourse of 'tradition' remains dominant is dependent upon the ability of an Orange and unionist elite to maintain power.

Rituals are by their very nature repetitive performances. They not only give the appearance of a lack of change but their imagined lack of change is often held by participants to legitimate the events. As Connerton suggests, commemorative rituals:

do not simply imply continuity with the past by virtue of their high degree of formality and fixity; rather, they have as one of their defining features the explicit claim to be commemorating such continuity. (1989: 48)

Yet every ritual event is a complex, unique occasion created by specific individual actions in specific social circumstances and interpreted and reinterpreted by all the actors directly or indirectly involved. The rituals have complex meanings that are not fixed. They are therefore, to an extent, adaptable to new circumstances despite their repetitiveness.

This research work is a conjunction of participant observation, ethnographic interview and text-based investigation. Whilst being aware of the specific problems with each resource it is not a question of necessarily privileging one over another rather of using them to cross-reference each other. It is in the process of cross-referencing that really interesting questions arise. When a young lad interviewed on radio explains that the Twelfth is all about throwing stones at Catholics it should not be dismissed because a senior Orangeman has told me personally that the Twelfth is primarily providing witness to the Protestant faith. But conversely it would be wrong to suggest that actually the young lad was telling us the truth and the Orangeman was hiding what he really believed. What is interesting is asking why these different discourses exist and how they work in relation to one another.

The whole distinction between 'knowledgeable' and 'unreliable' informants can be revealed for what it is: not a reflection of privileged access to 'real existing meaning', but a local construction put on a contest of interpretations. Why should anthropologists listen only to winners of that contest? If there is no single underlying meaning to 'reveal' then the anthropologist's account does not have to be consistent: to represent consistency when in fact there may be confusion and diversity has been a tempting short-cut to something which doesn't exist! In thinking of symbolism as a code, anthropologists miss the fact that in offering interpretations of a ritual their informants are actually being creative (Humphrey and Laidlaw 1994: 264).

Whereas many anthropologists who have approached ritual have been faced with a paucity of historical information or a relatively short time run, I was faced with sources on Williamite commemorations dating back to 1691 and have been able to spend five years watching a large number of events. What follows is an attempt to utilise diverse sources to allow a better understanding of some particular ritual practices.

2 NORTHERN IRELAND: ETHNICITY POLITICS AND RITUAL

From February 1967 a civil rights movement developed in Northern Ireland. The campaign concentrated on discrimination in employment and public housing allocation, and gerrymandering of local government elections, however, the major form of protest through which the campaign was conducted was the holding of demonstrations. A demonstration in the centre of Belfast, Derry or Dungannon had significance beyond particular issues; it involved marching in areas and on routes which since the founding of Northern Ireland in 1920 had been dominated by the parades of Orangemen and Apprentice Boys. Public expressions of Irish nationalism during this period had been restricted to predominantly Catholic areas, often to small country villages (Jarman and Bryan 1998). As such, civil rights demonstrations, whilst not directly proposing a nationalist agenda, publicly challenged the unionist political status quo through the holding of a form of political ritual which until then had largely been the preserve of unionism. Particular sections of the Protestant community, most notably groups organised by Ian Paisley, held protests, usually occupying town and city centres, the RUC – a proportion of whom were Orangemen – then blocked the civil rights marches and confrontations between the police and civil rights activists ensued. Between 1967 and 1969 these increasingly violent confrontations began to attract the attention of the world's media, to the increasing disquiet of the British government. By 1969, rather than asking questions about the nature of democracy in Northern Ireland, parts of the Catholic community were violently defending their areas from the state.

Political demonstrations are common all over the world but there are particular occasions, in particular circumstances when such protests question the fundamental nature of the state. The Northern Ireland civil rights movement was in part drawing upon political movements in the United States (Dooley 1998), but the context in which the demonstrations were taking place was quite different. The parade and demonstration carried with it resonances of particular importance to the majority Protestant ethnic community. To understand some of the dynamics involved I first want to explore ethnicity politics and ritual particularly with reference to Northern Ireland.

11

ETHNICITY AND POLITICAL COMMUNITIES

In the main, individuals in industrial society live more diverse, differentiated, lives than those in non-industrial and pre-industrial societies, and their identities cannot easily be defined in terms of a family group, village or tribe. Dispersed and diverse communities are defined through symbols – flags, songs, commemorative occasions, coins, passports, uniforms, football shirts, the wearing of insignia and so on. One could even argue that the more internally diverse the community, the more elaborate and regular the attempts to define it. It is not that communities have to share an understanding of these symbols, but simply that they share allegiance. These are 'imagined communities' (Anderson 1983), or 'socially constructed communities' (Anthony Cohen 1985). A political community will be constructed around a set of characteristics – geography, language, economic conditions, history, sex, etc. – which in particular social conditions allows that group to constitute itself over and above other possible groups. The 1991 census in Northern Ireland suggests that around 45.6 per cent of people identify themselves as Protestant whilst 38.4 per cent identify themselves as Catholics in a population of 1,600,000. Yet being Protestant and Catholic in Northern Ireland means more than simply identifying oneself with a particular Church or group of Churches, they are applied on the basis of the community one is born into, regardless of the specific religious belief an individual might hold. Indeed, an individual with no religious belief at all will still be perceived as coming from one or other of the communities unless they have particular characteristics that seem to exclude them, such as coming from one of the relatively small ethnic groups in Northern Ireland such as the Chinese. The Protestant community, or Protestant identity, is formed from a set of shifting characteristics including a particular history in Ireland and Ulster, a sense of being British in an Irish context, a sense of identifying with the reformed faith as opposed to Roman Catholicism, and a political identification with the United Kingdom particularly as a country with a Protestant monarchy. These characteristics are represented through a range of symbols such as the Union flag, the Northern Ireland flag, King William of Orange, the Protestant Martyrs, the six counties of Northern Ireland, the open Bible and crown, the harp with a crown on top, the red hand, the colour orange, the colours red white and blue, the blue football shirts worn by Glasgow Rangers and Linfield football clubs, the British national anthem, the hymn 'Oh God, Our Help in Ages Past', the Harland and Wolff shipyard, the Battle of the Boyne, the Battle of the Somme, the wearing of a poppy, etc. These symbols are utilised at different times, in a variety of contexts by some or most in the Protestant community and by those outside wishing to depict the Protestant community (Bryson and McCartney 1994). The meaning of the symbols varies, indeed is contested, throughout the community dependent upon age, sex, class, denomination, geography, political party, etc. All of these symbols appear in some form or another in Orange parades.

Ethnic identity is formed through internal definition and redefinition by the community and by external definition and redefinition in the processes of everyday interaction, both formal and informal (Jenkins 1997: 52–73). Burton's term 'telling' accurately describes the process that people in Northern Ireland go through. 'Telling constitutes the syndrome of signs by which Catholics and Protestants arrive at religious ascription in their everyday interactions' (Burton 1978: 4). People brought up in Northern Ireland learn how to 'tell'; those who come to live in Northern Ireland soon start to pick up the same skills. On rare occasions such a skill has been a matter of life or death. Usually it is undertaken so that conventions of politeness can be sustained amongst individuals who do not know each other well (Harris 1972: 148). The divisiveness of politics and religion means that conversations surrounding those subjects are usually only started when people are in an environment they are comfortable with and with people they know well. Individuals attempt to tell the religious and political background of people they meet so as to be able to conduct conversations that do not embarrass. There are many ways that people 'tell'. Most commonly they do so through names, but also by means of schools attended, speech and accent, home address, style of dress, occupation, sports played and teams supported.

The complexities and tensions within ethnic identification in Northern Ireland become clear when the heterogeneous nature of the communities is examined (Ruane and Todd 1996: 49–83). The Protestant community is divided by denomination, the largest being the Presbyterian Church making 21.4 per cent of the total population of Northern Ireland, followed by the Church of Ireland (17.7 per cent), the Methodist Church (3.8 per cent) and a wide range of smaller Churches. Major theological divisions exist not only between the Protestant denominations but also within particular Churches where historically liberal and fundamentalist groups have competed for control (Bruce 1986; Campbell 1991). As will be discussed, the Orange Order can be seen as having provided an arena in which men from diverse Church backgrounds can come together although pressure from fundamentalists to oppose ecumenical moves within the Protestant Churches has led to constant internal political tensions.

Research also points to a strong sense of local identity. This is particularly true in rural areas where individuals identify with their village or townland (Leyton 1974), and often attribute conflict to the influence of outsiders or particularly bad people who do not share community values (McFarlane 1986: 97). Suspicions within localities can be enormous and it would be foolish to argue that the sense of locality, even in rural areas, overrides ethnic divisions, nevertheless, locality can provide a sense of community which cuts across these divisions. In urban working-class areas the communities are not nearly as mixed and therefore the sense of locality is more closely linked to an ethnic and political identity (Boal 1982; Jarman 1993; Doherty and Poole 1995), but there is still a strong sense of locality in such areas. Protestants from the Donegall Pass area of Belfast may see themselves as different from Protestants from Sandy Row, despite the areas being separated only by a road (Holloway 1994).

By far the most important variable in ethnic relations is social class. The primacy of social class in understanding Northern Ireland may be debated, but no ethnography can ignore it (Coulter 1999: 61–100). Not only do class differences divide ethnic communities, and those class divisions within the Protestant community will be a central topic of this book, but they also clearly affect the relationships between communities. Most distinctly, the forms of expression and political engagement of the communities are very much dependent upon class interests (Bell 1990: 21). Working-class areas are more geographically divided with clearly visible boundaries. The more residentially mixed areas of Belfast tend to be middle class (Doherty and Poole 1995). Any tour around the streets of Belfast quickly reveals that the overt political expressions, such as flags, murals and graffiti are found almost exclusively in working-class areas (Rolston 1991; Jarman 1992, 1993, 1997a). Endogamy is a widespread and important feature of the ethnic divide in Northern Ireland (Harris 1972: 143–6; Ruane and Todd 1996: 65) but there is at least a suggestion, even if it is not backed up by much evidence, that mixed marriage is more common amongst the middle classes (Morgan *et al.* 1996: 5). The energies that have gone into setting up integrated education have tended to come from the middle classes although it is debatable what difference, if any, integrated schooling makes (Whyte 1990: 44–5). Leisure pursuits with a more middle-class basis tend to show less concern over ethnic identity. For instance there are all-Ireland rugby and hockey representative teams, and all-Ireland competitions. Soccer, on the other hand, has no all-Ireland team except, significantly, at university level. Within the Northern Ireland football leagues, most teams are clearly perceived as Catholic and Protestant, even in lower amateur divisions, and the support of rival Glasgow teams, Celtic and Rangers, is one of the most significant symbols of identity for Catholics and Protestants (Sugden and Bairner 1986; Whyte 1990: 38–9). In terms of socialising, the Belfast pubs liable to be most mixed are those in middle-class south Belfast. In short, there is considerable evidence to suggest that in terms of social interaction the middle classes are more integrated than the working classes (Larsen 1982a: 153–6; McFarlane 1986: 100; Whyte 1990: 38).

Much ethnographic and other social research has therefore sought to understand not a simplistic ethnic division, but the apparent divisions within communities and particularly those aspects of Northern Ireland, denomination, locality, class and the consequent value systems, that both cut across the ethnic boundary and create diverse political interests within ethnic groups. It will become clear in this book that any understanding of the ethnic boundary between what are termed the Protestant and Catholic communities requires an examination of the changing economic relationships between those communities and within those communities. The ramifications of changing interests are found in the terms used to describe political identification as well as the plethora of political parties particularly found in the Protestant community since the collapse of Stormont. I will use the term 'Protestant' to denote ethnic identification but closely related, and for some inseparable, are the terms 'unionism' and 'loyalism' which denote a claim to remaining part of the United Kingdom and showing loyalty to Britain or the British crown. But there are further complications. The term 'Unionism', was originally associated with the Ulster Unionist Party (UUP) but now there are other unionist parties: Ian Paisley's Democratic Unionist Party (DUP) and the Alliance Party, which were launched in the early 1970s, and numerous smaller unionist groups which have appeared subsequently. All unionists can be termed 'loyalist' while 'Loyalists' are supporters of the paramilitary groups the Ulster Volunteer Force (UVF), the Ulster Defence Association (UDA) and the more recent breakaway Loyalist Volunteer Force (LVF). By implication 'loyalism' carries with it a suggestion of being working class. Here I use only the general terms 'unionism', 'unionist' and 'loyalism' and 'loyalist'. The UVF and the UDA have political wings which have become more organised and more popular in the 1990s as the Progressive Unionist Party (PUP) and the Ulster Democratic Party (UDP) respectively. Political unity has often been problematic within the Protestant community and never more so than in the 1990s (Cochrane 1997). In June 1998, during the elections for the new assembly after the Good Friday Agreement, one senior Armagh Orangeman was so incensed by UUP leader David Trimble signing the agreement that he stood against Trimble in the Upper Bann constituency, on his own, under the ticket 'United Unionist'.

In practice the terms 'Protestant' 'unionist' and 'loyalist' are used in some discourses almost interchangeably, as are 'Catholic' and 'nationalist'. But, that is not to say the common use of these terms is without strategy. Actors may describe themselves as Protestant in particular social situations and loyalist in others. I heard one tale from Drumcree of a Church of Ireland minister asking a man on the hill what the situation meant to him as a Protestant. His indignant answer was that he wasn't a Protestant he was a loyalist. In contrast, on the Ormeau Road in Belfast where there has been an intense dispute over a number of parades since 1992 one spokesperson for loyalists in Ballynafeigh, when asked why Orangemen should be allowed down the road, consistently argues that the parades are simply part of the Protestant religion.

It is important to be aware of the heterogeneity that seems to be in conflict with ethnic identification. Ethnic identification exists at the level of the community but it is also part of the individual, or the 'self'. For it is in understanding the sense of self, and not assuming merely a simplistic automatic group consciousness, that one begins to understand the political ramifications of communal representations, the intensity of ethnic confrontations. Ethnic identification is of course social, but also very personal. Ethnicity is portrayed through common yet multi-vocal symbolic forms, allowing common allegiance where on other levels there exists heterogeneity (Cohen 1994: 121, 133–67) but it is precisely in the space between self and community that ethnicity is negotiated and where other forms of political community can develop. The ethnic categories of 'Protestant' and 'Catholic' dominate social relationships in Northern Ireland at all levels. Yet they are not all-encompassing and are constantly being worked, understood and developed by different interests. Bourdieu has described this process as the 'labour of representation' (Bourdieu 1991: 130).

THE LABOUR OF REPRESENTATION

The community is often understood in terms of fraternity and comradeship, nevertheless we cannot understand the development of a community – local, ethnic or national – without analysing the dynamic involvement with power relations (Abner Cohen 1969). Bourdieu has argued that in the social construction of reality we cannot construct anything we like but must construct reality within structural constraints. He argues that in the social space there are 'practical groups' which the social scientist can see as existing on the basis of a group's shared position. But that is not the same as an 'instituted group' (class, ethnic group, nation, etc.) which:

presupposes the construction of the principle of classification capable of producing a set of distinctive properties which characterise the set of members in this group, and capable also of annulling the set of non-pertinent properties which part or all of its members possess in other contexts (e.g. properties of nationality, age, or sex) and which might serve as a basis for another constitution. (Bourdieu 1991: 130)

Every group is the site of a struggle to impose legitimate principles of group construction. Any attempt at a new division must reckon on resistance from those who perceive an interest in presenting alternative relations.

The political labour of representation (not only in words or theories but also in demonstrations, ceremonies or any other form of symbolisation of division or opposition) gives the objectivity of public discourse and exemplary practice to a way of seeing or experiencing the social world that was previously relegated to the state of practical disposition of a tacit and often confused experience (unease, rebelliousness, etc.). It thus enables agents to discover within themselves common properties that lie within the diversity of particular situations which isolate, divide and immobilise, and construct their social identity on the basis of characteristics of experiences that seem totally dissimilar so long as the principle of pertinence by virtue of which they could be constructed as indices of membership of the same class was lacking. (Bourdieu 1991: 130)

Orange parades are part of a labour of representation. They are public events, frequently involving large numbers of people, frequently involving people from a wide range of social backgrounds, including people from diverse Protestant Churches and many non-church attendees, abstainers and heavy drinkers, young teenage girls dressed in the latest fashion and old men in dark suits and bowler hats, supporters of at least half a dozen different political parties, young men carrying paramilitary emblems and religious ministers carrying Bibles, politicians and party-goers. Individuals taking part claim the parades to be 'traditional' cultural events, religious, political and also carnival in nature. The banners carried support images reflecting on a wide range of historical, religious and political events and individuals, as well as pictures of different rural and urban, religious and secular, landmarks. Orange parades, the sash and the bowler hat, have come to represent the Ulster Protestant to the rest of the world, and within local politics the parades have been of such importance that even the unionist politicians who attempt to build a career without being in the Orange Order or participating in the events would have to treat the parades with respect. To understand how the parades work to represent a diverse community we need to consider how rituals work.

RITUALS

Rituals are good to study. It is no accident that they played such a prominent part in Durkheim's sociology, since they seem to exist beyond the individual and to represent the group (Durkheim 1915). Researcher, spectator and participant alike seem to be aware that they are involved in something, which is different from everyday action. But ritual is not easy to define (Lukes 1975), indeed, Goody (1977) argues that the diversity of uses for the term 'ritual' severely flaws it as an informative anthropological category. At one end of the spectrum ritual is seen as a form of standardised social action. As such a footballer may be described as ritually tying his left boot before his right boot. DaMatta (1991: 50–4) suggests that 'all social life is a ... "rite" ' and a ritual is that bit that is 'dislocated and thus transformed into symbols'. Alternatively, rituals are seen as occasions which always have reference to 'mystical beings or powers' (Turner 1967: 19). Why should a definition have remained so elusive? One suggestion that has recently come into favour is that ritual falls between two categories – action and meaning (Bloch 1986; Bell 1992; Parkin 1992; Humphrey and Laidlaw 1994). Ritual can be analysed as both an action and an expression, as something that is done and something that is said. It requires active participation, it entails individuals doing something – although they may not know why they do it – and yet it also seems to contain meaning, to say something. Ritual has been approached either by viewing its main function as developing group cohesion (Radcliffe-Brown 1952), in which case its meaning is of secondary importance, or as something that can be read as a text, as a form of communication (Leach 1976: 45).

The argument that ritual is a particular form of activity, falling between an action and a statement, has been made implicitly or explicitly by a number of anthropologists (Lewis 1980; Ahern 1981; Tambiah 1985; Bloch 1986; Parkin 1992; Humphrey and Laidlaw 1994). Ritual is a formalised, apparently standardised, and structured action – but then so is much of social life. It is invariably rule-bound and as such appears to be unchanging. Ritual gives the impression of continuity. Individuals taking part in a ritual subject themselves to rules – to the authority of the ritual. But then all social life is rule-bound (DaMatta 1991: 20–1). Are we suggesting the individual actors are not involved in creating the events, are they not active? What makes ritual different from other rule-bound action? Perhaps, that it has meaning? But then other actions have meaning, and it is possible for individuals to participate in a ritual without understanding a meaning (Lewis 1980). Does ritual have a particular religious or spiritual association? To suggest that it does is to argue that many secular, and nationalist, commemorations are not rituals when they clearly seem to be of the same order as religious events.

Humphrey and Laidlaw have attempted a way out of the impasse by trying to define ritual not by examining its function or interpretation but by seeing ritual action as 'a quality which action can come to have' (1994: 64). The key is *ritual commitment*. By this they mean that actors are prepared to commit themselves to a particular stance with respect to his or her action (1994: 88). They argue that ritualised action is non-intentional. Not that the actors do not intend to act, but the identity, or meaning of the act does not rely upon the intention or lack of intention of the actor; and those ritual acts are prescribed in a particular way, they are rule-bound and established. Or, as Humphrey and Laidlaw repeatedly put it, 'in ritual one both is, and is not, the author of one's acts' (1994: 99 and 106). 'Such acts are perceived as discrete, named entities, with their own characters and histories, and it is for this reason that we call such acts elemental or archetypal' (1994: 89). Crucially, 'because ritualised acts are felt, by those who perform them, to be external, they are also "apprehensible". That is, they are available for a further re-assimilation to the actors' intentions, attitudes and beliefs' (1994: 89). By distinguishing 'ritual acts', or 'ritualisation', from meaning or function we can see different sorts of ritual events, secular and religious, communicative and non-communicative (1994: 73), as part of the same category.

Ritual action can be religious, or not; performed by specialists, or not; performed regularly, or not; 'express the social order', or not. . . . there are life-cycle rituals, rituals of rebellion, imitative rites, rites of office, rites of commemoration, rites of purification, rites of affliction, worship, divination, sacrifice, namings, inaugurations, and so on. (Humphrey and Laidlaw 1994: 71)

As a clearly rule-bound, institutionalised action that actors engage in, it has a tendency to draw upon a sense of continuity. The actor is effectively buying in to something that 'exists'. Ritual action becomes comprehended by the actors as external, objectified, and thus 'apprehensible' – it can be understood, perceived and seized or appropriated.

RITUALS, SYMBOLS AND POWER

I am most interested in the way people exercise power, and resist power, by means of ritual, how ritual action becomes a political resource, part of the labour of representation. The link between ritual, political power and resistance is the focus of much recent work on ritual (Kertzer 1988; Kelly and Kaplan 1990). As part of the labour of representation, rituals are capable of turning the possibility of a practical group into an instituted group, or community, be it a social class, ethnic group or perhaps nation. Ritual helps to create solidarity within groups, often in the absence of consensus, provides access to political legitimacy and 'moulds people's understanding' of the political universe (Kertzer 1988: 14). Ritual action provides the objectification of politics, constituted and invested in symbols, in Bourdieu's terms, cultural or symbolic capital (Bourdieu 1990: 111–18, 1991: 72) that enables and sustains, but can also resist, the legitimisation of communities. Importantly, symbols are multi-vocal, multi-referential, multi-dimensional or polysemic, containing layers of meaning (Turner 1967, 1968). The multivocal qualities of symbols suggest that they do not communicate a single proposition, but rather a collection of meanings, and that those meanings are not static (Abner Cohen 1979; Morley 1980; Kertzer 1988). Symbols are invented, their political value or importance can rise and diminish over time, different groups can compete for ownership over them, and they can go out of existence (Harrison 1995: 255–72). Yet rituals and their associated symbols can give the impression of unity and continuity during periods of change and as such they provide a resource in relations of power.

Maurice Bloch in his thought-provoking analysis of ritual circumcision and politics amongst the Merina of Madagascar examines many of those aspects of ritual that I have already discussed. Rituals are formalised, they are repetitious, they are only weakly propositional, and have a 'fixity' or lack of adaptability (1986: 184). As such they construct an image of timelessness, and turn specific events into general occurrences.

Rituals reduce the unique occurrence so that they become a part of a greater fixed and ordered unchanging whole; this whole is constructed identically by every ritual performed in a hazy, weakly propositional manner; it appears to have always existed, and will always exist. Because of this, ritual makes the passage of time, the change in personnel and the change in situation, inexpressible and therefore irrelevant. (Bloch 1986: 184)

Bloch's analysis, focused as it is upon religious rituals in non-industrial societies, would have to be modified somewhat for the more secular events that I will concentrate on. For instance, the suggestion that ritual 'appears to have always existed' is clearly not strictly true of commemorative events, but the sense in which rituals defy time I think holds true (Myerhoff 1984; Kertzer 1988; Tonkin and Bryan 1996). I also believe that Bloch overestimates, or at least poorly defines, the 'fixity' of ritual by not paying enough attention to the polysemic nature of symbols. The ritual might appear to remain constant, and therefore defy time, but it is crucial to realise how the unchanging symbols are being understood. Bloch argues that it is striking that the transformation of the circumcision ritual, from village-based to state and royal event, 'did not much change the symbolic content' (1986: 140) and that 'the ritual has resisted direct modification in response to politico-economic change that many theories in the social sciences would have led us to expect' (1986: 193). Yet, as Bloch points out, whilst the symbols may remain the same they are being utilised to mean something different within the developing political relationships. Nevertheless, Bloch develops a persuasive argument around how rituals work politically to legitimate power and why different holders of power, in his case the elders in the villages, and later the Merina royal family, were able to appropriate that power and yet maintain ritual legitimacy over time. Ritual is 'a vague, weakly propositional, construction of timelessness' available for use by those in power (Bloch 1986: 191).

If ritual legitimises political power, and is therefore utilised by those in power, then we need to explain the imperative behind the relatively powerless taking part. To understand this we have to come to terms with 'identity' and 'self'. Bloch suggests that among the Merina 'Traditional authority implies a total order of which both superior and inferior are a part though in different degree ... [in accepting traditional authority] one is aligning oneself with a virtue that is believed to be, in the end, the source of one's own true self' (1986: 169–70). Within the ritual, all Merina, rulers and ruled, are depicted as conquerors as well as conquered (1986: 192–3). Do rituals that legitimise power in ethnic or national environments substantially differ from this?

Ethnic and national identity cuts across differentials of class and power. Unionist politicians repeat phrases suggesting a unity of identity time and again: 'We are the people', 'We are Protestant, we are British and we are from Ulster'. But those political mantras do reflect a sense of belonging that people in the community feel. It is therefore not surprising that people should make a ritual commitment to events that are understood to be part of an individual's own identity and sense of self. Rituals play a fundamental part in the creation of a sense of 'community'. But it is important to understand that in helping to 'create' or 'imagine' the community – 'the labour of representation' – we do not see ritual as simply functioning to bind an unthinking group.

In representational accounts of ritual, the events tend to be described as if their participants are so choreographed that the prescribed orthodoxy of their behaviour displaces their freedom or necessity to think for themselves – as if they have become automata. (Anthony Cohen 1994: 20)

I wish to stress that representations of the community through ritual are labour-intensive, involving individual actors in specific positions, some with more power than others, and reflecting their complex identities. Representations of the Protestant community have never been unproblematic and remain part of a worked process.

The power of ritual to represent has meant that it has remained at the centre of modern politics. Ethnic and national groups, as well as the state, utilise different forms of rituals, from carnivals to funerals, to represent the community. Possibly the most common form, and the form I will in the main be discussing, are commemorative events (Connerton 1989). It has been suggested that major public commemorations in Western society only really started to develop amongst urban middle and working classes towards the end of the eighteenth century (Gillis 1994: 70), and particular social and political changes led to a distinct development of 'traditional' rituals in the second half of the nineteenth century (Hobsbawm 1983: 263–307). The history of Orange parades does not contradict this to any great extent as early eighteenth-century Boyne commemorations in Dublin seem to be dominated by the upper classes. The development of Boyne commemorations in the north of Ireland are contemporary with both the American and French Revolutions and with the development of more capitalist social relationships, and there were further developments in the 1870s partly due to the enfranchisement of the working class.

Commemorative rituals are not organised by an elite or the state only to inculcate the masses with a collective ethnic or national consciousness. The relationship between the community and the rituals is not static but negotiated. Rituals that the state has originally opposed can prove so obstinate that states are forced to utilise them. This has been the case in Eastern Europe. Lane, viewing ritual in terms of social control, and Binns, preferring the term 'ceremonial', both examine the development of ritual in the Soviet Union, noting the changing relationship between the state and life-cycle rituals in the 1960s (Binns 1979–80; Lane 1981). Roth has noted similar developments in Bulgaria, suggesting that the life-cycle rituals are 'the result of a "negotiation" between the political elite and the folk' (Roth 1990: 10). Mach has examined the development of the May Day rituals in Poland, charting their pre-war working-class origins, their development and routinisation under the post-war communist state along with more popular ludic events, and their deroutinisation as open conflict developed in Poland in the 1980s. The communist state found it increasingly difficult to organise the May Day parade and the Solidarity trade union organised events utilising Catholic and national symbols. 'In Poland the communist state took over the workers' holiday and transformed it into a state celebration. Eventually, however, the workers managed to get it back as a form of anti-state protest'

(1992: 60). Jakubowska (1990) has noted a similar use of national rituals and symbols in Poland. The role of ritualisation in the political field, in the formation of ethnic and national groups, and in the legitimisation of the state, is dynamic. Not only can rituals be used to oppose power but even within state-organised events there may develop forms of resistance to power.

RITUAL AND RESISTANCE

In highly stratified societies, elites must work harder to foster symbolic systems among people whose experience insidiously undermines them, for the best that elites can hope to do is shore up a predominant symbolic construction of how society should work. They can never eliminate all loose ends, all contradictions in the symbols themselves, nor all vestiges of alternative symbol systems. Fragments of other systems, as well as internal contradictions, are forever threatening to replace discredited views of the political universe. (Kertzer 1988: 177)

Resistance, in the context of ritual, can either take place within events that apparently maintain a ruling elite or can develop through alternative rituals. Anthropology has long shown an interest in ritualised opposition to colonialism in the form of cargo cults and other millenarian movements. Scott has developed an interesting argument that the more dominant the power exercised, the more stereotyped and ritualistic the interaction between dominant and dominated becomes (1990: 3). He argues that what he calls the 'public transcript' of the relationship between the powerful and weak does not reveal the totality of that relationship. Disguise and surveillance play an important role in relations of power. Public appearance will be dominated by the self-image of the dominant and will rarely be opposed. This self-image in Orangeism is what I will consistently describe as 'respectable' Orangeism. The 'hidden transcript' will be found during off-stage performances by the less powerful. And Scott also suggests that there are elements of disguised and more anonymous forms of public resistance often in the form of rumour, gossip, songs, rituals and euphemisms. He describes these as low-profile forms of resistance (1990: 18). These elements of domination and resistance, of the discourse of the powerful and the resistance of the powerless, are particularly pertinent to understanding the Twelfth. As the power of elites and masses has fluctuated over the past 300 years, the nature of the Twelfth as a ritual occasion has changed. Scott argues that part of the discourse of the dominant is often the idea of unanimity amongst the elite and consent amongst the masses, helping to leave less political space for the less powerful to exploit (1990: 55–66). Indeed, Scott uses an analogy that is particularly apt for my present purposes.

Expanding the notion of unanimity, I then argue that dominant elites attempt to portray social action in the public transcript as, metaphorically, a parade, thus denying, by omission, the possibility of autonomous social action by subordinates.

Inferiors who actually assemble at their own initiative are typically described as mobs or rabble. (Scott 1990: 45–6)

The history of Orangeism is one in which elites, utilising parades, try to control autonomous social action, and, if unable to do that, then try to control the interpretation of that action. 'An effective facade of cohesion thus augments the apparent power of elites, thereby presumably affecting the calculations that subordinates might make about the risk of non-compliance' (Scott 1990: 56). In the chapters that follow some of the ways that the elite try to control events become clear, even to the extent of describing those not performing as they should as 'hangers-on', in other words a rabble. As much as possible, therefore, the elites will try to deal with anything that disturbs 'the smooth surface of euphemised power' (Scott 1990: 56). Sanctions and incentives are always brought to bear by those in a dominant position upon those who might resist (Scott 1990: 128–34). The parade has great potential for the legitimising of power, but large gatherings also suggest a potential, in anonymity and in the power of the collective, for those resisting power (Scott 1990: 66).

Strategic resistance to domination, utilising ritual, can take up many forms. For example, youth cultures can act to negotiate, subvert and oppose the dominant culture and meanings (Hall and Jefferson 1976; Willis 1977; Jenkins 1983). Des Bell (1990) has produced the most important interpretation of the complexities of parades and loyalist political culture. His examination of loyalist bands from the Waterside in Londonderry provides an insight into the dynamics of sectarianism and youth culture in working-class areas. Bell shows that the development of working-class cultural forms is based, not only on the sectarian division within Northern Ireland, but on class and generational lines. The creation of a particular style of marching and playing in parades by blood and thunder bands Bell sees as a reaction to the marginalised position of working-class youths in the Protestant community. Members of these bands do not simply copy 'respectable' Orangeism and indeed are often scornful of the Orange Order and some unionist leaders. Just as powerful groups maintain strategies of 'distinction' (Bourdieu 1985) so subordinate groups have strategies of resistance, albeit from necessity often disguised (Scott 1990). The form of that resistance will vary. Rituals, as well as providing an avenue for the powerful, also provide anonymity and disguise. They are not simply resources for the powerful and indeed at times may become a burden for the powerful.

No ritual occasions seem to encapsulate these possibilities better than the carnival (Bakhtin 1984; DaMatta 1991; Boissevain 1992; Poppi 1992; Cowan 1992; Abner Cohen 1980, 1993). Abner Cohen's analysis of the Notting Hill Carnival, held every August in west London, provides a good example of how rituals can be examined as complex and dynamic events within a diverse and changing political and economic environment (Abner Cohen 1980, 1993). Viewed historically, as well as ethnographically, the

Carnival developed in form from an English fair with poly-ethnic participation in the mid-1960s, to a Trinidadian carnival with steel bands and masquerading, incorporating in the mid-1970s the Jamaican reggae Rastafarian movements as part of the social and political development of London's West Indian community. In the later 1980s, commercialism and changing policing techniques effectively introduced new restrictions on the event, reducing the number of sound systems and the numbers following the masquerade bands. A report from accountants Coopers & Lybrand recommended that the event be run as a profit-making venture, raising suspicions amongst some organisers that the long-term effect would be to turn Carnival into a Lord Mayor's Show. Debate raged as to who 'owned' Carnival and there were consequent discussions on the origin of the event. By the early 1990s, there was a general feeling amongst some organisers that the Carnival had been contained and controlled. It had in a sense been lost to those people who originally saw it as belonging to them. All these developments in the Carnival related to local and more general social, economic and political changes. The development of the Notting Hill Carnival not only brought tensions with the state, particularly in the form of widely publicised confrontations with the police, but also produced internal tensions, specifically between the users of reggae sound systems and those in steel bands.

The struggle for power utilised existing cultural forms and introduces new cultural forms and 'as a result, nearly all cultural forms are politicised and contested' (Abner Cohen 1993: 126). Abner Cohen, rather than highlight only the integrative and harmonious Carnival, describes an event which appears full of Scott's hidden transcripts. Resistance can be direct but need not always be.

. . . as history repetitively demonstrates, a carnival's potentialities for fostering criticism, protest, subversion and violence are equally great, and at the best of times the celebration is poised between compliance and subversion. On the whole central authorities are always anxious to contain and even abolish it, but once tradition is established in a polity it becomes difficult for them to do so. (Abner Cohen 1993: 130)

Cohen's work on the Carnival provides an interesting comparison for a number of reasons. Orange parades show carnivalesque and ludic elements. This is despite the parades' Protestant cultural background, and despite their militaristic elements, and despite the popular image of the carnival as being all-inclusive as opposed to the Orange parades' Protestant exclusivity. The parades overturn many of the normal roles, they allow for play acting, for dance, for masked performance, for excessive drinking, for sexual licence, for mimicry and satire and for *communitas*. It is interesting that the more carnivalesque elements of the parades derive from the more working-class elements and are often those most criticised by 'respectable' Orangemen. Further, the relationships between the ritual, the state, and an ethnic identity, that are brought out in Abner Cohen's work are also present in the case of Orange parades. There are historical moments when the state and ruling classes encourage and control the events, and other moments when they abandon the events altogether or attempt to suppress them.

HISTORY AND 'TRADITION'

Bloch argues that to understand how ritual works it is not sufficient to understand its synchronic functions or its symbolic structure, but it is also important to understand its 'historical destiny' (1986: 11). Bloch proceeds to show, using limited historical resources, how the circumcision ritual, despite remaining relatively unchanged, served to legitimise different loci of power at different moments in time. In the late eighteenth century and early nineteenth century it acted to legitimise the position of village elders; through the nineteenth century it became important in legitimising the power of the developing royal state; towards the end of the nineteenth century Merina religion, under colonial pressures and Christian influences, took on a millenarian aspect, leading to the royal family abandoning the ritual; and in the 1960s it began to emerge within new political alliances in Madagascar (Bloch 1986: 157–67). 'Because the ritual can legitimate any authority, it actually legitimates the authority of those who have the coercive potential to insist on being considered as elders or kings' (Bloch 1986: 190–1). Such an historical analysis, when combined with a symbolic approach, reveals the relationship between ritual, its ideology and politico-economic circumstances. This allows Bloch to conclude that ritual's ability to be recovered by different forms of authority is due to its vague and weakly propositional construction of timelessness (Bloch 1986: 184).

Historians have been posing important questions in understanding ritual. The most pertinent and influential example was a collection of essays edited by Hobsbawm and Ranger on the 'invention of tradition' (1983). By 'invented tradition' Hobsbawm means 'a process of formalisation and ritualisation, characterised by a reference to the past, if only by imposing repetition' (Hobsbawm 1983: 4). Such 'invented traditions', argues Hobsbawm, are particularly prevalent when society is rapidly weakened and old social patterns are destroyed (1983: 4–5). Hobsbawm's invented traditions, particularly the development of parades and ritualised mass gatherings, are largely those in Europe after the 1870s, those connected to the emergence of mass politics and the growing influence of middle-class elites (Hobsbawm 1983: 267–8, 291–303). Twelfth parades were similarly affected by the growth of mass democratic politics and particularly the enfranchisement of some of the working class and involvement of the middle classes in the Orange Institution. Yet, although Hobsbawm does not rule out invented traditions in other periods, I am still left wondering about many rituals, such as the Twelfth, which had a clear existence before the 1870s. Hobsbawm distinguishes 'custom' – which is established practice, flexible in substance, depending upon conditions – from 'tradition' which is fixed and formalised calling upon historical legitimisation (1983: 2). In this sense custom is more like Weber's 'ingrained habituation' (Weber 1968: 25). Somewhat confusingly Hobsbawm and others suggest 'custom' is more common in 'traditional societies', these societies apparently being ones that do not change (Hobsbawm 1983; Cannadine and Price 1987). Is it useful to differentiate customary ritual from traditional ritual? Let me make a tentative suggestion. The important point seems to be the source of legitimisation. Tradition is being used in two senses. The first is as a term referring to a model of authority in the Weberian sense of appealing to principles of a geronto-cratic or patriarchal nature (Weber 1968: 226–41). These are Hobsbawm's 'traditional societies'. Here ritual might be more usefully described as customary; in Bourdieu's formulations, doxa – the naturalised way of under-standing – has not been opposed and therefore orthodoxy does not need to be developed to oppose heterodoxy (Bourdieu 1977: 167–9). For instance, where the rule of elders is not substantially questioned, the rightfulness of their power is doxa, therefore no discourse of orthodoxy – of authenticity – attempting to legitimate gerontocratic rule, has to be developed. When these relationships break down and are opposed, a more overt discourse of legit-imisation needs to develop. This is 'tradition' in the second sense, as a historical claim in itself; that is, a claim to authenticity. 'Tradition' in this sense does not imply age or continuity, although both might be present, but is rather a claim to legitimacy based upon the past. In line with Hobsbawm's 'invented tradition', it tends to be invoked in times of change when people's social relationships are being undermined. It is clearly also used to change the present by developing a political legitimisation for particular groups (Wright 1992: 21). It is in these second senses that I will be using the term 'tradition'. The common understanding of the word does imply objective age and continuity and it is for this reason that I will maintain the inverted commas around the term.

An historical analysis therefore clearly adds an important dimension to understanding the dynamics of ritual action, and particularly 'traditional' rituals. In the same Hobsbawm and Ranger collection Cannadine criticises both functionalist and Marxist sociology for failing to situate an under-standing of the ceremonies of the British monarchy in their historical context. From the standpoint of an historian he makes exactly the same observation as Bloch when he suggests that while a 'repeated ritual like a coronation remains unaltered over time, its "meaning" may change profoundly depending on the nature of the context'. However, Cannadine warns against reading any ritual in history simply as a text and argues that we should be aware of the context in which the ritual is performed and the quality with which it is performed before analysing its meaning (Cannadine 1983: 105–6, 1987: 4). Just because the ritual appears to be unchanged does not necessarily indicate that it means the same thing over time.

RITUAL IN NORTHERN IRELAND

Ritualised action creates events that provide a political resource utilised by interest groups within the political field. As such it appears as a dynamic force despite, and because of, the legitimation gained from the appearance of, and the claim to, 'tradition'. Ritual not only objectifies a sense of power and authority but also empowers those taking part. They are not simply dupes blind to domination but some are actively engaged, through the ritual, in resistance and this resistance takes place on a number of levels, both with the ritual experts, the ritual hierarchy, and with the state more generally. Ritual is an important site of negotiated hegemonic relationships, and anti-hegemonic battles. Yet despite the lack of a consensus within the ritual it still acts to objectify the group to the outside world; it still serves to mark boundaries and give an outward appearance of group consciousness.

> ritual emerges as a particular cultural strategy of differentiation linked to particular social effects and rooted in a distinctive interplay of socialised body and the environment it structures.... [This] argument suggests that ritualization is a strategy for the construction of a limited and limiting power relationship. This is not a relationship in which one social group has control over another, but one that simultaneously involves both consent and resistance, misunderstanding and appropriation. (Bell 1992: 8)

Bell has summed up four 'perspectives' that can be utilised in understanding ritual. The first is an examination of how 'ritualization empowers those more or less in control of the rite'; the second asks 'how their power is also limited and constrained'; the third considers 'how ritualization dominates those involved as participants'; and the fourth investigates 'how this domination involves a negotiated participation and resistance that also empowers' (Bell 1992: 211). Broadly speaking I will be utilising this formulation. I will try to identify the variety of interest groups, some working through the state, that utilise the Twelfth and the way that the rituals empower them. I will be suggesting that their power is limited and controlled; indeed, so much so that interest groups, particularly the upper classes and the state, at various times have abandoned and even suppressed the parades. I will try to show how Orangeism, through the Twelfth parades, provides ideological constructions clearly working in the interests of the powerful and masking alternative political strategies. But, importantly, I will be suggesting that the position of participants is not only negotiated, that the Orangeism is not always hegemonic, but that there are also clear lines of resistance and that the parades are used to oppose some of the powerful interests that also utilise the events. To understand these perspectives I will examine the complex, developing relationships between classes, between ethnic communities and between the state and those ethnic communities.

To understand the reaction of the state and sections of the Protestant community when the civil rights movement started to march into the cities and towns of Northern Ireland in the late 1960s we have to understand the social and cultural environment in which the marches were taking place. Whatever the specific messages of the demonstrations the ritual action itself raised questions of political identity and power. To comprehend the reactions of the Protestant community we need to place the parade, in particular Orange parades, in historical context.

3 APPROPRIATING WILLIAM AND INVENTING THE TWELFTH

... ritualized acts are 'apprehensible', waiting to be apprehended and, possibly, given meaning. (Humphrey and Laidlaw 1994: 101)

In studying the dynamics of this Protestant ethnic identity it is essential to analyse the way in which symbolic forms were and are competed for and the way in which political groups continue to attempt to exert control over them. The formation of a Protestant identity, amongst others, in the north of Ireland has been a complex, long-term political process. Rituals and symbols at some point are created – invented – and can be apprehended – appropriated – or opposed, by those in power. Commemorations of the Battle of the Boyne, the Twelfth of July, were created in the eighteenth century within particular economic and political circumstances and appropriated in the nineteenth century to become a 'respectable' representation of Protestant identity, part of 'the Protestant tradition' in Ireland. In this chapter I want to explore the invention of the Twelfth of July, opposition to it and then its appropriation by particular class interests in the second half of the nineteenth century.

THE BATTLE OF THE BOYNE

By the sixteenth century Ireland was more or less under the control of an English monarch and many landholders were English aristocracy. However, in the reign of Henry VIII the English establishment became Protestants, Anglicans, as opposed to Roman Catholics. At the end of the sixteenth century the area that English Protestant officials found most rebellious was Ulster, the nine counties in the north of Ireland. In 1601 the last great Gaelic Irish rebellion was defeated and, to maintain better control of the land, it was decided that it should be settled with people from England and Scotland. This process of settlement is now known as the Plantation. A large number of the migrants came from Scotland and were Presbyterians (sometimes known as Dissenters) settling predominantly in Counties Antrim and Down. The settlers from England, who were Anglicans, tended to move to Counties Armagh and Fermanagh.

Much fear and suspicion existed between the different groups and in 1641 there was a series of rebellions, including a massacre of Protestants in Portadown that is remembered and commemorated today. In 1649 Oliver Cromwell came and avenged earlier atrocities by committing atrocities himself. However, by the end of the seventeenth century the English monarchy had again become Catholic. Distrust between the Catholic aristocracy and Anglican aristocracy was great in both England and Ireland and eventually it was to lead to a battle that is still commemorated in Northern Ireland today – the Battle of the Boyne.

The Battle of the Boyne was a European battle. Louis XIV of France was at that time the dominant political power on the continent and Prince William of Orange was part of a grand alliance against Louis, which included the Roman Catholic King of Spain and the Pope, within which the position of England under James II became crucial (Murtagh 1993: 40; Haddick-Flynn 1999: 32–84). James, who had converted to Roman Catholicism, managed to unite opposition against himself in England. On 5 November 1688 William landed at Brixham, Devon, and proceeded unopposed to take the throne jointly with his wife Mary, the eldest daughter of James. James fled to France to seek help from Louis, and in March 1689 he landed at Kinsale in Ireland so as to use Ireland, with its predominantly Catholic population, as a stepping stone to the recovery of the English throne. In 1689 William sent relief to the Protestants under siege in Londonderry and in June 1690 he landed at Carrickfergus with a large European army and marched south through Belfast, where he appears to have received a welcome, on his way to the Boyne. William's own Calvinist background, and the promise of increased security for Protestant land ownership in Ulster, helps to explain this welcome. Eventually the two kings and their armies met at the Boyne on the 1 July (o.s.) and William led his troops across the river to victory.

In military terms the significance of the battle appears to have been limited, as the army of King James retreated relatively unscathed and William was unable to win a decisive victory and eventually returned to London. However, it did see the two kings in direct opposition and James did return to France afterwards. The decisive military event took place on Sunday 12 July 1691 at Aughrim and it remains the bloodiest battle ever fought on Irish soil (Bardon 1992: 165). The result was the treaty of Limerick, signed on 3 October 1691, which allowed 15,000 Irish soldiers to sail to France and those giving their allegiance to William and Mary to keep their lands. As part of the settlement Roman Catholics were assured freedom to worship. However, the Anglicans of Ireland did not prove so liberal. With Parliament winning rights over the monarch, William was unable to do much to curb the excesses of the newly victorious Protestant landowners, and, in addition, his interest in Ireland was mainly strategic. The Glorious Revolution had given new powers to the Parliament and they were used to enact penal laws against Roman Catholics and Dissenters.

For Ireland the Glorious Revolution meant not only a victory of some kind of parliamentary democracy over absolutism but also a political shift of power towards Anglican landowners who, through Parliament, produced what came to be known as the Protestant ascendancy in Ireland. For them, William's birthday, the closing of the gates of Derry at the start of the siege, and the battles of the Boyne and Aughrim immediately became events to be celebrated.

FROM WILLIAMITE COMMEMORATIONS TO ORANGE PARADES

The Orange Order was formed in Armagh in September 1795 and the first Twelfth parades under the new institution's auspices took place in July 1796. The *Dublin Evening Post* describes the Lurgan parade as containing fourteen companies formed of a motley group of turncoats, Methodists, Seceders and High Churchmen accompanied by a multitude of boys and 'country trolls cheering the lagging heroes'. Those in the march displayed banners showing William III on horseback and it appears that the marchers were clearly divided into lodges with sword-bearers, called Tylors, and baton-carriers. Marchers wore orange cockades and blue ribbons looped in the buttonhole. A large drum and fifes also accompanied the group (Sibbert 1914/15: 268; Loftus 1994: 15). The political environment, the type of people participating and the areas early Orange Order parades were held was in marked contrast to Williamite commemorations earlier in the century. Williamite parades that took place in the years immediately following the Williamite wars tended to be held in Dublin on William's birthday, 4 November, focusing upon a statue of King William in College Green, inaugurated on 1 July 1701 (Simms 1974). The parades were performed by the military and controlled by the state, a commemoration chiefly for the Anglican gentry and the companies and corporations of the city.[1] Jarman has argued that 'it was the role of the lower classes to observe and bear witness to the dignity of their betters' (Jarman 1997a: 34). Any popular celebrations took place around bonfires whilst the gentry retired to a banquet. The parades were part of an attempt to popularise William as a non-sectarian national figure by stressing the ideals of 'civil and religious liberty' and the Williamite campaign as a victory for parliamentary democracy (Jarman 1997a: 31–43). As the century had worn on the Dublin authorities had begun to find the commemoration a problem with bonfires and fireworks getting out of control (Hill 1984: 35).[2] Popular commemorations, including parades, also developed through Williamite societies, although Anglican gentry dominated many of them (Senior 1966: 2–3; Haddick-Flynn 1999: 92–107).

More influential for the development of the Orange Order was the Volunteer movement which, allied to the Patriot Party in the Irish Parliament, demanded constitutional reform, particularly greater separation from the English Parliament. Independent of the government, and convinced of their right to arm and defend themselves, the first Volunteers appeared in Belfast in 1778. They were broadly made up of Protestant merchants, tradesmen and farmers. On 1 July 1778, two companies of Volunteers paraded in Belfast and in Newtownards.[3] It was through the Williamite rituals, which commemorated the deliverance from arbitrary power, that their ideas could be expressed (Millar 1978: 27). Over the next few years parades were held on 1 July in places such as Coleraine, Cork, Dublin and Belfast, to commemorate the Battle of the Boyne, on 12 July to commemorate the Battle of Aughrim, 4 November to celebrate William's birthday and 7 December to commemorate the closing of the Gates of Derry (Simms 1974: 239; Millar 1978: 34). The state's celebrations and the Volunteers' celebrations were separate. Although these Volunteer corps did not recommend full Catholic emancipation, in some areas they did promote a new attitude towards their Catholic fellow countrymen (Bardon 1992: 217). The most often quoted display of liberalism by the Volunteers took place in Belfast in 1784 when its ranks were opened to all men 'whatever their religion',[4] and helped in the collection for a new 'Mass house' (St Mary's Chapel) to which they marched to hear Mass. On 12 July 1784 they presented Lord Charlemont, the titular head of the Volunteers, with an address favouring greater equality for Catholics, though he politely turned them down. The declining popularity of the Volunteers, after the reforms of 1782, may have forced them to widen their base by admitting Catholics and this caused tension between Catholic and Protestant groups, particularly in Armagh (Beckett 1979: 115–16; Jarman 1997a: 39–43; Stewart 1989: 130–1). There appear to have been no commemorative parades in Belfast for the centenary of the Boyne. However, some Volunteers quickly took on board the French Revolution. They marched in Belfast on Bastille Day, 14 July 1791, and it is possible that this was recognition of an alienation from the monarch. In 1792 there was a general refusal to attend the 4 November Dublin celebrations of William's birthday (Simms 1974: 240).

Whilst Williamite rituals and commemorations existed prior to the formation of the Orange Order it is also clear that they had not attained the wide appeal and participation that they were to after 1795 and the political utilisation of the events was in marked contrast to that which was to develop. Orangeism in its institutional guise helped to codify and control the Boyne commemorations in a form that had not previously existed. It could be said that Orangemen appropriated the events. The Orange Order itself developed in particular local economic and social conditions specific to County Armagh. Faction fighting had taken place for many years around the County and had taken on a particularly sectarian form with the formation of Protestant Peep O'Day Boys and rival Catholic Defenders (Senior 1966; Gray 1972; Gibbon 1972, 1975; Millar 1978, 1990; Frank Wright 1996; Brewer and Higgins 1998: 42–7; Haddick-Flynn 1999: 120–61). After a skirmish between Defenders and Peep O'Day Boys at the Diamond near Loughgall the victorious Protestant group marched to Loughgall and at the house of James Sloan decided to form a 'defensive' organisation. The new Orange Institution was structured around individual numbered lodges, regalia, rituals and symbols reflecting the Masonic background of some of its founding members and reflected the custom of public banding as represented in the Volunteer movement (Gibbon 1975). Although a number of Presbyterians were involved, there seems little doubt, particularly given the area we are discussing, that Anglicans predominated. What is generally agreed upon is that with a number of notable exceptions, few landowners joined at the start (Senior 1966: 20).

Despite this lack of widespread support from the landed class, early leaders wanted respectability and looked to distance themselves from the troublesome Peep O'Day Boys. Yet the immediate aftermath of the Loughgall 'battle' in September 1795 was a concerted attempt by groups of 'Orangemen' to run Roman Catholics out of the county. The demands that they take themselves to 'Hell or Connaught' were also accompanied by the smashing of looms or what has been called 'wrecking' (Gibbon 1975: 39; Bardon 1992: 226–7). Although Orange Institution leaders distanced themselves from such actions, an obvious effect was to alienate local gentry, merchants and the government from the new Institution, placing its early leaders in an awkward position (Senior 1966: 30).

We understand that on Tuesday last being the anniversary of the battle of the Aughrim, a great body of Orange Men, amounting to upward of 2000 assembled in Lurgan, and spent the day with the utmost regularity and good order. It unfortunately happened in the course of the afternoon that some words took place between Mr McMurdie, at Ahalee, near Lurgan, and one of the Queen's County Militia, when came to blows, Mr McMurdie received a stab of which he died.[5]

Gaining and maintaining respectability, in the face of public disorder associated with the Orange Order, was a problem for leading Orangemen from the organisation's first year onwards.

While the Peep O'Day Boys who preceded the Orange Order had the appearance of many of the agrarian secret societies, such as the Whiteboys and the Hearts of Oak, the comparatively highly developed nature of weaving in Armagh and the class of individuals from which the Peep O'Day Boys were drawn, mostly journeymen and weavers, suggests an early proletarian movement (Gibbon 1975: 34). Gibbon has argued that this makes the Orange Institution quite different from the previous agrarian-based secret societies. North Armagh, at that time, showed the most advanced stages of the capitalist linen trade, which resulted in the breakdown of rural relationships of labour patronage. A labour market developed in which Catholic labourers could compete openly with Protestant labourers. Faced with the breakdown of customary social relations, the journeymen, often young unmarried weavers, went about enforcing the penal code, against Roman Catholics, that had been won in 1691 (Gibbon 1975: 34). Frank Wright has argued that as conditions in, what he terms, the frontier society allowed a paternalistic relationship to develop between the ruling class of Anglican landlords and the Catholic natives, then the plebeian settler community, Anglican and Presbyterian journeymen and weavers, organised in such a way as to destabilise structures of authority. As the Catholic population began to organise as bands of 'Defenders', polarisation set in. The local elite was forced to co-opt some of the more controllable parts of the plebeian settler community (Frank Wright 1996: 27–38).

That the Orange Institution took up the Williamite banner, that of hard-won Protestant ascendancy, is not surprising. The Williamite anniversaries provided the newly formed Orange Order with a legitimised link to the Protestant sovereign (Millar 1978) as well as a rallying point that should have been readily acceptable, even respectable, to the middle and landed classes and the government, which in turn might have differentiated them from the disreputable Peep O'Day Boys. But even the first events were politically highly charged given the sectarian tensions, and it provided the government with the potential problem of civil disorder. With the rise of the United Irishmen and a predominantly Roman Catholic militia, the state's reaction to the commemoration immediately becomes important (Senior 1966: 41). Orange leaders became more overt in their politics and offered support to the state, describing themselves as Boyne Clubs. Increased gentry involvement in the Armagh area may also have stemmed the outrages against Catholics, by groups calling themselves Orangemen, that had followed the Battle of the Diamond, for they continued in areas where landowners had, up until then, taken little part (Senior 1966: 42–4). But outside developments were such that the growth of the Institution was to be assured. In September 1796 Parliament voted for the formation of a Yeomanry corps and Orangemen made up a substantial part of this force which was used to oppose the United Irishmen (McDowell 1979: 561–2; Campbell 1991). In short, a coalition between members of the lower class of Protestants and a section of the landed gentry was being established, and by 12 July 1797 the position of the Orange Institution had been significantly strengthened (Senior 1966: 68–9). The Twelfth of 1797 can only have reinforced the government's endorsement of Orangeism despite reservations. General Lake received a parade of artillery men, militia men, Orangemen and Yeomanry in Belfast then moved on to Lurgan where a crowd of 12,000 greeted them. Clearly, the appearance of General Lake acted to give important public legitimacy to the Orange Order and the Twelfth. Belfast, as the centre of radical thought at that time, had found it difficult to raise a Yeomanry corps. Neither did Belfast prove to be a hotbed of Orangeism for years after. Indeed, at the Belfast parade General Lake may well have perceived the event more as a show of strength in front of a disloyal town. This Twelfth in Belfast certainly appears to have had a unique level of government involvement. In Lurgan his appearance possibly completed the process of giving state legitimacy to the Orange Order, which started when Orangemen were drawn into the Yeomanry.

On 12 July 1797 a Grand Lodge of Ulster was formed and some of the early founders of the Order were moved aside (Dewar *et al.* 1967; Smyth 1995: 52–3). More significantly still, in April 1798, a number of prominent politicians in Dublin joined a city lodge and the Grand Lodge was moved there from County Armagh (Haddick-Flynn 1999: 175–90). Smyth has argued that 'the men of property hijacked the movement in order to control it' (1995: 53). The Institution's rules were rationalised and codified. The Grand Lodge was to be the ruling body, below which would stand the County Grand Lodges which in turn were divided into Districts composed of private Lodges. By 1798 senior political figures were attempting some sort of control over the mass of the lower-class Orangemen.

Two events at the end of the century had a significant effect on the new Institution: the Rising of the United Irishmen in 1798 and the Act of Union that came into force in 1801. Although direct involvement by the Orange Institution in countering the rebellion was limited, the government made further use of its membership, and stories of atrocities by the United Irishmen increased membership of the Order. Stories of Orange atrocities had the same effect on recruitment to the United Irishmen. The failed Rising completed the process of turning the Orange Institution from a small, geographically and politically limited group into a large, nationwide, influential organisation. Surprisingly, perhaps, in the light of its later role as defender of the Union, the Act of Union nearly split the Institution. Many Lodges feared the loss of the Parliament in Dublin as a diminution of local power and a forerunner to Catholic emancipation. Seventeen of the nineteen Orange MPs voted against the measure and Lodges in Dublin, Armagh, Monaghan, Antrim, and Down called for the Grand Lodge, which remained neutral, to better reflect the views of membership. One Lodge warned of the 'extinction of the Irish nation' (Sibbert 1914/15: 84–91).

THE BATTLE FOR 'RESPECTABILITY'

To understand the Twelfth parades in the early nineteenth century we need to recognise the relationship between the state, the government, the elite of the Orange Institution, and the lower-class, rural and urban, Church of Ireland and Presbyterian membership. I would agree with Smyth's argument that 'from the outset Orangeism had a respectability problem' (1995: 52). Early Williamite commemorations, particularly in Dublin, had the air of respectability. They were endorsed by the state. Even the Volunteer movement, patronised by middle-class Protestants, appeared respectable. But Orangeism was different, a popular culture that developed in shebeens and pubs, the site of much political resistance in early modern Europe (Burke 1978; Scott 1990: 120–4). It developed out of more direct lower-class sectarian confrontations that put at risk the economic and political stability of the country. Orange parades had quite a carnivalesque atmosphere and were occasions on which a mixture of drink and religious worship was not uncommon. The carrying of flags and banners, and the accompaniment of a band, or bands, and large drums seems universal. Parades either ended up at church services, at a field or at some general meeting point where a religious service was usually conducted. So whilst Orangeism provided possible security for local landowners and loyal defenders for the government the parades became sites for both drunken revelry and sectarian clashes. For much of the early nineteenth century those in power seemed unsure whether these local Orange parades should be encouraged or discouraged, whether they should be embraced by the establishment or put down as destructive for the well-being of the state. The parades became a resource for those seeking political control, but a resource with limitations.

The years from 1795 to the 1870s were turbulent ones for the Orange Order. Successive governments were ill at ease with the Orange Order, and that unease grew significantly after 1800. Parades increasingly became the site of conflict, with the first major disturbances in Belfast involving Orangemen taking place in 1813. The government's attitude to the Williamite anniversaries moved from one of encouragement, involvement or at least tacit acceptance, to one of discouragement and then outright opposition. This demanded a political balancing act of the senior Orangemen, who were by then well entrenched within the Dublin establishment; they had to try to keep control of these rituals, that went at least some way to providing them with legitimised political power, whilst placating those in government worried about the unrest caused by 'party' events. Hill has suggested one of the keys to these changes in her work on the Dublin Williamite anniversaries. To achieve national allegiance within the new Union, the state required a 'tradition' that would attract Catholics as well as both liberal and conservative Protestants. However, the Orange Order managed, over the thirty years from 1795, to become the sole bearers of the Williamite banner, and the state not only relinquished support for the 4 November celebrations in Dublin but eventually, in 1825, banned the Orange Order and its 'party' parades throughout Ireland (Hill 1984: 9).

Senior Orangemen attempted to sustain their position, while the government reacted to civil disturbances – commonly involving Catholic Ribbonmen and Orangemen as antagonists – and the formation of the Catholic Association by Daniel O'Connell to campaign for Catholic emancipation. Jarman describes this period as the era of riotous assemblies (1997a: 53–8). Leading Orangemen were desperate to stay within the law and there is some evidence of disquiet amongst brethren about the ineffectuality of the Grand Lodge of Ireland in protecting their interests (Senior 1966: 208). In 1824 the Grand Lodge was prepared to go so far as to suggest that members of the Institution desist from parading,[6] and this request was supported by the District Lodge in Belfast.[7] The evidence suggests that there was not great compliance with the Grand Lodge's request with at least eighteen Boyne commemoration parades being reported in the north.[8] In short, it appears that senior office holders in the Orange Institution had reached the point of not being able to sustain arguments for their political supporters to go out on parade, whether or not the resulting disturbances were the fault of Orangemen. Their position as large landowners, and as representatives of the civil authority such as magistrates, with most to gain from a peaceful land, meant that they had to take the dangerous political decision of abandoning the ritual events that acted as the focal point of their organisation and as cement for cross-class allegiances. In attempting to maintain the legality of their Institution, they were abandoning the very acts that gave it the appearance of such political unity. The only appeal that the senior Orangemen could make to their brethren was to their loyalty to the state. The rank and file was placed in a position of showing their loyalty by not partaking in a ritual that they believed showed their loyalty.

The strength of O'Connell's Catholic Association, and the disturbances involving Orangemen, Ribbonmen, and a number of other agrarian societies, persuaded Parliament, in 1825, to pass the Unlawful Societies Bill, despite stout opposition from Orange members (Haddick-Flynn 1999: 226). The Grand Lodge of Ireland had no choice but to disband, and on 18 March it did so, issuing an address which suggested that 'any lodges meeting after this day commit a breach of the law, and are liable to the consequent penalties'.[9] However, celebrations of the Twelfth remained widespread with disturbances at a number of them, including Belfast.[10] Orangemen continued to meet and parade despite efforts by the authorities and senior Orangemen to stop the commemorations.[11] The *Northern Whig* acknowledges the withdrawal of the 'respectable' portion of the Orange Institution and pointed out that 'the working classes in the town [Dromore] and neighbourhood are fully as pugnacious as those in any part of the empire'.[12]

The Unlawful Societies Act expired in 1828 and the government chose not to renew or replace it. There is certainly no doubting the strength of the Orange movement that July with at least eighteen large parades reported.[13] For members of the Grand Lodge the same problems remained: trying to wield the political force displayed on the Twelfth within the state, yet not appear to threaten the stability of the state and thereby lose the very force they were wielding. The next few years were to see their position becoming even more untenable. In 1829, despite a proclamation from the Lord Lieutenant suppressing the parades (House of Commons Select Committee 1835: 304), and proclamations by senior Orangemen, the parades went ahead and, with Catholics forming into Ribbon bands, trouble ensued. Magistrates in Belfast had a notice published dissuading participation in processions, despite remonstrations from local Orangemen that they could not be prevented from walking. A demonstration of fifteen lodges took place and later there was rioting in the Brown Street and Millfield areas (Bardon 1992: 247). There was trouble in at least eight towns with fatalities at Stew-

artstown (Sibbert 1914/15 vol. II: 343; Senior 1966: 240–1).[14] From 1830
to 1835 disturbances at parades were commonplace. Each year pressure was
brought to bear on Orangemen, from both within and outside the Institution,
not to parade; but the parades went ahead. In August 1832 a Party
Processions Bill was passed. But the parades continued despite the
prosecution of Orangemen.

In 1835 a Parliamentary committee was set up to look into Orangeism. Of
the three-volume report that resulted, the largest part was on Orangeism in
Ireland. The evidence of the Select Committee of 1835 provides a fascinating
window onto the Orange Institution and its celebration of the Twelfth. Not
only did those who were unsympathetic to the Institution throw scorn upon
the ability of the Orange elite to restrain their brethren, but some senior
members of the Institution expressed their role as offering leadership and
therefore controlling the rougher elements. Perhaps the greatest concern of
the Committee was the widespread existence of Orange lodges within the
British army. Added to this was the patchy evidence of a plot to put the Duke
of Cumberland on the throne. After the king had replied to an address from the
House of Commons pertaining to the discouragement of the Orange lodges,
the Duke of Cumberland was forced to dissolve the Grand Orange Lodge of
Great Britain. In Ireland there was much opposition to the dissolution, with
the Armagh District leading the way. Finally, on 13 April, the Grand Orange
Lodge of Ireland decided by 79 votes to 59 that 'the promotion of interests of
the Protestant population in Ireland – will no longer be served by the
continuance of that Institution' (Sibbert 1938 vol. II revised: 226).

THE RIGHT TO PARADE

A number of factors appear to be significant in the development of Orange
parades in the middle part of the nineteenth century. Party Processions Acts
were in force from 1832 to 1844 and from 1850 to 1872. The enforcement
of these Acts highlighted the clear class divisions over the celebration of the
Twelfth throughout this period. The rapid industrial development of Belfast,
with the consequential growth of a predominantly working-class population,
was also accompanied by persistent sectarian unrest. Whilst the gentry
distanced themselves from the mass of Orangemen, many leaving the
Institution, and despite the non-existence of a Grand Lodge for much of this
time, Orangeism persisted amongst the lower classes and its significance in
Belfast began to increase. For much of this period senior Orangemen, those
who did not leave the Institution, attempted to dissuade Orange lodges from
marching. The Lord Lieutenant also issued regular proclamations from
Dublin reminding magistrates, many being Conservative landlords, of their
duty to stop 'party' parades. The 1836 Constabulary Bill introduced
stipendiary magistrates as central government officials controlling a con-

stabulary. This allowed central government greater control of parades. Some magistrates were even dismissed for being unwilling to confront Orange parades (Frank Wright 1987: 13–14, 1996: 55–6).

In the 1830s, in areas such as Larne, Carrickfergus and Ballymoney, where there were few Catholics and a liberal Presbyterian population still opposed to Conservative landlords, Orangeism was very weak (Frank Wright 1996: 59). However, it appears there were still parades in staunchly Orange areas as well as the development of parades in areas such as Ballymena, County Antrim, which had not previously seen great numbers of Orangemen. Many Orangemen were dissatisfied with the sort of support they were receiving from MPs connected with the Orange Institution (BNL 16 July 1844). There were significant parades from 1836 to 1838, but, during the late 1830s and early 1840s, the parades appear to have become smaller and fewer in number with some Orangemen prosecuted (Sibbert 1938: 258).[15]

The Party Processions Act was not renewed in 1844, perhaps due once again to the government's need to use Orangeism in a time of growing crisis (Frank Wright 1996: 136). This relieved some of the pressure on the Orange Institution but senior members continued to advise against parades being held. There was no great rush by the landed classes back to Orangeism and 'respectable' members did not parade in public (Frank Wright 1996: 152).[16] The *Belfast News Letter* suggested that 'in these days of education and enlightenment, Protestantism and loyalty have discovered better modes of asserting themselves, than by wearing sashes and walking to the music of fife and drum'.[17] But large parades, often referred to as 'monster parades', were held; the ability to hold these was facilitated by the rapid development of the railway network in Ulster. The trains allowed Orangemen to gather in greater numbers and also had the effect of making the area around stations in Belfast common sites for sectarian clashes during July.

Limited government use of Orangeism became impossible once again in 1849 when a Twelfth parade over Dolly's Brae, County Down, saw a major confrontation between Orangemen and Catholic Ribbonmen, a confrontation which looms large in Orange folk history.[18] The confrontation resulted in a number of Catholic houses being wrecked, an estimated 30 dead Ribbonmen and three magistrates dismissed (Sibbert 1938: 351–6; Dewar *et al.* 1967; Bardon 1992: 302–4; Frank Wright 1996: 155; Haddick-Flynn 1999: 272–87). Landlords who had rejoined the Institution left once again and a new Party Processions Bill gained royal assent on 12 March 1850. Yet again the fundamental differences of interest within Orangeism were to be revealed in reactions to the ban placed upon party processions. The bulk of lower-class Orangemen perceived their loyalty as disregarded by the government. A few lodges in Armagh and Tyrone went so far as to burn their flags and warrants.[19]

Twelfth parades through the 1850s were patchy but not uncommon. Policing of Ulster's towns was heavy around the Twelfth, with reinforcements often travelling from southern areas to do the job. Some Orangemen were prosecuted for taking part in political processions. In Belfast, in particular, the July period was marked by the appearance of drumming parties comprising a fife and large drum, and decorations such as arches over the road covered in Orange lilies and a variety of Orange symbols. The local police were predominantly Orangemen and, although senior policemen were wary of Orange July displays, the displays were accepted so long as they took place within Protestant areas and did not threaten disturbances (Frank Wright 1996: 246–53). Generally, distinguished Orangemen, various government agencies and newspapers produced annual recommendations requesting that brethren desist from marching.[20]

If anything in particular seems to have characterised the period of the next twenty years it was the role of a number of conservative Protestant preachers who regularly gave sermons, not only in church, but also at demonstrations and in the centre of Belfast. Ministers such as Cooke, Drew, Hanna and McIlwaine became synonymous with just about every major sermon or demonstration that took place. The Reverend Henry Cooke particularly linked a Conservative brand of Presbyterianism with Orangeism and the belief that God had given the Protestants of Ulster an important role in the prosperity of the British Empire (Brewer and Higgins 1998: 57–60). Whilst the Twelfth as organised by the Orange Institution was, to a certain extent, in abeyance, many country Orange lodges and Districts continued to mark the occasion and there were informal commemorations, particularly in Protestant working-class areas of Belfast. Events remained peaceful so long as Catholics ignored the more provocative elements and the authorities managed to control them. But this was a strained status quo and parades often led to disturbances (Frank Wright 1996: 253–4). There were disturbances during July in Belfast in 1852, Lisburn and Belfast in 1853, and Belfast in 1855.[21] July 1857 saw some of the worst rioting in Belfast's history, with disturbances, particularly house expulsions, lasting right through until September (Sibbert 1938; Boyd 1969; Budge and O'Leary 1973; Gibbon 1975; Bardon 1992; Frank Wright 1996). The Commission of Enquiry blamed the street preachers, with sermons containing a heady mix of religion, politics and Williamite history, for some of the tensions and quoted a sermon by the Reverend Drew at an Orange Service in Christ's Church, Sandy Row.

> In the history of the maligned and indomitable Orange Institution, it will be found, when a great part of the aristocratic leaven was withdrawn from it, and by a majority the leaders consented to its extinction, the masses held together; and again, in times of treason and expected insurrection, the gentry once more flocked under the folds of the Orange banners.[22]

The divisive effect of the Party Processions Act for the Orange Institution remained apparent for the next decade. Despite efforts to stop them, parades remained relatively common. Whilst Belfast was heavily policed in the years following the 1857 riots, surrounding areas, particularly Lambeg and

Lisburn, were common venues for processions.[23] In 1858 people in Belfast left for a 10,000 strong demonstration although the *Newsletter* provides an unlikely observation that 'there was scarcely a man connected with the Orange Institution in attendance'.[24] In 1860 there were riots in Lurgan, Newtownards and Derrymacash following the Twelfth and the laws controlling party displays were made even tougher later that year with the Party Emblems Act; but it had little effect. In 1861 large meetings were again held around Ulster, some involving processions.[25] There may even have been some increase in the number and size of events. There were party riots during July in Belfast in 1863 and Belfast and Armagh in 1864.[26] More serious, however, were the disturbances in Belfast in August of 1864 after the foundation for O'Connell's statue was laid in Dublin. The riots lasted two weeks and the clash between Protestant 'ship carpenters' and Catholic 'navvies' showed a ferocity not previously seen (Gibbon 1975: 65–86; Budge and O'Leary 1973: 81; Frank Wright 1996: 260–8).

THE TWELFTH AND SOCIAL CLASS

When the Orange Institution formed in 1795, the use of Boyne or Aughrim ritual celebrations as the public expression of its existence acted to create the appearance of a visible Protestant unity between lower classes and the landed gentry. At first the celebrations were endorsed by the administrations in Dublin, not only because Williamite celebrations, in both their liberal and ascendancy veins, had become part of an accepted identity for the Irish state, but also because, pragmatically, the state needed counter-revolutionary forces. The state effectively endorsed the more conservative celebration of William's campaign in Ireland. However, the perceived interest of the state, the Ulster landed gentry and the lower-class Protestants were not always to remain so easily allied. Orangeism was very much based upon lower-class, rural groups of journeymen and weavers, many early lodges meeting in pubs. It developed in areas where significant economic changes were taking place disturbing previous social relationships. Early Orangeism, to an extent, can be seen as a site of resistance taking a reactionary form. What then follows is an interplay between those sites of resistance, local landlords and magistrates and the forces of the state.

The Orange Order did not invent the Boyne parades, but it did institutionalise, routinise and attempt to control them into the Twelfth. It also elaborated the physical and symbolic form of the ritual, although again it drew upon existing organisations and events. The Twelfth became an important contested political resource, utilised in different ways by Protestant classes with different interests, as well as by the state. The state's desire for hegemonic consent of the bulk of the population meant that in various stages it would abandon the Williamite celebration in favour of Saint Patrick's Day

(Hill 1984). Whilst this allowed the Orange Institutions to appropriate even greater control of the Williamite rituals and their meanings, it also increased the partiality of the events and created the possibility that they could be perceived as being threatening or even in overt opposition to the state. Attempts to 're-appropriate' the events were made by liberals. The *Northern Whig* in 1824 appealed to the spirit of the earlier celebrations of the Volunteers of Ireland and suggested that the Orangeman's loyalty 'was conditional, not permanent'.[27] O'Connell was not beyond appealing to the Orange faction, quoting the spirit of 1782 and toasting William with Boyne water (Sibbert 1938 vol. II: 73–4; Senior 1966: 249). However, in the main, those opposed to the Orangemen appeared to accept the new ideological role of the Williamite celebrations and attempted to undermine the events by using disturbances on the Twelfth as a political lever upon the government. This meant that support for the public parades by senior members of the Order, often themselves in positions of government, became a double-edged sword. The Grand Lodge of Ireland found it difficult to defend the parades and the consequent civil disorder, particularly during periods when emancipation and reform laws were on the agenda and tension was high. The regular claims that Orangemen were not involved, or at least not to blame, was in many ways irrelevant to the state. Neither state-sanctioned laws nor various degrees of persuasion from the Grand Orange Lodge of Ireland were particularly successful: the laws, because they were policed by a limited force and often a partial judiciary, and the Grand Lodge because the parades had become one of the few political resources the lower orders possessed. The fundamental differences between the Orange elite in Dublin and the bulk of the Orangemen in Armagh or Down explains why there was a readiness on the part of one, but not the other, to abandon the parades.

Class divisions that are in some ways effectively subsumed under the organisation of the rituals are immediately revealed when the ritual becomes oppositional to the state. Indeed, when the political ground had shifted so much that the government banned the organisation itself, divergent class responses become clear. The lower-class members continue to parade as best they can, while landowners and the elite in Dublin, who are effectively part of the state, reform their Orangeism within the boundaries the law has now set. The different interests of those that have taken part in the events are revealed. For both, the Twelfth events provide some sort of political power. For those senior Orangemen who are part of the state power structure, the rituals can only supply political legitimacy so long as those events are not seen to threaten the fabric of the state. At that point, it is no longer wise to be seen to be involved in or encouraging the Twelfth. However, from those lower down the social order, the Twelfth expresses relations of patronage and social closure reducing the ability of Catholics to move into particular labour markets. It also expresses a common identity by way of a display of physical force alternative to that of the state. That is, alternative in the sense that it is not controlled by the state. Thus, when the ritual itself threatens civil disorder, those higher in the Orange Institution are prepared to abandon it whilst those in the lower orders are not.

The Orange parades, as well as acting as political catalysts, reflected the changes taking place in the political environment. Their physical appearance tended to reinforce the structure of the Orange Institution. The routes and destinations of parades were affected, and thus developed, by a number of factors, including numbers taking part, the nature of the surrounding population, the law enforcement agencies and the legality of the events. The reaction of spectators in some ways depended upon the political environment surrounding individual parades, so much so that in Dublin Orangemen were forced to discontinue their public commemorations. Until the 1870s the political power of the Orange Order remained limited. Its greatest strength, even in 1835, was still predominantly in Armagh and Down and its infiltration into Belfast during that period was relatively limited. Only as political and economic structures in the north changed did Presbyterians join the Orange Institution in greater numbers, and, although this alliance was to become extremely important, the domination of the Established Church in the Institution's hierarchy was evident right up until the dissolution of the Grand Lodge in 1836. It was not until the second half of the century that political and social conditions would be conducive to Orangeism becoming a focal political institution.

4   PARADING 'RESPECTABLE' POLITICS

The continued popularity of the Twelfth among the lower classes, and perhaps the growth of Orangeism within Belfast's expanding Protestant working classes, had political potential which appears to have been recognised by William Johnston, son-in-law of Reverend Drew, with a small landholding at Ballykilbeg in County Down. He it was who, by organising large parades in the late 1860s and early 1870s, effectively questioned the role of the Grand Lodge of Ireland; he entered Parliament and in 1872 saw the Party Processions Act taken off the statute book. He not only appropriated the ritual Twelfth parades for his own political campaign, but in doing so forced elite Orangemen, who were conscious of losing political patronage, to show more active support for the parades. It was William Johnston who began to turn the parades into events that local politicians would find it necessary to be seen at and to speak at. It was during this period that the ground was laid for the type of Orangeism and unionism that was to dominate the north of Ireland for the next hundred years. The parades started to became 'respectable'.

WILLIAM JOHNSTON OF BALLYKILBEG

The details of William Johnston's rise and fall have been well documented (Wright 1972, 1996: 315–32; Gibbon 1975: 87–111; Patterson 1980: 1–18; Walker 1989; Boyce 1990: 137; McClelland 1990; Bardon 1992: 354–57). In 1864 the Belfast District Lodge broke from the Antrim County lodge to form its own County Grand Lodge. The Orangeism of landlord patronage in rural Ulster moved into Belfast but evolved in a new developed industrial environment amongst a Protestant working class attempting to control a developing labour market. The structure of Orange lodges allowed them to graft easily onto the fine status positions of the skilled craftsmen working in Belfast's industries. Lodges developed out of specific factories and particular trades with foremen frequently becoming Masters of the Lodge. Gibbon claims that 'the Order provided a means whereby the aspirations of almost any semi-organised form of occupational particularism could be incorporated' (1975: 96). What made this form of patronage and labour exclusivity so different was the increased independence of workers from their employers (Gibbon 1975: 94–101). This urban and industrial arena therefore still contained the structures of an Orange and Protestant ascendancy, but in a quite new form, a form with which the Grand Lodge of the Institution had yet to come to terms. Dominated by landlords and the clergy of the Anglican Church, it was most concerned with the threats that the Church might be disestablished; but, for many lodge members, more local political issues were uppermost. Disestablishment certainly mattered less, if at all, to the large number of Presbyterians in Belfast. Their power was expressed through the Twelfth of July parades and not only was the Grand Lodge doing little to fight the Party Processions Act but it often looked as though it was supporting it (Patterson 1980: xviii). Yet from the mid-1860s parades became more common, with the local police finding them harder to control. As the ability of the police and magistrates to deal with parades, particularly the more rowdy drumming parties, was reduced, so also was the ability of Catholic priests to control the Catholic population (Wright 1996: 269–83).

William Johnston was a political entrepreneur. Deeply committed to the Orange Institution he spent his life combating the Roman Catholic establishment. However, unlike many of his fellow Orangemen, Johnston appeared to believe passionately in equal procession rights for all, Catholic as well as Protestant (Wright 1996: 340–2; Jarman and Bryan 1998). After the prosecution of Orangemen in Gilford in 1864 Johnston started touring Orange lodges speaking against the Party Processions Act and tried to get the Grand Orange Lodge of Ireland to sanction a demonstration. When the Grand Lodge refused Johnston attempted to organise a meeting for 12 July 1865; he was threatened with expulsion from the Institution and forced to back down. The following year Johnston got around this problem by organising 'A Grand Protestant Demonstration' on his own Ballykilbeg demesne with regalia only to be worn on private property. The 9,000 strong parade proved successful although it received criticism from the *Belfast News Letter*.

Given the success of this parade, and with some support from the Belfast Grand Lodge, Johnston organised a massive parade for 12 July 1867 to go from Newtownards to Bangor.[1] He and twenty-five other Orangemen were charged with illegal assembly. Refusing to apologise, he was sentenced on 28 February 1868 to one month in jail (McClelland 1990: 41–2). With his martyrdom complete his support grew. Meetings were set up to push him forward as a working man's candidate for Belfast and red banners appeared with 'Johnston, the working man's friend' upon them (Gibbon 1975: 99). Johnston's position in the election campaign that followed probably owed more to his resentment of the elite that ran the Institution than to any strong feel for working class radicalism. He advocated land reform, but said little else on social issues. Importantly, Johnston's position was aided by the passing of an electoral reform act enfranchising more working men (Wright 1987: 43–4; Walker 1989: 60). At one meeting a speaker described

Johnston as 'the new leader of ten thousand Orangemen in Belfast, and of one hundred thousand in Ulster'.[2] William Johnston had effectively become the spokesman for popular Orangeism and he easily won a seat in Belfast in the 1868 election.

William Johnston's story is important because it marks a sea change in the relationship between the Orange Institution, conservative politics and the growing working classes of Belfast. Johnston appeared to understand that political power could only be assured under a hegemonic position in which the Protestant working classes felt that their political interests were being served. However, Johnston promoted an independent style of Orangeism which, although resolutely against the Catholic Church, was nevertheless supportive of the rights of individual Catholics, particularly their right to parade. But, as Wright has pointed out, 'letting both sorts of marches happen on the same ground meant accepting the ground was both Orange and Green' (Wright 1996: 342). With Johnston becoming Belfast County Grand Master in 1868, this independent, almost radical, and yet contradictory form of Orangeism briefly flowered (Wright 1996: 334–55).

Senior members of the Orange Institution and the Conservative Party could no longer rely on the patronage of the landlord–tenant relationship as they had in the countryside. Conservatism had lost control of Orangeism. As such, in the winter of 1869 the Conservative Working Men's Association was set up with the agreement of the Orange Protestant Workingmen's Association. More importantly there was a concerted attempt, led by Reverend Hugh Hanna, to purge the independent Orangemen from the Institution. Wright believes Hanna to be the first Presbyterian minister in Belfast to join the Institution. Hanna involved himself in the expulsion of some independents, in creating County Chaplains, and creating new Districts within Belfast County to try to obtain enough votes in the County Grand Lodge to depose Johnston. At the Twelfth in 1871 Hanna attacked Johnston for defending the rights of Fenians to march, and later that year Johnston was ousted as County Grand Master by the more conservative faction (Wright 1996: 353).

The conservatives had regained some control of the Institution, and Orangeism provided the means through which a new hegemonic relationship could be developed between the bourgeoisie and the Protestant working classes. Yet this was not so much the Orangeism of protecting the Established Church, whose concerns were those of the old establishment gentry, but an Orangeism that demanded the right for Protestants to parade, where workers expected the support and involvement of their 'betters'. Parades now took place openly, in spite of the law. In 1869 there were dozens of parades on 1 July, and over thirty parades on the Twelfth, although in some places banners were kept furled until a private field was reached. The railway system was used to bring Orangemen together for larger parades and the *Belfast News Letter* devoted pages to reports of the events. Platforms were erected at many fields for a religious service to be conducted and some political speeches were made. The Party Processions Act was shown to be inoperative and in 1870, at a parade out of Belfast, there were 249 banners on display. The parade was led by William Johnston wearing both orange and crimson sashes and at the Field the first resolution called for the repeal of the Party Processions Act.

On 27 June 1872 the repeal of the Party Processions Act gained royal assent. Parading on 12 July was now legal again and entering a new era of 'respectability'. County lodges attempted to impose their authority by issuing regulations over the parades, designating 'stewards', dictating when music should and should not be played and particularly warning against drunken behaviour.[3] Johnston's faction went to the Bangor parade but, significantly, most Belfast Orangemen, unable to get sufficient rail transport to the great demonstration in Antrim, resolved to have their own parade to Belvoir Park, whose grounds were offered by Thomas Bateson MP. The parade, reported at 20,000 strong, and in which there were 70 banners, a number of brass bands and the usual drumming parties, assembled at Great Victoria Street in the centre of the city and marched out along the Malone Road. Despite the platform collapsing, resolutions were read proposing loyalty to the Protestant throne, confidence in Her Majesty's present advisers, and a call for the Conservative Party to take care of Orange interests. A further resolution called for closer union amongst Evangelical Protestant Churches in opposing the Church of Rome.[4] This parade marked a shift from the countryside to the city and it was not long before the Belfast Twelfth would become the principal parade in Ulster.

THE TWELFTH AND 'RESPECTABLE' ORANGEISM

Over the remaining years of the century the presence of a significant number of Home Rule candidates at Westminster and significant agitation by the tenant right movement were to dominate the politics of 'the Irish question'. In the rural east of Ulster, politics was split between an old-style landlord Conservatism and liberal tenant farmers, a position not conducive to the development of Orangeism. Indeed, Orangeism varied quite widely in strength and practice, and enforcement of the right to march depended upon particular local political and economic conditions (Wright 1996: 383–431; Jarman and Bryan 1998: 15–40). In Belfast, however, the main division was between Catholic nationalism and developing unionism (Gibbon 1975: 119) and it was now the focus for Orangeism. In particular, almost all politicians in the north, supporting the Union, found it necessary to speak on Twelfth platforms. The Twelfth resonated with its new found importance. New Orange halls were built in many areas, more Orange arches appeared than ever before, the Twelfth effectively became a holiday in Belfast with nearly all of the factories closing, and, most of all, the Twelfth parade became bigger than ever before, attracting more well organised bands, and being led by many of 'the great and the good' in Belfast. Conservative Orangemen could still lose control to the more unbridled lower-class sectarian violence, July was still a period for many civil disturbances, and extra police often had to be transported north, but the ideological position that the Boyne celebrations had now achieved meant that there was never much chance of a Party Processions Act returning. The Twelfth was central to a new unionist hegemony amongst Protestants in Ulster.

The removal of the Party Processions Act from the statute book led to a marked increase in parades on all the commemorative days and significant civil disturbances, particularly in urban areas such as Lurgan, Lisburn and Portadown and parts of Belfast (Wright 1996: 385; Jarman 1997a: 61–79; Jarman and Bryan 1998). Extra troops were regularly drafted in from the south of Ireland as local magistrates attempted to control their district. Between 1872 and the first Home Rule Bill in 1886 the Twelfth developed into a more highly controlled and routinised political event. Smaller, more localised, parades disappeared in favour of larger District and County parades. In 1873 and 1874 magistrates in Belfast stopped parades in the Borough and the main parades had to start at the boundary; only in 1878 did a parade start from the centre of Belfast.[5] It is difficult to estimate the size of the parade; but it took up to an hour and a half to pass a given point with Orangemen marching up to eight abreast.[6] Joining in with the local Orangemen were often visiting Orangemen; particularly from Scotland, but also from England, Canada and occasionally Australia.

The meetings at the Field were developing into more formal political occasions. In the 1870s relatively few senior politicians spoke from the platforms, the majority of speakers being local ministers. Usually, although not always, there was a religious service at the start and the speeches themselves were given by way of proposing or seconding a series of resolutions. Although the number and content of these resolutions varied, in general they covered the need for Protestant unity and the Orange Institution throughout the Empire, loyalty to the throne and constitution, support for civil and religious liberties, support for the Union and opposition to Home Rule. Sometimes the Conservative Party would be thanked for looking after the interests of Empire and there was usually a vote of thanks to the landowner who had given the field in which they met. These speeches, some of which were very long, were reported in full by the *Belfast News Letter* in special editions which covered all the major parades in the north.

The disciplined and respectable nature of the parades was always in tension with the 'rougher' elements. The dominant musical accompaniment during 1870s and 1880s would probably have been the 'drumming parties'. In Portadown, in 1873, there were riots on both 23 July and 5 November over the rights of a drumming party to beat its way through the Catholic Tunnel area of the town, notwithstanding attempts by the local police to stop them. In general the drumming parties were looked down upon and restrained by the 'respectable' classes but Portadown was one of the few areas where the middle classes were prepared to show support for the rough drumming parties even against the forces of law (Wright 1996: 397–404; Jarman and Bryan 1998). By the early 1880s there were around half a dozen brass bands and between ten and twenty flute bands involved in the Belfast parade.[7] The shift away from the slow-moving, unmelodic and 'rough' drumming parties was applauded by reporters looking for a more 'respectable' and dignified event.[8] There were also attempts to control the amount of drinking that took place, with publicised bans on the sale of alcohol at the Field as well as regular reminders during the speeches at the Field that the behaviour of Orangemen on their return parade should not cause offence.[9]

It was not that these 'rougher' elements existed in a political vacuum. Wright (1987, 1996) has convincingly argued that during periods when Catholics were relatively disorganised it was comparatively easy for the state to control the more nakedly sectarian elements in lower-class Orangeism. But conservative landlords and the Belfast bourgeoisie, in utilising the ritual parades, were handling an inherently dangerous political resource which always had the potential of increasing civil disorder and instability within the state. When Catholics became assertive of their rights, such as during Home Rule agitation, then the ability, and maybe the will, of the state to control loyal parades was reduced. Political entrepreneurs could utilise these lines of resistance within the parades creating a 'thoroughly unbourgeois' political climate and setting 'the rule of law to nought' (Wright 1996: 503). The terrible riots in Belfast in 1886, lasting from June to mid-September, were the ultimate expression of this, with over fifty people killed (Wright 1996: 476–509).

In many ways the Orange Institution trod relatively carefully in trying to assert itself in Belfast. Each year the route and destination of the Twelfth parade had to be organised from scratch and, to begin with at least, the Institution attempted to minimise confrontation. It had after all been made aware of its political limitations in controlling brethren. At one level, senior Orangemen had the economic interests of a peaceful city to be aware of, whilst on another they were nurturing their relationship with a more independent-minded Protestant working class, the support of which was needed as a bulwark against Home Rule. As such, senior Orangemen continually attempted to portray the Twelfth parades as respectable and dignified occasions that could not possibly cause offence.

After a further widening of the franchise in 1884 and a redistribution of seats in 1885, the election of that year saw the liberals and Gladstone returned to power only with the support of Parnell's Home Rule Party. Gladstone embraced a policy of Home Rule. The very real threat of Home Rule had a galvanising effect on unionism in Ulster. For the liberals it meant a split between those who would side with the nationalists, and the majority, with a strong base in Belfast, who supported the Union. Working-class Protestants, during a period of economic decline, were reminded by

Protestant ministers, such as the Reverend Hugh Hanna, of the benefits of Protestant control of the labour market (Gibbon 1975: 126–7). There was a fusion of economic interests in the north that provided a powerful argument for Protestant opposition to Home Rule and the Orange Order was the obvious vehicle through which to express this political position. The Twelfth came to express in a much greater way the alliance of popular Orangeism and conservative and liberal interests as unionists. Not only were senior politicians joining the Orange Order, but they began to be seen regularly at the Twelfth. They would often ride in a carriage at the head of the parade and then make a speech from the platform. The resolutions reflected this more overt political relationship. The Conservative Party often received thanks for its support of the Union and in 1886 there was special congratulations for those Liberal Party members who helped defeat Gladstone's first Home Rule Bill. That year all the resolutions for the Belfast parade meeting at Saintfield were party political rather than religious.[10]

The closeness of the relationship between the fight against Home Rule and the Orange Institution meant that the Twelfth started to be used as a symbol of Protestant unity in the cause. Each year the parades were described as bigger and better than the year before. Each year it was reported in the unionist press that more members were joining the Institution and expressing 'undoubted enthusiasm . . . all over Ulster'. In 1900 the *Belfast News Letter* reflected that 'each year seems to witness an increase in the grandeur and magnificence of the turnout'.[11] Complaints were made about those businesses in Belfast that failed to close, so that by 1893 the Twelfth could be described as a complete and general holiday.[12]

Significantly, during the last two decades of the nineteenth century, there was a great increase in the range of people who were depicted on Orange lodge banners and Orange arches (Jarman 1997a: 65–71,1999b: 37–43). In 1884 the *Belfast News Letter* noted with interest that the image of Lord Arthur Hill, a large landowner and senior politician, appeared on a banner. In the years that followed images of local politicians such as Johnston, the Portadown MP Edward Saunderson and Gustav Wolff, partner of the rapidly growing Harland and Wolff shipyard, appear on the banners as well as conservatives from over the water like Lord Salisbury and Lord Randolph Churchill.[13] But the use of images on lodge banners showed an even closer relationship to industrial interests than that implied by the showing of conservative politicians. Many of the lodges existed within particular factories or trades. Factory owners and managers developed a system of patronage through the lodges whereby they would offer financial help in the building of a new lodge or the purchasing of a new banner. By the middle of the 1890s the *Belfast News Letter* was full of reports of banner unfurlings, which were occasions for political rather than religious speeches and took place in the weeks prior to the Twelfth. Sir Daniel Dixon, the first Mayor of Belfast and not an Orangeman, donated money to City of Belfast Loyal Orange Lodge (LOL) 373 and appeared on the banner, but decided it was too partisan to be seen unfurling it. Membership of the Institution was not a prerequisite for a banner portrait. Factory owner Robert Thompson appeared on the banner of Mullhouse Total Abstinence LOL 570, and his wife unfurled the banner. The lodge had formed out of Thompson's Mullhouse factory. However, the painting of living individuals on banners seems to have come to an unfortunate end in 1905 when one of the partners of Harland and Wolff shipyard, William Pirrie, who appeared on a number of banners, showed less than unanimous support for the Union as a part of a briefly revitalised liberal group (Morgan 1991: 52). The Grand Lodge passed a resolution that, with the exception of the monarch, only dead people could appear on a banner.[14]

By the end of the century the Twelfth had become more fully embraced than ever before by both the landed aristocracy and, importantly, capitalist industrial interests in Belfast. Nevertheless, their control remained limited and the 'respectability' of the events was always under threat. The continual complaints at the amount of drinking that took place on the Twelfth suggests that there persisted a strong element of drunken revelry in the day's celebrations.[15] The *Belfast News Letter* continued to treat with approval the demise of the drumming party in favour of better organised bands. By 1896 the number of these more melodic bands had risen to forty or fifty.[16] The continuation of drumming at the Field obviously caused annoyance to those interested in the religious and political agenda of the speakers, but the Field itself also held a few other attractions, such as 'itinerant musicians', 'impromptu dances' and carts selling refreshment.[17] The behaviour of some of the drumming parties and bands during the days and evenings surrounding the Twelfth was also not always met with approval. Above all the Twelfth continued to be the time of year in which rioting was most likely to take place at particular interfaces between Protestant and Catholic communities in working-class areas. Carrick Hill and other areas around north and west Belfast were regular arenas for July confrontations.[18] At the Drumcree church parade in Portadown on 12 July 1885 a Salvation Army band accompanied by 'roughs' followed the Orangemen through the Tunnel area playing party tunes and cursing the Pope, despite an apparent arrangement forbidding 'Orange bands' in that area. The result was a serious riot in which over forty people were arrested.[19] Of all the towns in the north however, Lurgan most often appears to have been the site for civil disturbances on St Patrick's Day and Lady's Day as well as around the Twelfth.

By the end of the nineteenth century, Orangeism and the Twelfth had become an important part of a more unified Protestant identity. They were appropriated and embraced by conservative politics, providing an ideal expression of a new hegemony between an enfranchised Protestant working class in Belfast and the more united unionist interests of the Protestant political elite. Nevertheless, this new hegemonic position was never stable and the first decade of the twentieth century was to reveal class frictions throughout Orangeism and militant Protestantism.

THE INDEPENDENT ORANGE ORDER

The more independent style of Orangeism, mobilised by Johnston, which resented the alliance of capitalist and landlord controlling the Institution, did not completely disappear at the start of the 1870s and indeed made a resurgence in the mid-1880s in Belfast (Patterson 1980: 12–18; Wright 1996: 484–95). But at the start of the twentieth century, when the perceived threat of Home Rule temporarily receded, the forces of independent Orangeism returned. For a short time, from 1903 until 1908, Orangeism, mixed with a certain amount of radical tenant-right and working-class politics, threatened the conservative establishment. Part of this threat was made through an attempt to criticise the Orange Institution as no longer standing for original Orange principles. Disenchanted Orangemen actually dared to take on the Orange establishment on that most public of occasions: the speeches at a Belfast Twelfth. When the Orange Institution disciplined the brethren for taking part some of the brethren formed a breakaway movement, the Independent Orange Order (IOO), and appropriated the Twelfth to their own diverse political interests.

The rise and decline of the IOO has been well documented (Boyle 1962–3; Patterson 1980; Campbell 1991: 348–60; Morgan 1991). The leaders of this Orange revolt, Thomas Sloan, Lindsay Crawford and Alex Boyd, reflected the different strands of opposition to the unionist elite: militant Protestantism, land reform and trade unionism respectively (Morgan 1991: 43–59). Their reasons for rebelling all differed but they had in common their Orangeism. Crawford's newspaper, the *Irish Protestant*, typified the line taken in arguing that 'Orangeism in Belfast has been made a tool to serve the wire-pulling of political organisations' (quoted in Patterson 1980: 45).

The discontent was apparently sparked by the suggestion that Colonel Edward Saunderson MP, Grand Master for Belfast, had voted against a clause in a Bill demanding inspection of convent laundries. However, this was most probably an excuse to express dissatisfaction over more fundamental issues and Saunderson and others were perceived as being ineffectual and too close to the government. In 1901 a party of Orangemen had been involved in disturbances in the small, mainly Catholic town of Rostrevor in County Down. The following year Rostrevor was selected for a Twelfth parade by Armagh Orangemen. In response the United Irish League, set up to agitate on the land question, organised a rally in opposition. The government decided to 'proclaim' (prohibit) both parades, having taken advice, it was suggested by some disgruntled Orangemen, from the Earl of Erne and Lord Arthur Hill, both senior Orangemen.

The Castlereagh meeting at the Belfast Twelfth provided a public forum for these issues. Resolutions were critical of the Rostrevor decision, but when Saunderson apparently defended the decision some Orangemen started heckling.[20] It was later in Saunderson's speech that, after some heckling from the audience, Thomas Sloan was hoisted onto the platform and demanded to ask Saunderson some questions. For someone of such a lowly class position to confront Saunderson in such a way was quite extraordinary. Saunderson denied that he had voted against the clause and Sloan left the platform. Later Sir James Haslett MP was also heckled. All the other Twelfth platform speeches included condemnations of the government over the Rostrevor incident.[21]

On 17 July William Johnston, the sitting MP for South Belfast, died, and Sloan decided to stand against the Conservative Association's candidate, Dunbar-Buller. Both candidates tried to claim to be the rightful heirs of William Johnston. Sloan argued that 'Johnston had beaten the wire pullers and history would repeat itself'.[22] On Sloan's victory the *Belfast News Letter* argued that the 'seat was won for their nominee largely by the Rostrevor proclamation, for it provoked the split in Orangeism which gave the candidate his chance'.[23] A few days prior to the election Saunderson introduced a resolution condemning Sloan's behaviour at the Twelfth platform and, some months later, refusing to provide a written apology, Sloan was suspended from the Institution for two years. Others were also suspended and three lodges had their warrants withdrawn (Boyle 1962–3: 124–5). At a mass meeting on 11 June 1903 resolutions were passed to set up the Independent Orange Order.

Consequently the Twelfth of 1903 had two competing Orange parades in Belfast. The IOO parade had about eight lodges and around five hundred men and the speeches at the Field were full of dissatisfaction with the ruling classes (Boyle 1962–3: 126–7). On the other hand, the 'official' Twelfth was reportedly the most 'imposing' ever seen in Belfast and on the platform at Cloughfern were all those members of the local business elite: Pirrie, Harland, Wolff and Dunbar-Buller.[24] The IOO gained support and the following year had twenty lodges in the Belfast parade. There was also a significant IOO parade in Ballymoney where Lindsay Crawford spoke in support of land reform.[25] The IOO was drawing support from two different interest groups: in Belfast it was working-class discontent and in north Antrim it was the demands for land reform by tenant farmers (Morgan 1991: 59). What they shared was populist fundamental Protestantism as expressed through a supposed return to the first principles of Orangeism (Crawford and Braithwaite 1904: 62). But such diverse interests were always going to make an alliance uneasy.

In 1905 the popularity of the IOO neared its peak. That year also saw the IOO release the *Magheramorne Manifesto*, surely one of the more remarkable documents in Irish history. On 14 July 1905 Crawford, accompanied by Sloan, introduced to a meeting in Magheramorne, County Antrim, attended by around 1,200 brethren, a political manifesto to which the IOO Imperial Grand Lodge had signed up. The document suggested that they should return to the banks of the Boyne to 'hold out the right hand of fellowship to those who, whilst worshipping at other shrines, are yet our countrymen – bone of our bone and flesh of our flesh'. It further argued that 'we consider it is high time that Irish Protestants should consider their position as Irish citizens and their attitude towards their Roman Catholic countrymen' (Boyle 1962–3: 134–5). It also attacked sectarian education and the landlord representatives of both Liberals and Tories. The Magheramorne Manifesto was not quite a call for Home Rule, but it sounded close enough to elicit support from the nationalist press and attacks from unionists (Boyle 1962–3: 135–8; Morgan 1991: 49–50). Despite some defections, the Manifesto was endorsed by lodges of the IOO and by the Banbridge District of the Orange Institution.

Soon afterwards, Sloan, concerned about retaining his seat in South Belfast, started to distance himself from the document. When the election arrived in January 1906 he defeated Arthur Hill with many of the tactics he had used previously, but not by pushing the *Magheramorne Manifesto*. The Liberals had some success in Ulster but importantly they had a massive majority in Westminster. Thus, although they did not have to rely on nationalist MPs to keep them in power, a Liberal administration was bound to raise Home Rule fears for unionists. A need for unity within unionism, a more unionist conservative opposition and a rather too radical-sounding Grand Master also played upon the diverse tendencies within the Independent Orange Order. In 1907 Crawford, influenced by Boyd, helped Larkin during the Belfast labour dispute and his advocating of a form of Home Rule and attacks on landlords and employers became more outspoken. Eventually, in May 1908, the Imperial Grand Lodge of the IOO, chaired by Sloan, suspended Crawford from the Order. In 1910 Crawford emigrated to Canada. That year Sloan, who had lost the support of temperance lodges, failed to win his seat (Boyle 1962–3: 149–52; Morgan 1991: 43–59). By 1909 there appeared to be only 230 members in Belfast and the base of the IOO had shifted up to north Antrim where the Institution has remained relatively strong right through to the present. Although the resolutions continued to appeal to the working man and political independence, it was very much fundamental Protestantism, temperance and the protection of the Sabbath day that were to become the focus of platform resolutions.[26]

THE ULSTER VOLUNTEER FORCE

In 1910 the Liberals were returned to power with the support of Irish nationalist MPs and Home Rule was again on the agenda. In November the Ulster Unionist Council started the process of obtaining weapons to arm the Protestants of Ulster and the Orange Institution started a register of brethren with military skills (Morgan 1991: 125). The two men at the political forefront of unionist action were Dublin-born lawyer, Edward Carson and a senior County Down Orangeman, James Craig (Buckland 1980). During the campaign against the third Home Rule Bill, the Twelfth became part of the general mobilisation that was taking place. The 'long and unbroken ranks of industrious and intelligent men, proudly wearing their regalia' were seen

as 'the household troops of the Unionist army'.[27] Carson called for preparations to be made for the government of a Protestant province of Ulster.[28] On
28 September 1912, 237,368 men signed Ulster's Solemn League and
Covenant pledging themselves 'to stand by one another in defending for
ourselves and our children our cherished position of equal citizenship in the
United Kingdom and in using all means which may be found necessary to
defeat the present conspiracy to set up a Home Rule Parliament in Ireland'
(Bardon 1992: 437). During a demonstration at the Ulster Hall, Colonel R.H.
Wallace, the County Grand Master of Belfast, appeared with a flag which
had apparently been carried at the Battle of the Boyne, although it was later
claimed by the *Irish News* to be a fake.[29] Ulster Day, 28 September, became
part of Orange folk history.

As the Home Rule Bill progressed through Parliament during 1912 and
1913, further preparations were made. In January 1912 the Ulster
Volunteer Force (UVF) was established. Not surprisingly a high proportion
of its recruits were Orangemen and local corps were soon training on the
demesnes of well-known landowners, much as the Volunteers had in the
eighteenth century (Bardon 1992: 440). The drills of the UVF were reflected
in the parades as 'tall, broad shouldered well dressed young men . . . marched
along with the steady step of soldiers'.[30] As such, by 1914 the public are
assured that 'the personnel, showed in convincing manner that the months
devoted to drilling have not been spent in vain'.[31] Carson was involved in
the presentation of UVF colours on the days preceding the Twelfth and there
are reports of UVF flags being carried in the parade.[32] The contradictions
involved in setting up the UVF, and a possible provisional government, to
oppose the forces of the Crown, whilst professing loyalty, was made clear in
Carson's Twelfth speech.

If they try we must resist them with all our might and main (cheers). Somebody may
well say I am talking a good deal of illegality. Well I am prepared for the consequences
(cheers). For my own part I know nothing about legality and illegality (laughter). I
mean as regards myself. All I think of is my Covenant (cheers). My Covenant to me is
the text and foundation of what is illegality and what is legality . . .[33]

Not for the first nor last time the Twelfth involved professing loyalty to the
Crown whilst acting to mobilise to opposition the forces and representatives
of the Crown.

In 1914 Britain went to war, and with this new situation the economic,
political and symbolic structures within which loyalist commemorations
took place were to change. At the outbreak of the war the Home Rule Bill
was put aside, despite having gained royal assent. Both the UVF and John
Redmond's Irish Volunteers were pledged for the cause. The majority of the
UVF went to become a large part of the 36th (Ulster) Division, the 16th (Irish)
Division being largely drawn from the Volunteers. On 1 July 1916 it was the
36th (Ulster) Division that spearheaded the attack at the Battle of the Somme.
Within two days 5,500 men were killed or wounded (Bardon 1992: 455),

and back in Belfast press reports of the glorious push were soon joined by the lists of the casualties. Orangeism had a blood sacrifice and renewed military and political legitimacy.

The speeches from the platform during the Belfast Twelfth in 1917 suggest the importance the Battle of the Somme was to come to play in the Orange Institution's commemorations. Colonel Wallace spoke of the new 'glorious first of July' since it coincidentally took place on the same date as the Battle of the Boyne using the old calendar. He recounted that men had 'sashes over their shoulders' and drove the enemy before them 'on the banks of the Somme, as their fathers had done 226 years before on the banks of the Boyne'.[34] The previous Sunday, 1 July, special services, organised by the Orange Institution, had taken place at churches all over the north of Ireland. The following year Carson made a thirty-five-minute speech at the Twelfth, connecting the sacrifice of the 36th (Ulster) Division with the unionist cause. Many Orangemen wore the decorations they had received during the war and at the Twelfth in 1919 a new lodge – Ulster Division Memorial LOL 977 – paraded for the first time and already there were banners depicting the recently fought battles (Jarman 1997a: 71–2, 1999b: 44–7).[35]

THE RIGHT TO MARCH

Disturbances at parades remained commonplace. In 1906 Carrick Hill saw rioting and in 1909 there was serious civil disorder on the Grosvenor Road which was followed by three days of riots on the Falls Road and disturbances in Portadown. This situation may well have arisen because of the increasing strength of the Ancient Order of Hibernians (AOH), which had 60,000 members by 1909 (Bardon 1992: 424). The AOH can be traced back to the Ribbonmen in the 1830s but grew in the first decade of the twentieth century and appears very much as a Catholic version of the Orange Order, organising parades, wearing green sashes and carrying banners. In the early 1900s it became more forthright in organising demonstrations and therefore contesting the control of public space. In 1905 swarms of police protected Lady's Day AOH demonstrations in Kilrea and Lurgan. In 1908 they paraded in Pomeroy three days after the Orange Order had paraded through the town, and were also forced to abandon a parade in Poyntzpass.[36] In 1909 over 600 police in Portadown were unable to prevent trouble as the AOH paraded to the railway station carrying a green flag and there were riots on the parade's return which spread to Lurgan. The official police report blamed 'an Orange crowd'.[37] On 29 June 1912 at Castledawson in County Londonderry, where an AOH parade attacked a parade of Presbyterian school children. Catholic school children were attacked in Lisburn the day after, but Castledawson caught the loyalist imagination: 'Remember Castledawson' became the watchword of the next few years. More significantly there was a wave of expulsions of Catholic workers at the Belfast docks and factories, and major disturbances in Belfast. There were other parading clashes in July and August involving the Orange Order and the AOH (Patterson 1980: 89; Morgan 1991: 128–30; Bardon 1992: 436).[38] The following year the AOH organised a parade in Garvagh, County Derry, the first Catholic parade in the town since disturbances at a Ribbon parade in 1813. Although the chairman of a meeting of Orangemen in Coleraine recommended that no opposition should be put up, members decided to organise a parade for the same day. In the end the government decided to 'proclaim' both parades.[39]

After the war disturbances at parades intensified. Easter 1916 had seen a group of Irish republicans stage a failed uprising, but the execution of its leaders gave the Irish republicanism movement unprecedented support. By 1918 Sinn Féin were winning by-elections in the south and the debate over Ireland was moving back to the top of the political agenda. On 3 July, in an attempt to maintain public order, the government introduced an order proclaiming all 'assemblies or processions in public places in the whole of Ireland', although this appeared not to include the Boyne parades.[40] But the politics of the north of Ireland was again expressed through the 'right to march'. The Apprentice Boys took part in the Relief of Derry parade and there were five Royal Black Institution parades on 12 August. The AOH insisted that their Lady Day celebrations should be allowed to take place. They attempted processions in Belfast, Garvagh and Omagh but all were obstructed in some way by the police. Members of Sinn Féin were arrested in Dublin and in Irvinestown, County Fermanagh, when they took part in a meeting and there were disturbances in Strabane.[41]

In January 1919 the Sinn Féin members set up a Parliament of Ireland, the Dáil Eirean, and shortly afterwards military actions took place under the name of the Irish Republican Army (IRA). Unionist MPs were prepared to settle for a six-county state within the province of Ulster. Of more immediate concern, however, was the impending armed conflict with republicans. Between April and June 1920, Derry had seen serious rioting and gun battles between the UVF and IRA, with the army intervening in support of the UVF (Bardon 1992: 468–9). All parades within 5 miles of Derry were proclaimed. Extra military forces were brought in for the Twelfth to be held in Belfast. There were disturbances in Sandy Row in late June and additional precautions were taken by the police. The parade appears to have passed off without incident as the Orangemen walked at a brisk pace 'proving themselves to be endowed with a physical stamina which makes them worthy representatives of the sturdy British race'.[42] There was much excitement as Carson spoke from one of two platforms, threatening to reorganise the UVF to defend 'the Province', although he received criticism in the British press for this. When workers returned after the July holiday, Carson's threat seemed to be brought into effect as Catholics were expelled from many of the major docks and factories (Bardon 1992: 472–4). By the end of August the army was operating a curfew in Belfast.

RESPECTABILITY

It is always difficult to tell the exact strength of the Orange Institution at a particular time. It is estimated that between 1908 and 1913 the numbers of Orangemen in Belfast more than doubled from 8,834 to 18,800 (Bew *et al.* 1995: 24). There was apparently an 'Orange revival' in 1907 and 1908 with a return to the 'old fervour'. There was a clear and continuing attempt by senior Orangemen to marginalise the less reputable elements of the parades. Drumming parties were continually derided and seem to play their part more on the days leading up to the Twelfth, particularly at the Eleventh Night bonfire, rather than on the Twelfth itself. Many of the bands, brass, flute and pipe, were connected to, and funded by, local factories, Orange lodges and Conservative Associations.[43] Also in the parade were plenty of dignitaries in open carriages.[44] In other words, the parades would bring all classes together, as long as they were not too rough, and the upper class did not have to walk. Indeed, the size and decorum of the Twelfth was used as an index of the vitality of Ulster Protestantism.

In recent years strong measures have been taken to expunge from the ranks what might be described as 'undesirables' – members who bring disgrace on their colours – and each year the Order is becoming stronger in a better class of member. Indeed one of the features of yesterday's procession was the manly upset bearing of the men, their respectable appearance, and their evident determination to show by their example that they are true Orangemen in deed as well as in name. . . . Several of the lodges were largely composed of young men – tall, broad shouldered, well dressed – and as they marched along with the steady step of soldiers they were heartily cheered at different points.[45]

This relationship between the 'respectability' and 'stirling manhood and character' of the men taking part in the Twelfth was a strong feature of the way the *Belfast News Letter* covered the event through this period. Belfast, 'Ireland's greatest city', saw thousands, 'bone and sinew, the brain and muscle', 'unite to commemorate . . . the Boyne'. The procession demonstrates strength, and 'is a proclamation of power and influence'.[46]

The middle of the nineteenth century saw Orangeism reflect many of the processes of modernisation that Ulster itself was going through. There was a shift of power from rural proto-industrial areas to Belfast, from country landowners to industrial entrepreneurs, from tenant farmer to labour aristocracy. Industrial Ulster became dependent upon British imperialism (Gibbon 1975: 103). The fifty years from 1870 to 1920 saw the Orange Institution develop from a relatively localised, rural and politically marginal organisation to one that dominated the political and economic structures of the urbanising north of Ireland. It proved to be an institution capable of supporting a system of labour patronage. More importantly it was utilised by both the land- and industry-owning classes to create an identity around which unionism could develop in opposition to Home Rule. If the factory owners patronised the Institution with money for lodges and banners, unionist politicians used the Twelfth to try to express a cross-class, Protestant and unionist identity. There was an ongoing attempt to make the event 'respectable'. The discipline and behaviour of the ranks of men marching with their Orange sashes was contrasted with 'the rebels' who would lay siege to Orange parades. Those elements of the parades which did not conform to this image, such as the drumming parties, were marginalised. The consumption of alcohol was either disapproved of or ignored. After William Johnston revealed the political potency of the Twelfth of July, the ruling class set about attempting to control the event.

The control however, was constantly being undermined by class divisions. The interest of tenants and landowners, workers and employers, as expressed through their unity as Protestants, were always diverse. Not only did the Twelfth have a carnivalesque and sectarian aspect that could always embarrass those seeking political control, but Orangeism itself could be utilised for limited class confrontation and resistance to the Orange elite. As such, the actions of William Johnston, and later Thomas Sloan and Lindsay Crawford, served to remind the ruling elite of the fragility of Orange unity. If the Protestant workforce felt that its interests were not being looked after, the July celebrations could also be used to make that dissatisfaction clear.

As a resource for political power the parades had their limitations. Use of the parades was limited by the practical employment parades were put to in the displaying of dominance by one community over another – William Johnston's attempt at 'equality of parading' reached those limits. Use of the parades was limited by the internal ideological structure of Orangeism – Lindsay Crawford took it to those limits. They were limited by the relationship of the different class interests within Orangeism – Independent Orangeism reminded the Grand Lodge of those limits. Political utilisation of the parades was also limited by the unpalatability of Orangeism to English liberals and some conservatives. The consequence of reaching those limits was that parades could be prohibited. The Orange Institution was used by the state and by different upper-class interests when it served their purposes. When it did not serve those purposes, the parades continued to be utilised by the lower classes in particular areas.

Organisations which have this kind of significance, however manipulable they may be, or appear to be, do not just disappear or fade away when the calculations of their manipulators dictate that they are expendable. (Wright 1996: 151)

After 1920, with formation of Northern Ireland, new relationships of control were formed and the limitations changed. The Twelfth could now become a celebration of the new quasi-state.

5   RITUALS OF STATE

When a political group gains power its symbols join the symbolic structure of the state. In contemporary nation states there usually exists a standard set of national symbols (emblem, flag, national anthem) which are officially recognised, unambiguously defined and protected by law. (Mach 1993: 106)

From 1921 to 1972, the period during which Northern Ireland had a local Parliament, the Orange Institution was in a position of great political power. The Orange Institution had 122 of 760 seats on the Ulster Unionist Council – the ruling body of the Ulster Unionist Party (UUP) – and the majority of the other seats would have been taken by members of the Order. Of the 149 unionists elected to the Northern Ireland House of Commons between 1921 and 1969, 95 did not make the cabinet, of whom 87 were Orangemen. All Northern Ireland's Prime Ministers were Orangemen and only three members of the cabinet during that time were not in the Orange Order although three others resigned or were expelled after achieving their post. During much of this period Orange halls were used as meeting places for unionist constituency associations (Harbinson 1973: 90–3). Although it is not possible to produce statistical evidence, it is also clear that many civil servants and policemen were in the Orange Order (Weitzer 1995: 34). Under these conditions the Twelfth parades became rituals of state.

The Twelfth of July demonstrations which Ulster stages every year form in a general way a grand inquest at which political and other matters affecting the whole community come under review.[1]

Senior politicians spoke on many of the platforms and what they had to say was effectively government policy. The speeches made at the Twelfth by James Craig or Basil Brooke, Northern Ireland's first and third Prime Ministers, reviewed the previous year in government and set out an agenda for the future. In doing so they were drawing on the legitimacy of the ritual occasion. They were demanding support and loyalty by staking a claim to be conforming with the principles of Orangeism. On the majority of these occasions the resolutions prepared by the Orange Institution congratulated the government and the Prime Minster on their service to Northern Ireland. Since those in government were not so different from those in the Grand Lodge, such mutual political reinforcement was not surprising. In this sense it is difficult to argue with Farrell's general description of Northern Ireland during the period as 'the Orange State' (Farrell 1980).

In contrast to the dominance of Orange parades, emergency powers under the Civil Authorities (Special Powers) Act 1922 and a Protestant-dominated police force meant that public displays and demonstrations by constitutional Irish nationalism, such as those by the Hibernians, were restricted, and republican events, particularly the Easter commemorations, were routinely banned. Whilst this situation eased somewhat in the 1950s, the unionist government still saw it as necessary to introduce legislation in 1951 to control parades through the Public Order Act (NI). The legislation required that the police be given 48 hours notification of a parade unless the procession was 'customarily held along a particular route'. In other words, 'traditional' Orange parades were exempt whereas nationalist, and particularly republican events, which had been restricted or used irregular venues, had to give notification (Bryson and McCartney 1994; Hadden and Donnelly 1997: 19–21). As such, the development of nationalist and Catholic and unionist and Protestant parading 'traditions' was closely related to their power within the northern state (Jarman and Bryan 1998: 41–58).

THE TWELFTH IN THE NEW NORTHERN STATE

Many reasons can be put forward for the particular form which the state of Northern Ireland took. Any vague ideas concerned with tolerance and the protection of minority views, that the new Prime Minister, James Craig, may have had do not seem to have been sustained for long (Bew *et al.* 1995: 12). Whether it was fear of a Dublin administration, or British policy on Ireland, or the attitude of northern Catholics, or the internal dynamics of Ulster unionism, the government of Northern Ireland made little effort to tackle the alienation felt by the Catholic minority. Government policy continued with a sectarian populist strategy so often appealed to by unionists over the previous fifty years. The B-Specials, a part-time armed police force drawn from the UVF and Orange Order, was never likely to win support in the Catholic community. By abolishing proportional representation and re-drawing local electoral boundaries, unionists even controlled councils with a majority Catholic population. Catholics were also effectively excluded from any important roles within the civil service. Although it was not until 1934 that Craig notoriously spoke of a 'Protestant Parliament for a Protestant people' such a position was broadly implicit from 1921 (Farrell 1980: 81–5; Buckland 1981: 24–5; Bardon 1992: 474–500; Bew *et al.* 1995: 21–54).

The Twelfth soon became a ritualised focus for the unionist government. The speeches from the Twelfth platform became a 'state of the nation' occasion with the unionist politicians being thanked in the resolutions for their work. Even by 1923 there was a sense of security returning to the events, the *Belfast News Letter* claiming that there was a reduction in 'party tunes' compared to the past. Bew *et al.* have suggested that there were two unionist blocks, one under Craig was 'populist' in that it was generally keen on state intervention and, in particular, encouraging the close relationship of government with the Protestant working classes. The anti-populist group were keener on maintaining stricter control of finance and were uneasy with the developing sectarian nature of the Northern Ireland civil service. The role of the Orange Institution, as part of the populist armoury, was to ensure the non-employment of Catholics in public services (Buckland 1981: 63; Bew *et al.* 1995: 55–63). The economic situation, however, particularly within industry, was worsening and unemployment headed upwards. As a result, with unionism becoming more secure, class interests became more distinctive. Under these conditions there was a shift in the politics of the Twelfth. For a short time the new enemy was not republicanism, but Socialism and Bolshevism. The resolutions in 1924 contained one which criticised the 'insidious attacks through socialist propaganda' and speeches attacked the 'followers of Marx'.[2] In 1925 three candidates of the Labour Party, Northern Ireland, were elected in Belfast and this, along with the return of some sitting independent unionists, reduced the number of UUP MPs from forty to thirty-two. Also that year Dawson Bates, the Home Secretary, decided to ban a mass march through Belfast being organised by the Unemployed Workers' Committee, the Belfast Trades Council and the Labour Party (Farrell 1980: 122–3). By 1926 and 1927 anti-socialist rhetoric dominated the speeches with much talk of 'Russian hirelings', 'Self-advertising Socialists', 'Bolshevists', and 'Communists'. At the same time Craig was prepared to talk about the Free State as the 'friendly neighbours'.[3]

The Twelfth parades however remained events at which diverse political interests – albeit unionist interests – could express themselves. The interests of senior Orangemen were usually, but not always, the same as those of the government, whilst the interests of particular sections of the Orange Order could differ on specific issues. For instance, policies and legislation on education during the 1920s and 1930s were regularly the cause for contention which could reveal itself in speeches critical of the government from platform speakers at the Twelfth or in the form of heckling from the brethren. In 1931, government suggestions that the Protestant clergy should not have control of primary teacher training at Stranmillis College produced a clear split amongst platform speakers. Where government ministers were in attendance criticism of the government was reasonably polite and deferential, but in rural areas such as Coagh, Dunloy and the Clougher Valley, where no government ministers were present, speakers were outspoken. One Orangeman demanded 'leaders who were not ashamed to march with the ordinary rank and file', a criticism of the Prime Minister who had not been seen at some recent Twelfths.[4]

The relationship between the governing elite and sections of rank and file was not always harmonious and the parades could provide a vehicle for limited resistance in spite of the pressures for deference that existed. In 1937 there were a number of critical speeches made at Cloughmills, Dungannon and Glenarm, about the unionist government in general, whereas again at platforms where government ministers were present there were speeches strongly in defence of the administration's policies. The reaction to the critical speeches indicates the way the government could use a call to unity to stifle other voices. The *Belfast News Letter* editorial on the following day is typical.

Those who profess to be staunch unionists and yet deliver speeches which tend to discredit the government might well ponder the reason for the enthusiastic reception of their criticisms by political enemies.

Anything therefore which is calculated to cast discredit on the Ulster government and can be regarded as 'a significant portent of its downfall' is the utmost value for Republican Party purposes, as it revives the party's hope that it may yet secure control of the Province and make it part of a 'Gaelic and Catholic State' owing no allegiance to the crown.[5]

Tensions derived from class interests, from the diversity of Protestantism and from different understandings of Orangeism itself were always capable of revealing themselves. The stock answer for the political elite was always that divisions or any perceived lack of support for the government was effectively support for Irish nationalism. Control of the Twelfth as an event remained difficult even though the UUP, and through it senior Orangemen, had achieved an unprecedented position of power. The populist nature of the Twelfth parades meant that, at least to a certain extent, unionist politicians could appear to be held to account for their actions when they made appearances. As such, discourses of 'respectability', ritual pressures of deference and calls for unity were clearly key strategies for senior political figures remaining in the ascendancy.

In 1926 the Twelfth was made a Public and Bank Holiday in Northern Ireland, giving it the sort of official state recognition that it had not enjoyed since the demise of the Dublin commemorations over a hundred years earlier. The following year the Grand Lodge of Belfast purchased a field at Finaghy, in the south of the city, which meant that the Institution's largest parade began to develop a set annual route. Although the County lodge specifically pointed out that it would go to other parts of the city, difficulties in obtaining alternative venues meant that only in 1928 and 1934 did the main parade take a route anywhere but south out of the city, along the Lisburn Road. The number of lodges in Belfast had also grown from 210 in 1912 to 243 in 1922 and 268 in 1927. Whilst this is not necessarily an indicator of a growth in membership it suggests at least a sustained popularity within the city.

The July commemorations show some changes during the later part of the 1920s and into the 1930s. Forms of street decoration, such as Orange arches and wall murals, flourished (Jarman 1997a: 72–4) and there seems to have been an increase in the number of bonfires on the Eleventh Night when bands paraded to the bonfire and children danced around singing 'patriotic songs'. There were even gramophone records played. Drumming parties were by now rare during the Twelfth parade itself and also less common on the preceding nights, although they were still found on the Shankill and complaints in the press about their behaviour continued. There was also a suggestion that there were fewer party tunes at the Twelfth, with the introduction of some modern tunes and military marches. There were a wide variety of bands – brass, flute, pipe, concertina, bugle and accordion – which, according to reports, showed a definite improvement in quality.[6]

Orangemen attended Somme commemorative services that took place on a Sunday near 1 July, with some lodges parading to the service. There were some local parades for the unfurling of new banners or to take a banner to the house of a new lodge Master. Orangemen also marched from lodge halls to church services on the Sunday before the Twelfth. On the Twelfth, the Orangemen in Belfast paraded four abreast, generally dressed in a suit, although far from all wore a dark suit and bowler hat. Many wore brown, grey or tweed suits, with a soft felt hat, trilby or a cap. Sometimes the banner-bearers would break into a sort of 'dancing walk', setting the banner swaying 'gaily from side to side'.[7] Apart from the Union Jack, there were also a number of Canadian and American flags carried in recognition of Orangeism over the Atlantic.

During the 1920s and 1930s there was rarely any question over whether an Orange parade should take place. Indeed, in 1930 there was a Twelfth parade in Rostrevor, the first since 1903. The last Saturday in August was added to the Twelfth and 13 July, and 12 August as an important parading occasion. The Royal Black Preceptories, or Black Institution, had grown in respectability and importance from the middle of the nineteenth century. It developed into a more exclusive organisation than the Orange, and concentrated on the religious aspect of Orangeism. The banners tended to depict stories from the Old Testament rather than the political events and figures more common on Orange banners (Buckley 1985; Jarman 1997a: 184–7). Specific 'Black' parades became more common in the early 1900s. The parade and Sham Fight at Scarva on 13 July appears to have become an event specifically for the Blackmen of Down, Armagh and Belfast in the first quarter of the twentieth century. There were also Black parades in the middle of August to mark the Relief of Derry. The 'Black' 'Last Saturday' in August may have developed first in Scotland and then become more common in Northern Ireland after the Great War (Jarman 1997a: 73). By the 1920s there were parades at six venues reflecting the geography of Northern Ireland, and senior politicians made important and well reported speeches just as they would for the Twelfth. The Junior Orange Lodges were formed from the First World War onwards, holding parades and coming under the control of the Grand Lodge in 1925 (Grand Orange Lodge of Ireland 1995: 43). During the 1930s the Apprentice Boys of Derry started a new parade that took place on Easter Monday to counter the republican Easter parades that had developed (Apprentice Boys of Derry 1989).

Any sense in which the parades were proving uncontentious in the late 1920s seems to have dissipated in 1931 and 1932 as a number of factors raised the tensions between north and south. The Twelfth of 1931 had a resolution warning of 'the insidious propaganda of the Roman Catholic Church' and this was followed by conflict over Orange and Black parades in the south. Orangeism in the Free State had not been strong for many years but there were Orange lodges in counties such as Donegal, Monaghan and Cavan. As the new Irish state began to settle, there were Orange parades. In Clones, County Monaghan, forty lodges paraded in 1923 with the County Grand Master claiming, perhaps bitterly, that they owed nothing to the British and that as Orangemen in the Free State they would be good citizens and good neighbours.[8] There were parades in Monaghan and Cavan up until 1931. That year the IRA stopped a parade in Newtowngore, County Leitrim, and there was trouble at parades in County Monaghan (Bardon 1992: 535–6). In Cootehill, County Cavan, the local IRA issued a proclamation to stop a Black parade in the town commemorating the Relief of Derry, describing the organisers as the 'Imperialist agents of Great Britain'.[9] Reaction in Northern Ireland was predictable with serious disturbances taking place in Armagh and Lisburn. In Portadown the B-Specials were mobilised after two buses full of Hibernian members were attacked on their way to and from a demonstration in Armagh. Disturbances continued over the next few days with the *Belfast News Letter* blaming republicans and the Hibernians for provocatively parading through a loyalist area in Armagh, and pointing to the superior way the police had dealt with these incidents compared to the actions of liberal administrations prior to the formation of the northern state.[10] In following years Orangemen from the south tended to come north to attend demonstrations.

Tension was further raised when the Fianna Fáil Party, led by de Valera, came to power in the Free State in 1932. He immediately set about removing the oath of fidelity to the Crown and refused to make the payment to Britain which had been agreed under the Treaty. In return Britain put duties on Irish imports, thus instituting an economic war (Bardon 1992: 436). Further, the political battle between parties in the south was often conducted by trying to gain legitimacy from the Roman Catholic Church. It was not unusual for policies to be defended with reference to papal encyclicals (Lee 1989: 157–74). Such politics reinforced the fears of northern Protestants and played into the hands of unionist politicians.

On St Patrick's Day 1932 two people were injured when an Hibernian parade in South Derry was fired on (Farrell 1980: 136). From 22 to 26 June the Roman Catholic Church held an International Eucharist Congress in Dublin. Catholic areas in Northern Ireland prepared by decorating the streets and many people travelled down to the event. On their return, however, many of the special trains and buses were attacked. Incidents took place in Banbridge, Kilkeel, Larne, Lisburn, Loughbrickland, Lurgan and Portadown (Farrell 1980: 136–7; Bardon 1992: 537–9). A few days later the North

Belfast Accordion Band was attacked on the Crumlin Road during a Somme commemoration and a riot ensued (BNL 2 July 1932). Unusually, one parade to an Orange church service, through the predominantly Catholic town of Coalisland in County Tyrone, was re-routed, as the local police chief thought they were not taking their usual route. An angry local lodge Master was quick to point out the relationship between the Orange Institution and the government.

The government has been placed in power with the assistance of Orange brethren, and if that government could not afford them reasonable protection the sooner a change was made the better. (Thomas Nevin, Master of Coalisland LOL 93)[11]

On the Twelfth they were allowed to march right through Coalisland.

Orange arches appeared with 'Ulster will not submit to De Valera' written on them and the *Belfast News Letter* warned that dignitaries 'of the Roman Catholic church have gone out of their way to attack Protestantism'.[12] At most of the demonstrations there was criticism of the southern state and particularly of de Valera's attempt to get rid of the oath of allegiance. At Poyntzpass, Prime Minister Craig expressed a theme that was to be much repeated in later years: 'Ours is a Protestant Government, and I am an Orangeman'.[13] There were riots in west Belfast after a party of men had apparently attempted to bring down an Orange Arch and Catholic pubs in Dungannon were attacked (Farrell 1980: 136).[14]

Despite these incidents there was considerable working-class cooperation in Belfast in demanding greater measures to relieve the poverty that so many people were suffering. There may have been few questions over Orange parades, but the same could not be said for other forms of public demonstration. During October 1932 working-class agitation was so great that the police banned a demonstration that was to have starting points in all parts of Belfast. When the ban was enforced, rioting broke out in parts of the city, particularly on the Falls and Shankill. As the rioting continued over a number of days the government attempted to blame Catholics for their disloyalty and to point the finger at the IRA (Farrell 1980: 127–30; Bardon 1992: 527–9). As so often in the past, working-class solidarity was quickly broken. The year of 1932, that had started with the election of de Valera in the Free State, ended, rather aptly, with the opening of a splendid new Parliament building at Stormont to the east of the city (Officer 1996). In between times unionist control of public space was obvious. Whilst Catholics had been attacked in June and workers batoned in October, the Twelfth allowed the full expression of a Protestant state.

'A PROTESTANT STATE FOR A PROTESTANT PEOPLE'

I can assure you that the policy of the future will be the policy of the past, and that will be no surrender to the disintegrating forces of this country. I am an Orangeman to the heart and always an Orangeman . . . (James Craig, the Twelfth 1933)[15]

The period leading up to the Second World War saw little within unionism by way of a challenge to the relationship between the Orange Institution and the administration. Twelfth demonstrations contained consistent calls for unity. De Valera's position in the Free State was strengthening. His introduction of a new constitution in 1937, including articles laying claim to the six counties of Northern Ireland and enshrining the Roman Catholic Church as having a 'special position' within the state, provided legitimacy for the northern government in its constructed Protestant state. Craig saw it as quite suitable that the southern government should govern for Catholics and that the northern government should recognise 'Protestant ideas and Protestant desires' (Bardon 1992: 543). Indeed unionist politicians had been quite blatant about the nature of the state of Northern Ireland. Future Prime Minister, Sir Basil Brooke, at a platform speech at the Twelfth in Newtown-butler, Fermanagh, in 1933, argued that since Roman Catholics were out 'to destroy the power and constitution of Ulster' then loyalists should only 'employ Protestant lads and lassies'. Craig was quick in support of his Cabinet Minister's views (Bardon 1992: 538).

During the marching season in 1935 sectarian bitterness culminated in the worst rioting in Belfast since the 1920–2 period. Parades by Orangemen and Protestant bands were heavily implicated and for four days Dawson Bates, the Home Affairs minister, actually banned all parades. Sectarian attacks had become more frequent in Belfast since the early 1930s, the Ulster Protestant League had been particularly active in promoting militant Protestant issues since 1931, and, as suggested above, senior politicians attempted to sustain unity by scapegoating Catholics as the real enemy. It appears that the celebration of George V's Jubilee increased tensions still further. Dock ward, a small area of tightly packed terrace houses just north of the city centre, felt the tension most keenly. The area contained both Protestants and Catholics though they were divided locally at street level. Attacks on houses and workers took place in May and, after a shooting on 17 June, Bates introduced the parade ban. His decision was all the more surprising as Dawson Bates was known as one of the more 'Orange' of unionist politicians. It has been suggested that the decision was a 'knee-jerk' reaction under pressure from Sir Charles Wickham, the Inspector General of the RUC (Hepburn 1990: 79). Belfast Grand Master Sir Joseph Davison warned that they were going to have their demonstration 'no matter what restrictions were placed upon us'.[16] In fact, it only took four days before Dawson Bates ended the ban and even during the ban, on 23 June, an Orange parade took place unimpeded by the police (Hepburn 1990: 79).

The returning Twelfth parade ended in clashes along York Street, blame for which was disputed. By the end of the night two Protestants and two Catholics had been shot dead. The following days, from 13 to 21 July, saw serious rioting in Belfast, particularly in the Dock area, with many Catholics being burned out of their homes. People in 430 Catholic and 64 Protestant houses had been forcibly evicted. In some areas these pogroms were clearly systematic. Seven Protestants and three Catholics were dead and 55 Catholics and 28 Protestants seriously injured. Even after a return to work on 22 July, some Catholics were expelled from their work places (Hepburn 1990: 83). Such trouble was not confined to Belfast, with similar disturbances also taking place in Coleraine, Lisburn and Portadown, and there were also some attacks on Protestants in Limerick.[17]

Explanations for these particular disturbances can range from 'land hunger' (the need for housing), to specific local politics, poor policing and sectarian tensions. What is indisputable is that, yet again, the July parades provided the focus. As with major riots in the previous century, senior Orangemen distanced themselves from events over which they clearly had little direct control. The Grand Lodge of Belfast issued a statement blaming nationalists for boycotting the Silver Jubilee celebrations thus raising tensions in the city.[18] Nevertheless, a certain amount of organisation went into the evictions and certainly in the Donegall Road area, in south Belfast, a local 'prominent Orangeman' was involved (Hepburn 1990: 91). In Britain a report by the National Council for Civil Liberties looking into the Special Powers Act expressed damning views on the actions of the Stormont government. Efforts by nationalists to get Westminster to intervene proved fruitless (Farrell 1980: 140–1; Hepburn 1990: 90–6).

Events in the lower Dock area seemed to have been aggravated by the activities of a Glasgow 'Billy Boys' band who also brought a considerable number of strangers into the area (Hepburn 1990: 82). Even before the Twelfth, fourteen members of the Beresford Accordion band and fifteen members of St Mary's Accordion band had appeared in court on charges of a breach of the peace following disturbances after a Somme Anniversary parade. A nationalist politician particularly singled out the bands and their followers parading in the city as being highly provocative.[19] A letter to the *Belfast News Letter* the following year also gave that impression.

In contrast to the quiet and dignified marching of the Orange lodges we had various juvenile bands with female followers who waved party emblems and sang and shouted provocative expressions towards Roman Catholics. It is scandalous that these irresponsibilities should be allowed to parade on the streets at all. . . . I could not help wondering what a visitor from the wilder portions of New Guinea would think of 'white superiority' if he could be transplanted to such a scene. (T.H. Mayes, Ulster Reform Club)[20]

Indeed, during this period accordion bands, rather than drumming parties, seem to have been the dominant form of musical expression, considerably outnumbering brass and flute bands on the Twelfth. A lot of small local bands formed with little in the way of uniforms except that they might have all worn the same type of cap.[21] In Belfast they appear to fulfil the role in working-class areas that the drumming parties might have played thirty years earlier, and blood and thunder bands filled forty years later.

The Twelfth of 1936 was heavily policed with armoured cars, and the B-Specials were mobilised. The *Belfast News Letter* suggested that the Orangemen would be as disciplined as always, but warned loyalists who were not Orangemen to leave it to the police to deal with attacks upon processions.[22] In fact, the Twelfth for this year, and the next three years, was relatively free of incident. By 1938 and 1939 the renewed threat from the IRA and the prospect of war with Germany started to dominate the speeches. As ever, the unionist press claimed record numbers.

The outstanding feature of the procession yesterday was the excellent 'marching discipline' that prevailed. A quicker pace than usual was maintained and some lodges displayed uniformity of dress – dark clothes, bowler hats, white gloves, black boots or shoes – which gave them quite a soldierly appearance.

There were many fine bands – turned out like guardsmen – and the musical standard was excellent.[23]

During the Second World War, as during the Great War, senior Orangemen decided that the war effort was more important than customary celebrations. With the odd exception, Twelfth commemorations were abandoned from 1940 through to 1944. There were church services in commemoration of the Somme and the Boyne, but the July period, particularly in 1940 and 1941, passed by almost unremarked upon in the press.

THE GOLDEN ERA?

The post-war period is particularly interesting because it comprised the formative years of many of those senior within Orangeism during 'the Troubles' (from 1969 onwards). It is well within living memory and thus forms a backdrop to many of the arguments over the 'tradition' of parading that came to prominence in the late 1960s, mid-1980s and again in the mid-1990s. The post-war Twelfth is remembered as a relaxed, good-humoured time when politics was of secondary importance during what was perceived as a religious event. It is recalled, by way of anecdotes: that Protestants and Catholics, the Orange Order and the Hibernians, shared instruments and banner poles in country areas; that whole communities shared pride in, and collected money for, the local bands; and that Roman Catholics went to watch the pageantry of the Twelfth parade. However, whilst Catholics will confirm some of these stories, and an analysis of the period confirms it to be untroubled compared with the previous 150 years, parades still provided a focus for local politics and could still prove divisive. In 1951 Stormont introduced a Public Order Act that effectively allowed for the suppression of nationalist parades, normalising what had been the position under the Special Powers Act (Jarman and Bryan 1998: 41–58). That was followed, in 1954, by the Flags and Emblems Act which effectively protected the Union flag wherever it flew in Northern Ireland and allowed for the removal of the

Irish Tricolour if the RUC felt good public order required such action (Bryson
and McCartney 1994: 144–8).

The idea that the period from 1945 to the mid-1960s was a golden era for
Orangeism also resides in memories Orangemen have of the happy and
unfettered nature of the parades themselves. The hegemonic dominance of
'respectable' elite or middle-class Orangeism, the development of which I
have traced above, may well have reached its zenith but it was never totally
dominant. It relied upon the ability of the unionist elite to sustain its relationship with the Protestant working class. Resistance still appeared in the
form of more 'rowdy' and 'informal' elements within the parade and
opposition from nationalists. Limits imposed on how Orangemen and
bandsmen should behave were questioned and, just occasionally, parades
that even the state found difficult to legitimise took place in nationalist areas.

Initially the Twelfth in Belfast after the war reflected the lack of material
and finances. Bands were less numerous, lodges were depleted, transport to
the parades restricted, collarettes – rather than sashes (the older style sash
was larger and worn over one shoulder running down to the hip and up the
Orangeman's back) – were becoming even more common, there were fewer
arches, smaller bonfires, and there were no lambeg drums. Nevertheless,
even in 1946 the *Belfast News Letter* was yet again claiming there would be
a 'record Twelfth'.[24] In 1948 121 bands took part, with pipe and silver bands
apparently more popular than ever.[25]

The big drum has gone down before them, the flute band, though those that remain
toot as defiantly as ever, are fewer and fewer, and further between. The accordion band
seems to be a spent force, which is a merciful dispensation indeed. ('The Roamer')[26]

By 1952 there were complaints that there were so many pipe bands that 'the
Sash' was heard less often since it is more easily played by flute and accordion
bands.[27] The Lambeg drum remained relatively common in areas of Armagh
and Down, but disappeared from the Belfast parade, although it could still
be heard on the Eleventh Night or at semi-organised drumming matches in
which the object was almost to physically intimidate one's drumming
opponent (Scullion 1981: 19–38). These drumming matches were not
appreciated by all in the unionist fraternity.

After a few drunken brawls, much foul language, and serious traffic congestion, the
incessant din comes to an end well after midnight.
    Does Mr. Forrest think that traditions like this are a firm foundation for a
progressive Ulster? Surely if the ability to beat a drum were the mark of an advancing
civilisation the most primitive natives of Africa would by now be masters of the world.
I should hate to think that Ulster's strengths depend upon the revival of past and long
worn out traditions. ('Young Unionist')[28]

Some Orangemen argue that the Lambeg drum is no longer used in the
Belfast Twelfth because it is too slow and difficult to carry for such a distance.
However, I suspect that its association with a more rowdy 'Twelfth' has as

much to do with it. And the Lambeg drum was not the only 'tradition' to come under critical scrutiny from 'respectable' Orangeism. Amongst the musical accompaniment, one section receives particular attention:

the popular 'Sash' seems to have dropped down the scale like many other party tunes. I have heard it said that some visiting bands overdid 'the Sash' in recent years. ('The Roamer')[29]

The 'visiting bands' referred to were those from Scotland who had a reputation for giving lively, exuberant performances. They would often arrive off an early boat on the Twelfth morning and start 'tirelessly living it up' for the rest of the day.[30]

As always, the bands from Clydesdale provided that touch of abandon which appeals to the spectators. One, at least, enlisted the services of two drummers whose combined efforts served to emphasise the louder passages of the music. As the auxiliary drummer had recourse to walk backwards his performance evoked outbursts of laughter.[31]

Not for the first time in the recent history of the more 'respectable' Twelfth such behaviour did not meet with unanimous approval.

The dignity of the walk was highly impressive – except perhaps for the performance of numerous Scottish bands whose spirits were often over-exuberant.[32]

Criticism of Scottish bands appeared in the *Belfast News Letter* in 1959 and was rebuffed by a letter from the Thornliebank Amateur Accordion Band which pointed out that none of its members did anything out of place such as 'jazzing to party tunes or sloppy marching'.[33] I take 'jazzing' to mean the weaving and dancing up the road which is relatively common in the Belfast Twelfth of the 1990s, particularly on the return from the Field. Thankfully for the *News Letter* 'there is still a murmur of appreciation in the crowd when a correct lodge in Sunday go-to-meeting clothes comes along'.[34]

  Not only was the behaviour of certain types of band questioned but some of the influences on the Orangemen and spectators were not always appreciated. In 1949 the Belfast County Grand Lodge issued statements that there should be no 'jazzing' of banners and that brethren should not wear their regalia in a public-house.[35] The contradictory attitude towards alcohol that is an ever present feature of the Twelfth in Belfast was summed up in a report of the Twelfth by an English visitor in 1958.

Although so many banners proclaim 'Temperance' or 'Total Abstinence' there seemed no rabid teetotalism about it all. One marcher I met afterwards, as he handsomely refreshed himself, explained that the banners proclaimed what they did at the lodge, elsewhere they did what they liked. That seemed a neat definition of Ulster's independence of outlook.[36]

Some fashionable elements were also introduced into the Belfast parade with some Orangemen in 'Teddy Boy' gear in 1956, and teenage girls 'wearing slacks' and doing 'the twist' walking alongside the parade in 1963.[37]

There was a slow development in what became known as the 'wee-Twelfth', the 'little Twelfth', 'miniature Twelfth' or 'mini-Twelfth'. Whilst it was common for individual lodges to have a small parade in the week or so before the Twelfth, sometimes to take a banner from the lodge building to the lodge Master's house, the wee-Twelfth was a collection of local lodges parading in their particular District. In Belfast this type of parade seems to have developed from a small number of east Belfast lodges marching on 1 July to commemorate the Somme. There appear to be no reports of this parade prior to the Second World War. Rather, it seems to have been a parade organised by one or two lodges that effectively became a Bally-macarrett District parade in the 1950s. There are also reports of a 'miniature Twelfth' at Leckpatrick, near Strabane in 1955,[38] and at some point in the 1950s or early in the 1960s pre-Twelfth parades started in Sandy Row District in south Belfast and also in west Belfast, encompassing the Shankill. Whilst to begin with these parades have a relatively low profile, they seem to proliferate around and after the start of 'the Troubles' in 1969.

POLITICS AT THE FIELD

Early post-war unionist politics was dominated by the relationship between the unionist government and the Protestant working classes within the new economic and political environment provided by the welfare and education reforms of the Labour government in Westminster. The conflicting interests of business groups, the political elite espousing popular Orangeism, and the increased role of the wider British state proved decisive within unionism. Initially, significant sections of the UUP were hostile to 'socialistic' reforms, although a deal with the Labour government that gave financial backing to the reforms helped mollify some of the objections. Nevertheless, the attraction of the Protestant working classes to the Northern Ireland Labour Party and other left-of-centre candidates proved to be a constant dilemma for senior unionist politicians (Bew *et al.* 1995: 111–15). At the same time, national education reforms yet again threatened to undermine the denom-inational structure of the education system in Northern Ireland, once again giving the more fundamentalist wing of Orangeism one of its favourite causes to fight (Bardon 1992: 595).

The threat to the Orange Institution from both socialism and fundamental Protestantism (Bruce 1986: 64) demanded constant calls for unity during Twelfth demonstrations. Twelfth resolutions and speeches attacking Communism were made every year from 1948 through to the mid-1950s. The speeches at Sixmilecross in 1953 in rural Tyrone, with a local election beckoning, are typical and revealed many of the fears over Labour and socialist advances.

Mr Beattie (Co. Grand Treasurer) said that he had been told about great arches in Sandy Row and the Shankill. The people of the border counties would rather see West Belfast returning a unionist to Westminster than putting up elaborate decorations at the Twelfth.

The Orange lodges believed it was a shame that places like Sandy Row and the Shankill should send Mr J Beattie [Independent Labour Party] to Westminster. The unionists of Tyrone and Fermanagh were better loyalists than either Sandy Row or the Shankill because they were not only Twelfth of July loyalists, but also loyalists at election time.[39]

In the main, of course, the Twelfth continued to be a day at which members of the government reiterated policies after resolutions had congratulated them on their good work. In 1951 the *Belfast News Letter* described the Twelfth of July as 'the day for the annual re-statement of Ulster's first principles'.[40] In 1956 the same newspaper described it as 'Ulster's Red Letter Day' which 'affords an opportunity to all to declare their unity on the fundamental issue in the political life of Ulster'.[41] However, the use of the Twelfth as an overt party political platform was not welcomed by everyone. Perhaps not surprisingly, some of the unionists, such as Norman Porter, who stayed independent of the Ulster Unionist Party, particularly resented it. Porter was a prominent local MP and independent unionist, with a fundamentalist background. At a local parade in 1956 he complained about the resolutions for the forthcoming Twelfth and the likely platform speeches of politicians.

With the greatest respect to my Parliamentary colleagues I wish . . . to deplore their remarks at Orange gatherings when they discuss such matters as agriculture, transport, unemployment, and industrial development, especially when these matters are in no way connected with the defence of Protestantism. (Norman Porter)[42]

Porter consistently repeated this argument at Orange events in the years that followed. In fact, there seems to have been a tendency, by the mid-1950s, in some rural areas of Ulster, particularly mid-Antrim and mid-Derry, only to have religious services at the Twelfth.[43] In Bellaghy, County Derry, in 1956, they decided to 'follow recent practice' and hold only a religious service with the resolutions simply being read out and seconded. Yet on the same day, at Finaghy, speakers were giving a rousing defence of the government's policy on health, power and employment.[44] By 1960 the 'religious' as opposed to the 'political' nature of the Twelfth was central to a number of the speeches on the Twelfth. The debate was summed up in *Belfast News Letter* editorials.

The religious services are preferred by many within the Orange Order, who believe that they are more in keeping with the occasion. The 'Twelfth' platform they claim, is not the most suitable place for political speeches. . . . But those who have carried on the Order know . . . that their aim can only be made good through political action and consistent vigilance on the political front, and history proves the soundness of that view.[45]

Some speakers that year argued that by interfering with politics the Institution weakened itself, and people confused the objects of the Unionist Party and the Orange Order. This feeling probably arose for two different, though connected reasons. First, there is some evidence to suggest that inter-communal tensions were particularly low at this time. For instance, there was an ongoing debate in the UUP over allowing Roman Catholics to join and stand as candidates for the party (Bardon 1992: 609–10). As the issue of the border seemed to fade, and perhaps a more permissive society started to intrude, many of the more religious brethren saw the Institution, unlike the UUP, as being a Protestant, moral, guardian. The UUP was always liable to be tainted by its involvement in mundane everyday politics and some brethren would have liked to see the Orange Institution able to act more freely as a moral pressure group. This view of the Twelfth was challenged both by senior members of the Institution, who of course were also often senior in the UUP, and also by brethren who saw the Institution as a sort of democratic forum through which their own political views could be made known. Second, there was significant disenchantment with the UUP. This partly stemmed from the development of left-wing politics, as represented by the Northern Ireland Labour Party. But also of growing significance was pressure from fundamentalist or ultra-Protestant groups, in which both Ian Paisley, from 1956 involved in a group called Ulster Protestant Action, and Norman Porter were involved (Bruce 1986: 66–7; Moloney and Pollak 1986: 88–9). These groups attempted to take the 'religious' high ground which could elude the Orange Institution because of its 'political' involvement.

These divisions to an extent represent the battle for ideological control within the Protestant bloc suggested by Bew *et al.* The unionist elite's retention of hegemonic control, using popular Orangeism, became increasingly difficult due to a number of factors. Bew *et al.* accept that one of these was the pressure from British business interests to improve relations with the south, an increasingly important market, but they also argue that economic decline and rising unemployment allowed secular labourite responses to attain greater force, and also eventually moved unionism under O'Neill, in the 1960s, into more reformist regional economic planning (1995: 111–15). These economic and political forces reveal themselves in both the development of the Northern Ireland Labour Party and also in reactionary Protestant fundamentalism. The Twelfth during this period is not a politically static event but rather an arena through which political forces could play out their relationships.

CONTROLLING THE 'RIGHT TO PARADE': DUNGIVEN AND THE LONGSTONE ROAD

In spite of the period 1945–65 being one in which inter-communal tensions were relatively low, there is still a catalogue of incidents where parades, demonstrations and political rallies ended in disorder, particularly in the late 1940s and early 1950s. In the main this involved the RUC attempting to stop the Irish Tricolour being displayed at a variety of republican or socialist events. This led to the introduction of the 1951 Public Order (NI) Act and the 1954 Flags and Emblems (NI) Act. These legislative changes only sought to 'normalise' the *de facto* control on nationalist and republican events and displays that had existed prior to the war. In practice, by the late 1950s and early 1960s, restrictions on such events were becoming less and even republican Easter commemorations were more often taking place without police interference (Jarman and Bryan 1998: 51–8).

In contrast to the treatment of nationalist parades, Orange parades were rarely stopped or re-routed. However, there were a number of revealing incidents, most notably on the Longstone Road in County Down from 1952 onwards and in Dungiven, County Londonderry from 1953 onwards. The Longstone Road dispute erupted when Orange lodges applied for permission to parade to a new Orange Hall that had been built in the area. The planned route for the Orangemen took them through a predominantly nationalist area. Home Affairs minister, Brian Maginess, had recently banned nationalist parades in Derry and Enniskillen and initially banned the Orange parade. The ban was lifted on 3 July, after an outcry, and a second parade took place which was halted by nationalist protesters. These acts of weakness were held against Maginess and he very nearly lost his seat to an independent unionist in the 1953 election. At the start of 1954, a vote of no confidence in the government was passed at a big rally held in Belfast's Ulster Hall by the Ulster Orange and Protestant Committee at which independent unionist Norman Porter was the main speaker. Eventually Maginess was replaced by G.B. Hanna who upheld the Longstone Road ban for that year. At the Belfast Twelfth the Ulster Orange and Protestant Committee handed out leaflets criticising appeasement by the UUP, and quoted the 1947 Education Act and the recent successful IRA attack on Gough barracks, in Armagh, as examples of weakness. The leaflet argued that there were traitors in Stormont and that 'brass hats of our loyal Orange Order must face facts or face the consequences'. There was some limited heckling of platform speakers and one man was asked to leave the Field.[46] By the Twelfth in 1955 the Longstone Road ban had been removed. A day before the Twelfth three bombs went off on the Longstone Road and on the day of the parade hundreds of police lined the route. As L.P.S. Orr MP, Norman Porter MP and Brian Faulkner MP joined 15,000 Orangemen on the Longstone Road, G.B. Hanna made a speech at Finaghy pointing out that the Hibernians had, a few weeks earlier, paraded in the same area. Two weeks later a Gaelic festival parade in Newtownbutler, County Fermanagh, was banned, resulting in a serious riot.

The Dungiven dispute seems to have developed after a loyalist band, wishing to celebrate the coronation of Queen Elizabeth II, was prevented from parading through the town by a group of nationalists. Tension in Dungiven rose again in 1958, when, on 3 July, the loyalist Bovevagh (or

Boveva in some papers) band caught locals by surprise and marched through the centre of the town. On the following Sunday police were asked to remove a Union flag from an electricity pylon in the grounds of a Roman Catholic church. Some reports suggest the flag was then wrestled from police and burnt. Certainly there were some disturbances during the afternoon. Nationalist MPs described the use of the Union flag as 'provocative' and suggested that it would not be respected if it was used for 'party purposes'. A unionist MP retorted that by 'displaying the Union Jack, the members of the Orange Order showed that they were positive, active adherents of the Crown and of the Protestant faith – nothing to do with politics'.[47]

The following year Home Affairs Minister, W.W.B. Topping banned an Orange parade which planned to go through Dungiven to mark the visit to Northern Ireland of Princess Margaret. A few days afterwards the Bovevagh band organised another parade which was also banned. This time the loyalist reaction was more widespread. In particular Ian Paisley, and Ulster Protestant Action (UPA) – a militant Protestant organisation based in Belfast, with which Paisley was closely associated (Moloney and Pollak 1986: 81–2) – organised a parade and rally at the Queen's Island shipyard. Topping was condemned and further action was threatened. Topping replied the next day that the band had just been re-routed and that there was support from significant elements of the Protestant population of Dungiven for his decision.

At the Twelfth platform in Belfast Topping was heckled by UPA supporters who handed out leaflets. Chairman, John Bryans, Grand Master of Belfast, demanded that they conduct themselves as Orangemen, but interruptions continued with some Orangemen holding their own impromptu meeting at the end.[48] In Coleraine, at the meeting attended by brethren from Dungiven and Limavady, there was an attempt to submit a resolution protesting at the government's actions. The chairman refused to accept it and suggested that the Order should not descend to the level of ragamuffins. As the chairman tried to pass the resolutions there were shouts of 'No they are not passed.' At the end a man came up and read the alternative resolution.[49] A couple of months later Topping lost his ministerial job and was replaced by Brian Faulkner.

The following year, on 10 July, Faulkner allowed an Orange parade in Dungiven led by the Bovevagh band and with Norman Porter MP and Robert Chichester-Clark, a Westminster MP, taking part. There were scuffles during the parade, although nationalists had decided against a counter-demonstration. There were disturbances involving police and locals for three days following (Farrell 1980: 222; Moloney and Pollak 1986: 90–3). William Douglas, Bovevagh band leader and District Master of Limavady, was given a rousing reception at the Coleraine Twelfth. Faulkner later defended his decision on the basis that they were only parading to a church service.

In the two main parading disputes involving the Orange Institution during the 'golden era' an attempt by the state to restrict a loyalist parade resulted in senior politicians losing their jobs. They were replaced by men keen to return to a populist line. At the same time nationalist parades were often restricted and rarely took place anywhere but in the most Catholic areas, and even then they were sometimes stopped. Hard-line unionists such as Norman Porter and Ian Paisley had successfully flexed their political muscle in ways in which Paisley, in particular, was to do increasingly through the 1960s.

The 1950s are remembered as a 'golden era' for Orangeism but a closer analysis of the period reveals some of the frictions within Orangeism that were to become more obvious by the mid-1960s. In September and October 1962 there were major celebrations, including a large parade in Belfast, to commemorate the signing of the Covenant fifty years earlier, with the usual support for the government being pledged. But a few liberal voices within the UUP were beginning to speak up and there was increasing criticism of the government's economic policies (Bardon 1992: 620). This criticism arose not only from the political left, in the form of increased support for the NILP, but also from local industry. In 1963 Captain Terence O'Neill took over from Brookeborough as Prime Minister. To begin with he showed little in the way of reform on civil rights and discrimination and his economic policies were driven by political conflicts within the Protestant, unionist bloc (Bew *et al.* 1985: 128–40). For the Twelfth in 1964, the editorial in the *Belfast News Letter* proclaimed a familiar message.

Fashions may change; political ideologies may be dented and policies bred to meet new situations, but fundamental principles, as we acknowledge them on this anniversary in Ulster, are forever. . . . Men from many different levels of society will proclaim, propose and acclaim them. . . . men of all ranks are happy in brotherhood.[50]

Orangeism appeared to be in a dominant hegemonic position. The Twelfth appeared more paternalistic and less threatening than at any other time in its history. But I have tried to suggest that even in this 'golden era' there was resistance from both within and outside unionism. Scott argues (1990: 4), that the dominant are never completely in control although the public transcript more often than not reflects the position of the dominant. It is in public that those in subordinate positions are most likely to appear to endorse the hegemonic values. Yet resistance to the position of the dominant can be seen even in the public transcripts I have studied above – a close look at the Twelfth revealing the tensions that were to become so acute. In retrospect it is clear that the Orange and unionist elite were in an untenable long-term position.

6 'YOU CAN MARCH – CAN OTHERS?'

> The struggle between political forces is exceedingly abstract and distant from the everyday experience of most people. One of the primary ways it can be made palpable is through the symbolic dramatizations of conflict that such mass demonstrations make possible. Individuals can then identify abstract political principles with actual people, and they can identify political positions with tangible symbols. The sight of people who are peacefully parading these symbols being physically assaulted by police can have a powerful emotional effect on onlookers. (Kertzer 1988: 120–1)

In 1972, after three years of violent confrontations that had required the introduction of British troops to police the streets of Northern Ireland, the British government decided to close the Stormont Parliament and replace it with direct rule from Westminster. The result was to take away the Orange Institution's main source of political patronage and, therefore, to significantly reduce its avenues to power. The Twelfth, the ritual that symbolised the Northern state, also underwent significant changes. From the mid-1960s onwards the hegemonic position of Orangeism was questioned not only by the civil rights movement, not only by nationalists, socialists and republicans, but also, to a certain extent, by the British state and the Northern Irish bourgeoisie. Orangeism, which had appeared so appropriate for the cause of opposition to Home Rule, and which had provided the state of Northern Ireland with a distinctive identity, no longer held attractions for significant numbers of the middle classes of Belfast. The industries in which it had held sway were in decline, and increasingly owned, or supported from, outside the six counties. Some senior unionist politicians, grappling with increasing economic problems, became less inclined to issue populist Orange clarion calls. In particular, the new Prime Minister, Terence O'Neill, who came from an aristocratic and landed background, was clearly a politician first and an Orangeman second. How reformist he actually was in economic and social spheres is open to question (Bew *et al.* 1995), however, his actions further divided unionism and allowed an increasing number to question his Orange credentials. Suddenly a Twelfth platform became a hostile place for some in the unionist elite and when the civil rights movement literally 'marched' into the arena parades and public demonstrations once again became the focus for political action (Purdie 1990).

78

PAISLEY: 'MAD MULLAH' OR SUPER ORANGEMAN?

Protestant opposition to O'Neill coalesced around a number of personalities, but by far the most pro-active and successful was the Reverend Ian Paisley. Two factors make him of particular interest in terms of understanding parades. First, he has not been a member of the Orange Institution since 1962, and second he was, and is, a fine exponent of the counter-demonstration. The distrust of Paisley felt in the higher echelons of the Institution can be traced back to the early 1950s. The friction caused when Paisley set up the Free Presbyterian Church was such that it was never given any real recognition within the Orange Institution and its ministers were prevented from becoming chaplains in Orange lodges. In 1958 a fellow Orangeman, Warren Porter, brought the charge of 'unbrotherly conduct' against him, after Paisley published an attack on Porter. He finally left the Order when angered by the Mayor of Belfast's attendance at a Roman Catholic funeral Mass. It was on his resignation that he apparently accused certain Orange chaplains of having 'a Romeward trend in their philosophy' (Moloney and Pollak 1986: 51–5). Although by leaving the Institution he was cutting himself off from the normal route into political influence, his outspoken attacks and his skill at theatrical, public political demonstrations allowed him to become an increasingly important figure in unionist politics. In October 1964 he infamously threatened to march up the Falls Road to remove a Tricolour that was sitting in the window of the Sinn Féin office. This forced the RUC, under the Flags and Emblems Act, to go and remove it and a week of rioting followed on the Falls. By the mid-1960s Paisley had already gained renown for organising demonstrations against various liberal Protestant figures or on occasions such as when the Union Jack over the City Hall was lowered on the death of the Pope in 1963 (Bruce 1986: 72–4). Court hearings, fines and eventually imprisonment only added to his populist appeal. Despite no longer being an Orangeman, Paisley spoke at Orange functions and retained some significant support amongst rank-and-file Orangemen, so much so that there was even talk of the Orange Order splitting. Opposition from Paisley and others helped to give the Northern Ireland government and the RUC excuses to stop the civil rights demonstrations that took to the streets. But in stopping some of Paisley's forays into Catholic areas they also positioned themselves to be accused of weakness in the face of republicanism (Purdie 1990: 23–6).

In January 1965 the Taoiseach, Seán Lemass, held talks with O'Neill at Stormont. The following month O'Neill visited Dublin. On 25 February, Paisley was part of a parade to Unionist Party headquarters which included loyalist bands from all over Belfast (Moloney and Pollak 1986: 120–1). An examination of the Twelfth platform speeches also suggests discontent. At the Belfast demonstration in Finaghy, leaflets from 'Protestant unionists' were handed around, and a number of speeches were interrupted, including that of the Grand Master of the Grand Orange Lodge of Ireland, Sir George

Clark. Ringleaders apparently kept their sashes under their coats as Clark called for their sashes to be taken from them, threatening 'a strong right arm'.[1] However, these interrupted platform speeches were just the start. There were disturbances at different platforms almost every year from 1965 through to 1977. The exceptions were 1969 and 1970, when resolutions and speeches were highly critical of the government and many politicians failed to turn up, and in 1974 when the success of the Ulster Workers' Council strike might have given an added sense of unity and confidence to proceedings. But in general the formality of the ritual occasion could no longer hide the divisions that existed. The diversity of interest groups involved in the Twelfth had started to reveal themselves in a much starker way and the Boyne celebrations were now reflecting the growing crisis in Northern Ireland in general and in unionism in particular.

By the time the 1966 Twelfth arrived that sense of crisis was growing. The British Prime Minster, Harold Wilson, had impressed upon O'Neill the need to look at community relations, especially the issue of discrimination in housing. For his part O'Neill at the very least showed a greater willingness to meet the Catholic community with visits to schools and hospitals. However, agitation from Paisley meant that a train bringing participants from the south up to the celebrations for the Easter Rising of 1916 was stopped. He organised a parade to the Ulster Hall that included part of the route of the republican parade (Jarman and Bryan 1996: 57–8). The County Grand Lodge in Fermanagh, whose County Grand Master was former Prime Minister Brookeborough, passed a resolution calling for the banning of Easter republican parades. A cabinet meeting decided to put a number of restrictions on the republican parade. Paisley was involved in setting up the Ulster Protestant Volunteers, which seemed to model itself on the Orange Institution with members wearing a white sash with red and blue fringe, and marching with bands (Harbinson 1973: 94; Moloney and Pollak 1986: 124–31). On 6 June Paisley organised a parade, to demonstrate against the 'Romanising tendencies' at the Presbyterian General Assembly, which went right past the mainly Catholic Markets area and left a riot in its wake. He was prosecuted for this and on 20 July went to jail. A few days later a large parade, with his support, went to the centre of Belfast where attacks were made on Catholic-owned pubs (Farrell 1980: 234–5; Moloney and Pollak 1986: 131–5; Bardon 1992: 634–6). Unionist MP Nat Minford questioned Paisley's Orange credentials.

If this person thinks his strutting like a bloody turkey cock and that his slabberings on public platforms are going to make me tremble he is around the bend. . . . Where will he be on the Glorious Twelfth? Will he be wearing the colours? Where will he parade unless it is to his own advantage? Will he make the Twelfth glorious?[2]

Paisley's agitation was in part aimed at the ecumenical wing of the Presbyterian Church, with its connections with the World Council of Churches. The Grand Lodge decided to make a resolution that year that was critical of ecumenism, but there were calls for the resolution to be withdrawn and one deputy Grand Chaplain refused to go to Finaghy because of it.[3] O'Neill was supposed to be speaking on all three resolutions at Cullybackey. This plan was changed when it was realised it meant him speaking on the second resolution critical of ecumenism and the third resolution, which although congratulating his government on economic successes, implied some criticism as it called for greater protection for the 'constitutional position of the Province'.[4] Nat Minford and Phelim O'Neill were not invited to the Twelfth; Phelim O'Neill was openly critical of the resolution. The Grand Master, Sir George Clark, introduced the resolution at Finaghy along with an attack on Paisley suggesting that he should not be invited to Orange meetings. At Newtownards the resolution was not even introduced. However, there was heckling of speakers at five platforms with Prime Minister O'Neill's name being greeted with cries of 'traitor'. At Ballynahinch, Faulkner was shouted at and had copies of Paisley's newspaper, the *Protestant Telegraph*, waved at him. At Kilkeel, Roy Bradford MP and two Stormont Senators were jostled and kicked.[5] In its editorial the *Belfast News Letter* suggested that heckling 'where it did occur was predictable, unoriginal, and reflected the level of intelligence of those who indulged in it'.[6] During the Last Saturday Black parades there was trouble at Castlederg, where police broke up a counter-demonstration, at platform speeches at Dromore, where Nat Minford was surrounded and abused, and at Ballymena, when Home Affairs Minister Brian McConnell was shouted at by a group wanting to know about 'Protestant Ministers in jail'.[7] There had even been a suggestion by a group called 'The Orange Voice of Freedom' – set up to highlight the lack of leadership in the Orange Institution – that MPs should not be invited to the Field.[8] The plan by this group that it should have a march on the Shankill, with Orangemen in regalia, was an obvious threat to the authority of the Orange Institution. The government's banning of this parade explains the heckling McConnell received at the Black parade in Ballymena (Moloney and Pollak 1986: 146).

A *Belfast Telegraph* editorial recognised the struggle for power taking place in the context of the Twelfth and also attacked Paisley.

Not long ago speeches on the Twelfth of July were the dullest part of proceedings. But not today. What the Orange platforms have witnessed is a critical round in a struggle not only for control of the Order but for the possession of Northern Ireland's soul. Is this statement too strong? We do not think so. Orangeism is again in a key position. It is the first to have to make the choice between responsible Government through the present unionist leadership or a form of dictatorship through a religious war led by a latter-day 'Mad Mullah'.[9]

Perhaps most significantly a new paramilitary organisation, styling itself the Ulster Volunteer Force (UVF), shot three Roman Catholics in Belfast, one of them fatally. The government immediately banned the UVF under the Special Powers Act (Boulton 1973; Bardon 1992: 635).

The Twelfth of 1967 showed all the hallmarks of the growing divisions. The usual resolution paying tribute to the Prime Minister was criticised by Harry West, a recently sacked government minister, and eventually caused an uproar at seven venues. At Coagh the Westminster MP for Mid-Ulster, George Forrest, was pulled from the platform, kicked and left unconscious, after he had threatened demonstrators with his chair when they jeered at O'Neill's name. In Tandragee, County Armagh, hecklers shouted 'O'Neill must go' and 'Up de Valera'. At Enniskillen, the MP supposed to propose the O'Neill resolution did not turn up and instead Harry West and the former Prime Minister, Lord Brookeborough, delivered critical speeches. At Fintona, the resolution was changed to omit O'Neill's name and in Lisburn the meeting was disturbed by a heckler using a loud hailer. At the Belfast parade the Grand Master, George Clark, was heckled and there were cries of 'objection' as the resolution was read out. A number of government ministers were noticeable by their absence and O'Neill only spoke at Portglenone for a few minutes.[10] In October, George Clark resigned 'due to ill health' and the uncontroversial John Bryans was voted in to the post (Moloney and Pollak 1986: 148–9).

The Twelfth of 1968 was not as dramatic as that of the previous year but divisions were still apparent. At Finaghy there was heckling as the Reverend Martin Smyth gave the chairman's address. Clearly there was some disquiet over the expulsion of Phelim O'Neill. Captain L.P.S. Orr, Imperial Grand Master of the Orange Order had suggested, a few days earlier, that it was up to individual Orangemen to interpret the rules and that he personally did not think that it was necessarily wrong to attend a Roman Catholic funeral. Orr, however, came under attack at the Ballyclare platform from Reverend William Thompson who argued that an Orangeman should refuse an invitation to any Roman Catholic ceremony.[11]

CIVIL RIGHTS AND 'THE RIGHT TO MARCH'

It is beyond the scope of this book to examine in any detail the development of the civil rights movement, but its activities, particularly its organising of mass public rallies, clearly played an important role in exposing the inadequacies of the Northern Ireland state and revealing the divisions within unionism. Disquiet over discrimination in housing and employment, as well as gerrymandering in local council elections, had been growing during the 1960s. The Northern Ireland Civil Rights Association (NICRA), a coalition of republican, socialist and other interest groups, was founded in February of 1967. At Easter NICRA held protest rallies in Armagh and Newry after Craig had banned a republican rally in Armagh due to a threat from Paisley to organise a counter-march. But it was during the second half of 1968 that the tactic of having public demonstration really developed (Farrell 1980:

245–7; Nelson 1984: 67–75; Moloney and Pollak 1986: 153–4; Lee 1989: 420; Purdie 1990; Bardon 1992: 651–4; Ó Dochartaigh 1997).

In August 1968 the Campaign for Social Justice, based in Dungannon, organised a parade from Coalisland to Dungannon. When Paisley's UPV organised a counter-march the RUC decided to block the path into Dungannon, beating back the few that tried to continue. The thousand-strong opposition march sang 'The Sash' and 'God Save the Queen'. Developing against the backdrop of the civil rights campaigns and anti-Vietnam War protests in America and Europe, the civil rights movement began to gain publicity and support both inside and outside the Catholic community. However, given the historical significance of parades in the north of Ireland, given the powerful position of Orangeism, and given the ethnic territorial divisions of city, town and country communities, it was always likely that it could be depicted as a nationalist threat. And although the call for a united Ireland was at this point muted, the parades were, of course, a threat to the state of Northern Ireland as it was then constituted. Even in places such as Armagh, Derry, Dungannon or Enniskillen, where the population was predominantly Catholic, the town centres with their war memorials, town halls, Orange halls and Protestant-owned businesses, were perceived as Protestant. As such, the organisers of counter-demonstrations were able to play upon existing fears and utilise the territorial perceptions many people held. Town centres were not neutral areas; the centre of Dungannon was no Speakers' Corner.

Over the months that followed confrontations between civil rights demonstrators and the police became world-wide television news. In Derry on 5 October 1968 demonstrators tried to take the route into the city usually taken by the Apprentice Boys in August. The march was banned and they were baton charged by police when they started off (McCann 1974; Farrell 1980: 246–7; Bardon 1992: 654–5). On New Year's Day 1969 about eighty students of the People's Democracy, set up after Paisley had demonstrated and effectively stopped students marching into Belfast in October, set off on a march from Belfast to Derry. Police offered little protection as marchers were attacked at Burntollet Bridge on the road from Dungiven to Derry. It was later discovered that a number of those conducting the ambush were themselves in the B-Specials. When they finally arrived in Derry they were given a hero's reception and there was further rioting.

When Faulkner resigned from the government, O'Neill's position was becoming more untenable. Twelve unionist MPs met in Portadown, at what became known as the 'Portadown Parliament', to plot his downfall. A General Election was called for 24 February 1969 and unionists were split into 'pro-' and 'anti-' O'Neill camps. Despite doing reasonably well, forming a government and introducing a new Public Order Bill, O'Neill could only stumble on until the end of April. That month Paisley was in jail, and further civil rights demonstrations ended in riots. Derry was approaching a state of civil war. A number of bombs exploded at an electricity station and a reservoir, and were blamed upon the IRA, although it was later revealed to be the UVF attempting to destabilise the government. O'Neill was succeeded by Chichester-Clark, who beat the more hard-line Faulkner by one vote. Chichester-Clark announced reforms, including 'one man, one vote', an amnesty allowing for the release of Paisley, and at the same time gave Faulkner a place in the cabinet (Farrell 1980: 254–8; Bardon 1992: 661–9).

As a result of the government changes, the civil rights demonstrations eased up, but the summer was approaching and that meant the 'traditional' marching season. As far back as February loyalists had blown up the Long Stone, at the Longstone Road, the scene of the parading dispute in the 1950s (Moloney and Pollak 1986: 183). In June an Orange church parade in Dungiven was attacked. On 29 June another Orange parade took place in Dungiven for the unfurling of a new banner led by the Bovevagh flute band. Protesters held placards reading 'You can march – Can others?'[12] The Orange parade commemorating the landing of William at Carrickfergus was reintroduced for the first time in seventeen years.[13] By May and June areas in north and west Belfast were particularly tense. The Connolly Commemoration Committee announced a parade for 15 June that would carry a Tricolour into Belfast; the newly formed Shankill Defence Association (SDA) announced a counter-demonstration. Both marches had restrictions placed upon them but the SDA parade was allowed into the city centre whilst the Connolly parade was not. The UVF also issued a threat to the 'provocative' Connolly parade. In the end three members of the Connolly Association took a walk down Royal Avenue and the SDA called off the counter-demonstration although crowds stayed in the area singing 'The Sash' and the national anthem.[14] There was a tense civil rights demonstration in Strabane on Sunday 29 June and another in Newry on 5 July.[15] Although the Newry march passed peacefully, and a senior Orangeman had appealed for it to be allowed to proceed unhindered, Paisley later announced that he would lead a parade through the town in the near future.[16] There was rioting in Armagh after a People's Democracy march on the 7th, and there were more clashes in Lurgan on the 11th over disputed flags.[17]

The Twelfth was punctuated by violence. In Derry, a parade was attacked and police fought running battles in the Bogside for the following three days. In Lurgan the disturbances of the previous day continued. In Belfast the display of a Tricolour from Unity Flats provoked rioting and Orangemen were held back by police as they tried to enter the flats. In Dungiven an Orange parade was attacked and in the afternoon the flag outside the Orange Hall was burnt. The next day B-Specials fired over the heads of a crowd attacking the Orange Hall, but eventually it also was burnt (Farrell 1980: 258; Bardon 1992: 665).[18]

It was noted that a number of unionist MPs were absent from the Field demonstrations. The recently installed Prime Minister, Chichester-Clark, was spared direct attention but the general unionist establishment was not. In

Markethill, the Secretary of the County Grand Lodge of Armagh, J.A. Anderson, described unionists in Stormont as ineffective.

Either our members have not the ability to reply or else they are too lackadaisical, but one thing is certain – they will not refuse their salaries or expenses.[19]

Most of the various speakers' venom was reserved for the civil rights movement. L.P.S. Orr in Banbridge argued that the Orange Order was the oldest civil rights movement in Ireland. Rafton Pounder MP suggested at Finaghy that he did not speak as a politician but as an Orangeman 'as he did not approve of politicians using Orange platforms to fly political kites'. Nevertheless, he then went on to argue that the civil rights movement was undermining the very existence of the state. It is also interesting to note that, at this point in time, the republican movement was not singled out as being behind the civil rights campaign.[20]

It is ironical to hear the cry from the streets from people who denied the freedom of speech, whose political theories are mixed up with Communism and anarchism, a political creed which, wherever it had succeeded, deprived the people of these freedoms. (Capt. John Brooke MP, the Twelfth platform, Enniskillen)[21]

For the first time in many years Paisley spoke at an Orange Twelfth demonstration, but significantly it was that held by the Independent Orange Institution at Castlereagh and the Ulster Unionist Party came in for strong criticism.

Members of the People's Democracy were arrested in Enniskillen on 26 July when the parade was banned and on 2 August serious rioting started around Unity Flats when rumours circulated, later denied by the police, that a Junior Orange parade coming down from the Shankill had been stoned from the Flats. Riots continued for days afterwards and eventually the stretched police force in the area were replaced by the B-Specials and Orangemen conducted 'peace patrols' wearing their sashes.[22] Significantly, some Catholics living up near the Ardoyne were forced out of their houses (Farrell 1980: 259). The situation was so tense that there were growing calls for all parades to be banned. Even the *Belfast News Letter* suggested that the Apprentice Boys might alter their 12 August parade route and that Paisley's proposed parade in Newry on 16 August should be banned. Paisley had already called for Orange regalia to be worn at his Newry demonstration. Concern within the Orange Institution at the violence connected with Orange events was also growing and the Grand Lodge Secretary, Walter Williams, reminded brethren that Orange regalia was only to be worn during parades under the auspices of the Institution. He also pointed out that brethren were obliged to keep the rules of 'the statute book'. John Bryans, Belfast County Grand Master, urged Orangemen to back the police.[23] There was clearly a worry among the officers of the Institution that they were losing control.

The Apprentice Boys' parade in Derry on the 12 August 1969 is popularly seen as the start of 'the Troubles'. Tension built throughout the day and by the time the main parade moved out of Magazine Gate a large crowd from the Bogside had collected in Waterloo Place. A battle ensued involving Bogside residents, the RUC and B-Specials, and loyalist groups that effectively kept the Bogside under siege for three days. Discontent quickly spread to Armagh, Coalisland, Dungannon, Dungiven, Lurgan and inevitably to Belfast. The police became unable to deal with the situation as groups of Catholics and Protestants clashed in west Belfast. In some cases the RUC, and particularly the B-Specials, were supporting loyalist groups. Houses were wrecked and hundreds of families forced to move out. Eventually, on 15 August, it was decided to call in the troops. So fearful of the police were some in the Catholic community, that the army, to begin with at least, were a welcome sight. In July and August 1969 ten people died, nearly 1,000 were injured and 170 homes were destroyed and 417 damaged. Of 1,820 families forced to leave their homes 1,505 were Catholic (Farrell 1980: 259–62; McCann 1974; Buckland 1981: 129–31; Lee 1989: 428–9; Bardon 1992: 665–72).[24]

Only on 13 August did the government place a ban on marches and demonstrations. The Grand Orange Lodge immediately announced that there would be full compliance, but that time of year their major parades were over. As *The Times* put it:

By waiting until now to ban the parades, by waiting until the Orange faction has had its fling, the Stormont Government convicts itself of partiality in the eyes of the minority.[25]

In fact, the Last Saturday Black parades were affected but significantly the Hibernians' parades of 15 August were also covered. Nevertheless, the Hibernians' parade in Dungannon went ahead, as did the Apprentice Boys' Burning of Lundy in Derry in December although the normal parade seems not to have taken place.

The last few months of 1969 were relatively calm. However, the position had been set which was to dominate the future of Northern Ireland. Particularly in urban areas communal boundaries were strengthened by house-wrecking and intimidation. Catholic working-class areas became hostile to both the police and shortly afterwards the army and came to be known as 'No Go' areas. As the war against the state of Northern Ireland developed, the strength of the largely dormant IRA grew. The Northern Irish and British authorities acted and reacted with increasing force at this questioning of British control. Nevertheless, a greater involvement from the British government also brought into question the nature of the government of Northern Ireland. In the long run this was to lead to the downfall of the Stormont Parliament but in the short term it meant changes which included the disbanding of the B-Specials and the disarming of the RUC. Disillusionment within Protestant areas with the ability of the state to protect their interests grew and the unionist establishment continued to fall apart. Local defence organisations formed into what became the Ulster Defence Association (UDA). Paisley's Ulster Constitution Defence Committee, which had played a part in opposing republican Easter parades since 1966, also became a rallying point. On 2 October there was a gun battle between the security forces and loyalists with two loyalists and a policeman being killed (Moloney and Pollak 1986: 197–201). The forces of the state were still predominantly on the side of the loyalists, but Northern Ireland began to look less like a safe 'Protestant State for a Protestant people'. The hegemonic position of Orangeism was under siege from all sides.

THE DEMISE OF STORMONT AND THE STATE RITUAL

It would be just as impracticable to suggest that the USA should give up Independence Day as to suggest that the Orangemen should give up the Twelfth. These things are traditional and not provocative. (John Andrews, Northern Ireland Senate Leader)[26]

The lead-up to the Twelfth of 1970 revealed all the new stresses within the political structures of the state and on the streets. In April Paisley stood in a local by-election in a seat vacated by O'Neill. Mainstream unionism did its level best to oppose him. Even the Imperial Grand Master of the Orange Order, Laurence Orr, was brought in to appeal to the Orange vote for unionist candidate Bolton Minford. Paisley won with 7,980 votes to Minford's 1,200. On 18 June Paisley won the seat of North Antrim in the Westminster General Election. At the other end of the unionist scale the Alliance Party was formed to reflect a more liberal and reformist position. The unionist bloc, reflected in the Ulster Unionist Party, symbolised by the Orange Order, had finally disintegrated.

A large republican Easter parade in Derry on 29 March ended in violence. On 31 March a junior Orange parade returning along the Springfield Road, west Belfast, was attacked by Catholic youths as were the soldiers that interceded. The riots in the Catholic Ballymurphy estate over the following nights were some of the first major confrontations with the army in Belfast. Farrell suggests that for the first time the army 'appeared in the RUC role of protectors of triumphalist Orange parades' (1976: 272). On the other hand, on 2 June when a loyalist band parade was directed away from the Ardoyne, north Belfast, there followed two nights of rioting in the Shankill (Bardon 1992: 667–78). On 15 June there was more trouble in Dungiven after an Orange church parade attended by Orangemen from all over Northern Ireland. A Methodist Church conference called for all parades to be halted for the love of the nation, and there were calls for the Church of Ireland to sever its links with the Orange Institution. It has also been suggested that the new RUC Chief Constable, Sir Arthur Young, former London police commissioner, wanted the parades banned (Moloney and Pollak 1986: 208).

Even Windsor Park, home football ground of Linfield Football Club, refused to hold a Sandy Row District Orange service.[27] Chichester-Clark was caught between the growing strength of Paisleyite politics and the growing involvement of the security forces and British authorities less sympathetic to Orangeism. On the one hand, the parades looked like they would inevitably lead to major civil disturbances, on the other hand, banning them would be political suicide: the parades went ahead. On 27 June a 'mini-Twelfth' parade in west Belfast, passing the Catholic Ardoyne area, ended in rioting and a gun battle in which three Protestants were killed. Another Orange parade in east Belfast led to confrontations around the Catholic Short Strand area. A Catholic Church was attacked and four Protestants and an IRA man lost their lives in the disturbances. The IRA had begun to defend Catholic estates and Protestants perceived the army as facilitating these new enclaves by its relative inactivity. At the opening of the annually erected Orange Arch in Sandy Row, County Grand Master Martin Smyth suggested that 'if the troops were unable to ensure the security of Northern Ireland let them say so and the men of Ulster will rally again, as they did in bygone days, to maintain the welfare of their own homes'.[28] Yet early in July the army undertook an operation in the lower Falls area, imposing a curfew and using a large amount of force, that greatly increased recruitment into the IRA (Bowyer Bell 1989; Farrell 1976: 271–3; Moloney and Pollak 1986: 207–10; Bardon 1992: 277–9).

The Orange Institution did announce that all private lodge parades, with the exception of two to the Cenotaph, were called off with only District, Somme and Church parades being sanctioned by the Institution. The Prime Minister announced that some parade re-routes had been agreed with the Orange Institution. For instance, Sandy Row District were re-routed away from the Grosvenor Road. Chichester-Clark himself refused to be drawn as to whether he would parade. In the end he did not march. The resolutions contained no reference to the government. The third resolution was the same as a 1922 resolution and called upon 'the authorities to give full, proper and immediate protection to law abiding citizens'. Government ministers were, in the main, absent from the platforms and many of the speeches were highly critical of them. At Finaghy the Deputy District Master, Charles McCullough, of No. 9 District on the Shankill, listed all the grievances, including the disarming of the RUC and disbanding of the B-Specials.

All this has come about with the connivance of the government, which represents itself as being unionist, yet frequently expresses itself in terms that fall short of the traditional unionism with which we have happily identified ourselves over the generations. . . . Our traditional principles have been shattered, our beliefs questioned and maligned, our physical defences weakened and we have endured the humiliation of watching a bloodless government acting in our name conceding demands under pressure from urchins and hooligans.[29]

There were, of course, criticisms of rioters, particularly from Rafton Pounder MP who yet again 'did not approve of Orange platforms being used to fly political kites'. Most of the speeches, however, were typical calls for Orangemen to close ranks in a time of crisis.[30]

A report in the *Belfast News Letter* from Angela Storer described how the Twelfth in Belfast seemed to lack life, gaiety or spontaneity compared to previous years. She also noted that a number of Orangemen wore 'I'm supporting Paisley' badges. In Maghera there was heckling of speakers by John Wylie, Free Presbyterian and Paisley supporter, and there were calls for William Douglas, District Master in Limavady and member of the Bovevagh band, to speak.[31]

Despite suggestions by the Apprentice Boys that they would not be going near the Bogside, the government announced a six-month parade ban on 23 July. This effectively meant that three successive Apprentice Boys parades in Derry had been affected. Only war memorial services were excluded. The Prime Minister suggested that 'Peace is at stake here . . . and so is economic progress and the future of responsible government in Northern Ireland.' A band parade in Garvagh was stopped but an Orange service parade in Kilsherry, County Tyrone was apparently allowed because the marchers 'did not walk in organised files'.[32]

Debate raged within unionism and within the loyal orders over how to react to the ban. The Black Institution decided it would march on the Last Saturday, some Apprentice Boys walked to a new hall in County Down where Paisley spoke, there were summons served on six Blackmen after a parade in Maralin, County Down, a Protestant Unionist Association in Londonderry said it would defy the ban on 12 August and Paisley led a parade in Enniskillen and called for Parliament to be recalled. There were votes of no confidence in the Prime Minister from local Orange lodges and the County Grand Lodge of Belfast criticised the 'continuing ineptitude of the government'. Some unionist backbenchers suggested limited parades. The Apprentice Boys of Derry organised a service, but did not have a parade. However, a group did try to march over the bridge and there were distur-bances on the Waterside and in the Bogside.[33]

On 26 August, three days before the Last Saturday parades should have taken place, the Home Affairs Minister, Robert Porter resigned due to 'ill health', possibly another ministerial casualty of the parading issue. Also, cabinet minister Brian Faulkner, who once led Orangemen down the Longstone Road, was thrown out of the Ballynahinch Branch of the Apprentice Boys 'No Surrender' Club for his support for the ban. On the Last Saturday there were parades in Ballymoney, Belfast, Omagh and in Rathfriland. Although Lundy was burnt in December in Londonderry, there were no reported parades.[34]

A now rejuvenated IRA developed a military campaign designed to undermine the state (Bowyer Bell 1989: 373–92). Members of the security forces were attacked, town and city centres were bombed, and working-class

Catholic areas were effectively turned into 'No Go' areas for the forces of the state. The long-term goal may have been a united Ireland but the demise of Stormont and the consequent introduction of direct rule was seen as a step towards that goal. The unionist government, frustrated by their inability to deal effectively with the situation, was under continued pressure from hard-line politicians. Over the next few years a large number of loyalist organisations appeared to try to galvanise unionist politics. In September 1971 Ian Paisley founded the Democratic Unionist Party (DUP), whilst continuing the call for a 'third force', and around the same time a number of Protestant community vigilante groups formed into the Ulster Defence Association (UDA). The following year the Vanguard movement was formed by William Craig within the Ulster Unionist Party, and connected to Vanguard were the Orange Volunteers consisting of Orangemen and ex-servicemen (see Nelson 1984; Bruce 1992). Many of the new groups expressed their presence by holding parades. There are no published figures for the number of loyalist parades during this period, but frequent reports appear in the press of different types of parades.

By March 1971, after a large demonstration by shipyard workers, Chichester-Clark succumbed to pressures and resigned to be replaced by Brian Faulkner. Given the ongoing military campaigns, the issues surrounding parades and demonstrations did not appear as central as they had over the previous five years. Nevertheless, they continued to provide occasions that led to inter-communal violence. The marching season got under way at Easter with a large republican parade on the Sunday, and shots were fired on a crowd watching a junior Orange parade in east Belfast a few days afterwards.[35] In early June the government announced that an Orange parade in Dungiven was to be banned. Faulkner argued that the government wished to preserve 'the right of peaceful procession but a distinction must be drawn as far as possible between major traditional parades and others'.[36] William Douglas once again rose to the occasion and announced the parade on and called for support. In a situation that was to be repeated in Portadown and Belfast in the 1980s and 1990s the police blocked the route and Orangemen and their supporters confronted them. Violence became inevitable and rubber bullets and CS gas were used. William McCrea, later to become a DUP Westminster MP, was arrested. Officials of the Orange Institution had not been able to control the situation. As they pleaded for the crowd to disperse there were cries of 'What did you bring us here for?' The following day even the *Belfast News Letter* was critical, describing the Order's handling of the situation as confused and suggesting that 'it was pointless for leaders to suggest that, at the eleventh hour, they counseled against the parade through the town'.[37]

In Belfast the Whiterock parade that took in the Springfield Road as part of its route again became a cause for concern. The security forces pressed for an alternative route to be taken and eventually the parade went down Ainsworth Avenue, rather than Mayo Street where there had been riots the previous year. Nevertheless, confrontations still followed as Catholic and Protestant youths clashed and troops fought with Catholic youths.[38] A week later Paisley warned that if any parades were banned he would call loyalists out onto the street. A parade in the predominantly nationalist town of Coalisland was slightly re-routed. At another parade near Ardoyne the army split the crowd from the parade but there were still clashes in Ardoyne.[39]

The day before the Twelfth a series of IRA bombs went off in Belfast raising tensions still further. Nevertheless, although there were a few incidents in Belfast and a sit-down protest in Annalong, County Down, the day passed without major problems. The resolution read from the platform expressed admiration for policemen and soldiers but called for stronger law and order measures. Yet again speakers on Twelfth platforms were heckled, this time in Portadown and Rathfriland. In Portadown the platform speakers threatened to call the police unless calm was restored. Hecklers were complaining about the World Council of Churches and climbed the platform at the end to continue their protest. In Rathfriland the Imperial Grand Master of the Orange Institution, L. P. S. Orr, was heckled for not doing enough to counter terrorism. In Augher, County Tyrone, the Grand Lodge was criticised over its hostility towards the Free Presbyterian Church.

On 9 August the conflict intensified when the British government introduced internment and yet larger parts of the Catholic community came to resent the presence of the army. Over 300 individuals were seized and held without trial resulting in widespread civil disturbances. Yet again it was announced that marches and parades were banned. The Ancient Order of Hibernians had decided much earlier to call off its August demonstrations, but large anti-internment rallies took place in September supported by the SDLP and People's Democracy. More illegal marches took place towards the end of the year, the SDLP withdrew from Stormont and the IRA campaign intensified still further. In the main, loyalists held to the new ban, although Paisley still led Apprentice Boys on a parade to Stormont on 13 August (Farrell 1980: 285–90; Bardon 1992: 679–89).

On 30 January 1972 the Civil Rights Association organised a mass anti-internment rally in Derry that was to enter the Guildhall. It ended with the Parachute Regiment opening fire on the crowd and killing thirteen people in what became known as Bloody Sunday. On 18 March the British Prime Minister, Edward Heath, decided to suspend Stormont and introduce direct rule from Westminster. William Whitelaw became the first Secretary of State for Northern Ireland. On 28 March a huge loyalist demonstration ended at Stormont.

Protestants, unionists and the Orange Order, were entering a new era in terms of their relationship with the state. It was now no longer a unionist government based at Stormont that would make judgements on whether particular parades should take place, but the RUC, under the watchful eye of the Northern Ireland Office, the Secretary of State, and a not quite-so-distant

British government. One of Whitelaw's first moves was an amnesty for illegal marchers (Farrell 1980: 293). To begin with, the British government's relationship with the nationalist community appeared to improve as some internees were released and tentative negotiations were started. First the 'Officials', then on 26 June the 'Provisional' IRA called cease-fires. However, at the same time loyalist groups had started to take a yet more hard-line approach. Amongst other actions the UDA set up 'No Go' areas to mirror those in nationalist areas. The debate over these areas had come to symbolise the more general questions of legitimacy and authority in Northern Ireland. For loyalists the control of 'No Go' areas by republicans was indicative of the weakened and ineffective state that appeared to allow the IRA to move with impunity. These new UDA 'No Go' areas were not directly related to intercommunal insecurity but rather directed at the British army. They were as much symbolic as they were of practical use. On 21 May there were confrontations between the army and loyalists in east Belfast and on 3 July a potentially even more serious confrontation developed around the barriers in the areas of the Springfield and Woodvale Roads, Protestant areas of west Belfast. Eventually, after a large number of UDA men, perhaps up to 8,000, paraded around the Shankill area, the army agreed to joint patrols (Bardon 1992: 694–5; Bruce 1992: 60–4). It was to facilitate the Twelfth that the UDA 'No Go' areas were relaxed.

In Portadown the IRA had set up barriers in Obins Street, the area known as the Tunnel, through which the Drumcree Orange church parade was due to pass. On Sunday 9 July the British army removed the barriers and after some disturbances a large number of UDA men lined the route up to the tunnel and threatened to go further if the parade was attacked. The UDA were again in attendance for the Twelfth with masked men collecting money in the town. The Twelfth in some other areas was just as tense. One of the three resolutions called for the re-instatement of Stormont, and many speeches called for unity. At least one speaker in Belfast called for more support for the UDA. In Ballymena William Craig suggested that 'when we speak of organising ourselves for every contingency that means if necessary using arms to defend the right of the majority'.[40]

The Twelfth had gone through significant changes over the previous years. In particular, it had changed from being an expression of the state of Northern Ireland and its unionist government to an event utilised by an increasingly divided and disillusioned unionist community for its own 'defence'. Belfast and other large towns in the late 1960s and early 1970s had seen a vastly increased sense of anger at the inability of the Orange and unionist elites to deal with the advance of Irish republicanism, economic decline and the involvement of the British government. One expression of this appears to be the development, in working-class areas, of what became known as 'blood and thunder', 'kick the pope' or 'fuck the Pope' bands with names such as 'Defender' and 'Volunteer', drawing on a Protestant and loyalist heritage. These bands had only limited musical skills, playing one-key flutes, and were dressed in simple uniforms of grey slacks, a white shirt, a coloured V-neck jumper with perhaps a cap to match. They were often accompanied by groups of teenage girls who also transported alcohol to the Field. The large bass drum that formed the centre of the band was often painted with loyalist insignia and the band was led by a baton-thrower. They introduced a more rowdy and carnivalesque atmosphere to the proceedings. One band, in 1969, when it was asked what music it would be playing apparently answered 'three hymns: The Boyne Water, Derry's Walls, and The Sash'.[41] This growing element in the Twelfth parade did not find particular favour with all the onlookers and Orangemen. In 1971 Faulkner particularly criticised the hooligan element which the *Belfast News Letter* editorial explained 'so gratuitously attached themselves to many otherwise well conducted and orderly parades and whose sole purpose has frequently been at odds with the high principles of the lodges'.[42]

Restraint by the bands, restraint by those following on the footpath – and particularly the young girls who do little to endear themselves to the crowd by the songs they sing – will only enhance the reputation of the Order and the strength of its support. (*Belfast News Letter* editorial)[43]

At the opening of the Sandy Row Orange Arch in 1971 local Orangeman George Watson condemned 'the young people who follow a parade and sing obscene songs'.[44] It is also interesting that in 1969 after Ulster Television (UTV) showed a film about the Twelfth, Norman Porter and William McCrea complained about the drinking scenes. McCrea argued that the Twelfth appeared as a 'drunken festival'.[45]

This more 'rowdy' element has always been present at the Twelfth, particularly in Belfast. It would appear that during the 1950s it was not as prominent, but towards the end of the 1960s once again assumed a higher profile. In a sense the Twelfth was losing its 'respectability'. Not coincidentally, many people both inside and outside of the Institution believe that it is around this time that many of the middle classes left the Orange Institution. By the mid-1990s it was widely believed that membership of the Orange Institution had fallen from a high of 100,000 to nearer 45,000. In the 1930s membership of Belfast lodges was so large that Orangemen would march up to four abreast. By the 1990s the majority marched with just two abreast. It is not unreasonable to suggest that this decline started in the late 1960s. The Twelfth was no longer symbolic of the state and, particularly in Belfast, it was no longer patronised by all Protestant classes.

FROM RESPECTABILITY TO RESISTANCE

In the 1920s many Orangemen joined the B-Specials and became defenders of the state of Northern Ireland. In the 1950s and 1960s the B-Specials were used to maintain the dominance of Orangeism and their right to parade, but by 1970 the only involvement of the B-Specials was in the form of a lodge, Ulster Special Constabulary LOL 1970, marching in Belfast in commemoration of the now disbanded part-time police force. From the first years after the forming of the state of Northern Ireland senior politicians had attended Twelfth parades and non-attendance could be held against them. By the end of the 1960s many were not appearing at parades and they were even banning some parades. From the mid-1920s until the 1960s the speeches from the Twelfth platform were formal, predictable events with resolutions congratulating the unionist government and ministers for the past year's work. Only occasionally was an Orange platform used to criticise actions and policies. From the mid-1960s onwards the Twelfth platform became an arena at which various unionist factions attempted to claim to be the legitimate protectors of the Protestant community. Speakers were heckled, leaflets were passed around and on a few occasions proceedings were reduced to physical confrontations.

The development of the Twelfth into a ritual symbolising the state of Northern Ireland reached fruition in the 1950s when the relationship of Northern Ireland with the state in the south became easier, and when community relations within Northern Ireland were relatively untroubled. In the main, senior members of the Orange Institution were at one with the unionist government and were able to convince the Protestant working classes to continue with what was effectively a form of economic and political patronage. The relationship between the UUP and the Orange Institution could hardly have been stronger.

Given the closeness of the relationship between the state, the government, the Ulster Unionist Party, the Orange Institution and the Twelfth rituals, during the period from 1920 to the mid-1960s, it is not surprising that some of the tensions within the state revealed themselves through the Twelfth. Whilst Farrell (1980) examines the relationship between the business community and the state as the origin of the crisis, Bew *et al.* (1995) view the crisis as developing out of the relationship between the different classes within the Protestant community and the relationship between the Northern Irish and British states. Whatever the reason for it, the crisis had a dramatic effect upon Orangeism. For much of the post-Second World War period the greatest threat to the UUP came from the attraction of working-class Protestants to the Northern Ireland Labour Party. This was countered on the Twelfth platform either by appealing to Orange unity or by aligning socialism with Catholicism. A much more serious and complex threat came from fundamental Protestantism, most clearly represented by Ian Paisley. There has always been a tension between the 'religious' and 'political' aspects of the Twelfth. Initially, Paisley was only a relatively insignificant voice claiming that the political actions of unionists, supported by Orangeism, were undermining Protestantism. This led to the possibility that the Orange Institution could be accused of a 'Romeward' trend. As O'Neill's government, under growing scrutiny from London, was forced to consider liberalisation in some social and economic spheres, Paisley's arguments began to attract support. Further, he was also prepared to defend an Orange domination of the streets in a way that the government became less inclined to do. The Orange Institution, and its public rituals, were torn between a defence of the elite in the Ulster Unionist Party and the more robust defence of perceived Protestant interests being undertaken by Paisley. The dynamics of the situation were further complicated by the growing public pressure from the civil rights movement. The type of forthright attack upon civil rights parades advocated by Paisley inevitably started to lead to civil disturbances which also brought Northern Ireland under scrutiny from the outside. The greater involvement of Britain would almost certainly mean an undermining of the Protestant state with greater reforms and eventually the collapse of Stormont altogether. The Orange and unionist elite could no longer defend the independent form of the state of Northern Ireland and the perceived Protestant interests of the time, at the same time.

The major changes in political relationships that took place between 1968 and 1972 were in part articulated through parades. In 1968 and 1969 the civil rights movement used demonstrations as a medium to ask questions of that nature of the Northern Irish state by demanding the right to public expression in areas that for fifty years had been the preserve of Orangeism. Opposition to civil rights demonstrations by Protestant protesters and the police served to symbolise the inequality of rights that existed. Yet the dominant elements of the civil rights movement were still demanding rights within Northern Ireland rather than a united Ireland and there was little in the way of nationalist communities questioning the rights of Orangemen to hold their parades. But in 1969, as confrontations become increasingly violent, the situation changed. Instead of trying to march into town and city centres, nationalist communities in the Bogside, in Derry and west Belfast increasingly sought to exclude the police. Communal confrontations led to more clearly defined ethnic territorial areas. In these conditions opposition to Orange and Apprentice Boys parades grew as they were viewed as transgressions of boundaries. This was not only because Orangeism represented for nationalists the unionist regime, but also because those parades inevitably brought the RUC and particularly the B-Specials with them. The confrontations that surrounded the Apprentice Boys parade in Derry on 12 August 1969 were significant not only because they set in motion a train of events that led to the introduction of the British army onto the streets, but because many in the nationalist community in Derry were now opposing a loyalist event that came into a city with a predominantly Catholic population. From 1969 to 1972 the nature of political opposition to unionism shifted from civil rights to more overt Irish nationalism and the armed struggle of republicanism. Orange parades that transgressed boundaries became the site for confrontations and disturbances. Leaders of the Orange Order were caught between helping to maintain the peace whilst not being seen as capitulating to the enemy. For many in the Protestant community unionism and Orangeism seemed unable to defend their interests. In many working-class Protestant areas it was not the Orange Order but the UDA that appeared as the defender of the community.

The Twelfth could no longer be a ritual of state. Rather it became the site for a political struggle. In working-class areas, where the communal conflict was most intense, blood and thunder bands developed and a lively, more overtly sectarian and yet carnivalesque, form of parade started to dominate. Senior members of the Orange Institution – never quite sure whether their loyalties lay with the state, the government, with Orangeism or with working-class loyalism – lost control of the rituals. 'Respectable' Orangeism was in retreat. Sarah Nelson in her work on loyalism in the early 1970s vividly describes the anxiety felt by 'respectable' Orangemen and she quotes a senior Belfast Orangeman:

We could understand that because the Government were not taking action people would be tempted to form vigilantes . . . but it worried us. The lawlessness could escalate . . . the criminal aspect greatly increased, especially with this change of values in Ulster now. We were a force for peace in those troubled times, touring the streets and keeping people calm, maintaining respect for the law. The security forces had to take command in the province – not just to stop republican disorder but to stop this slide into anarchy on the Protestant side. (quoted by Nelson 1984: 90)

Parades through Catholic areas both looked more like invasions and were treated as invasions, and with the police and army working to some new agendas they became less likely to ensure the safety of the rituals wherever Orangemen wanted to go. The possibility arose, for the first time since the middle of the previous century, that a large number of Orange, Black and Apprentice Boys parades might be banned. Calls seemed to increase for the right to hold 'traditional' parades, indeed, some parades started to become almost oppositional to the forces of the state.

7 THE ORANGE AND OTHER LOYAL ORDERS

In the previous four chapters I have considered in some detail the development of the Orange Institution, or 'Orange Order' as it is more commonly known. Of particular importance in its development have been its relationship to the state and the class and denominational make-up of its members. To understand the role that the organisation plays in the modern politics of Northern Ireland, and the significance of specific parades, its present structure and membership must be examined. There are also two other important loyal organisations involved in parading, the Royal Black Institution and the Apprentice Boys of Derry. The Orange and Black Institutions and the Apprentice Boys, are commonly termed 'the loyal orders'. Also related to the Orange Order, the Royal Arch Purple has a large membership but parades infrequently. There are smaller loyal orders: the Independent Orange Institution, the Junior Orange Institution and the Association of Loyal Orange Women. These will be briefly considered at the end of the chapter.

THE ORANGE INSTITUTION: STRUCTURE AND DISSENT

The Orange Institution is structured, hierarchically, into a series of geographically based private, District and County lodges. The governing body is the Grand Lodge of Ireland although, as I will explain, it has only limited authority. There is also an Imperial Grand Orange Lodge with representatives from all countries in the world which have Orange lodges, but this body has no local authority.

The Private Lodge

In Ireland there are approximately 1,400 private lodges, each one in existence on the basis of having a document called a 'warrant' giving its number, which is issued and owned, by the Grand Lodge of Ireland. A warrant number can be passed from one lodge to another. If a lodge goes out of existence, then a new lodge can take over that number. A new lodge can be formed when a number of present members make an application and are issued with a warrant and number. Lodges meet about once a month, usually on a regular fixed day at the local Orange hall. In rural areas one might find only one lodge in a hall, however often a number of lodges use an Orange hall, and in urban areas a large hall will be used by a considerable number of lodges. There are about 800 Orange halls in Northern Ireland.[1]

Each lodge elects a number of officials annually, usually in September. The most important of these is the Master, the symbolic head of the lodge, but the lodge also has a Deputy Master, a Secretary, a Treasurer, a Chaplain, a Lecturer and a number of 'Tylors'. These roles can change on a regular basis although it is not uncommon for an individual to hold a position for a number of years. The 'Tylor' controls entry to and from lodge meetings, with movement to and from the lodge room being allowed by the use of a password or a particular knock on the door. The Orange Order still has many of the trappings and rituals of what might be described as 'a secret society'.

Lodge meetings can vary in form depending upon the lodge, although in recent years attendance at meetings has become notoriously poor. A meeting always involves a religious service at some point, and much of the rest of the meeting is made up of private ritual events such as initiations and installations, and of the business of running the lodge. Indeed, most of the discussion entails lodge finances, lodge membership and the organisation of forthcoming parades. For most lodges the focus of the year is the parades that take place on and around the Twelfth and many brethren only turn up at the July parades. Lodge meetings are therefore usually sustained by the hard core of officials. There are continual complaints from the more active membership about the poor attendance at lodge meetings. Although lodge halls are the focus for social events such as Orange balls and dinners, the Twelfth is the day on which everyone appears.

Each lodge keeps a lodge book recording its membership, the dues paid by brethren to the Institution (which may be a few pounds a month), attendance at meetings and the minutes of meetings. The lodge book provides a resource through which the history of the lodge can be traced. In recent years many Orange Districts have published small local histories of the Orange lodges in their area. These invariably list the Masters of the lodge from its foundation and mention significant individuals and war veterans, as well as repeating the stories of local battles along with Derry, Aughrim, Enniskillen and the Boyne.

Each lodge has its own identity, and is felt to have a specific character. Their names might identify with a particular historical figure, political or religious – Cromwell, William of Orange, William Johnston, Edward Saunderson, Edward Carson, Winston Churchill, St Patrick, Reverend Cooke or Hugh Hanna. Alternatively, an individual of specific importance to the lodge, such as an ex-member, might appear in the name. The name might commemorate an event, particularly a battle – the Siege of Derry, Enniskillen, the Boyne, Aughrim, the Somme. The name might incorporate a particular work place – the Great Northern Railway, the shipyard, the Post Office. The name might invoke an idea – 'True Blue', 'Temperance', 'Total Abstinence', 'Crown and Bible', 'Defender', 'Loyal', 'Royal'. Perhaps most commonly, particularly in rural areas, the name recalls a sense of place – a townland, a village, or a district. Indeed, sometimes it can be a place that members used to be connected with. In the country there are lodges connected with the house of the local landlord or gentry. Since some lodges in Belfast were set up by people who moved from the countryside in the second half of the nineteenth century, they carry names such as Fermanagh and Tyrone United Loyal Orange Lodge (LOL) or Donegal LOL.

Nearly all Orange lodges have a lodge banner. These are expensive and ornate items which are carried at the head of a lodge on mini-Twelfth parades and on the Twelfth. Far and away the most popular image is that of King William riding a white horse at the Battle of the Boyne. The other most commonly used images are those of the Crown above an open Bible or a reigning or past monarch. It is quite common to see ideas of Empire represented by a picture of a young Queen Victoria handing a Bible to a kneeling Indian prince with the motto 'The Secret of England's Greatness' below it. However, there is a whole range of images which reflect the themes mentioned above such as the portrait of a historical figure or the depiction of particular events. Sometimes a particular building such as a local church or the Orange hall might be depicted, or even a train or the shipyard, suggesting the industrial roots of the lodge (Jarman 1997a, 1999b).

Each lodge has a number of financial commitments. A banner can last for thirty years or more although many are replaced more often. A new banner can cost £2,000 or more and must be decided on well in advance as the few banner painters in Northern Ireland have very full order books. For most parades, but particularly the Twelfth, a lodge will want to hire a band, which can cost over £300. It is also quite common for the lodge to provide catering for the band they have hired. Add to this the upkeep and heating of the Orange hall and there is clearly a significant financial commitment over the year. If this financial commitment is spread over many brethren then a lodge can be reasonably financially comfortable. For instance, some lodges have forty or fifty members, and some of the largest lodges used to have hundreds. But many lodges are much smaller than this and may even be reduced to under ten active members. Orange lodges are not usually well-off.

Private lodges can also make local bylaws, though these regulations require approval from the Grand Lodge before they come into operation. There is usually no problem as long as they are consistent with the laws of the Institution. Decisions at lodge meetings are made on the basis of a majority vote. Any member dissatisfied with a decision can take his complaint to the District lodge.

Lodges therefore capture much that is local and particular. Their membership, and the position members hold in the lodge, may reflect class relationships and relationships of patronage both urban and rural. They

reflect movements in population, and they reflect religious and political particularities in an area. Just as one lodge might act as a social club with
members willing to share a drink, others would be teetotal and highly
religious. Just as one lodge would be politically active, so others would not be
involved at all in overt politics in the narrower sense of the word. Just as one
lodge might be full of local conservative farmers so will another contain trade
unionists and labour supporters. Just as one lodge may be drawn from a Presbyterian Church so another might be drawn from the Church of Ireland or
Methodist congregations. Many lodges contain a diverse range of men who
simply live in the same area. At the level of the private lodge the Orange Order
is a diverse organisation.

District and County Grand Lodge

Each private lodge sends six representatives to the District lodge. There are
126 District lodges in Ireland. The District lodge is usually in a larger lodge
building, but often meets in the same building as the private lodges, about
once every three months. For instance, Portadown No. 1 District is based at
the Carlton Street hall in Portadown and, although quite a few of the lodges
meet at the relatively large building, there are also a number of outlying
Orange halls, there being at least three other Orange halls within a couple of
miles of Carlton Street hall. In Belfast the situation is slightly different. There
are nine Districts in Belfast, although they are numbered up to ten since
Districts 7 and 8 recently combined due to their small size. All of the District
halls date from around the last quarter of the nineteenth century, which saw
such a great expansion of Orangeism in Belfast. The largest Districts, with
over thirty lodges each, are Sandy Row, District No. 5, in the south of the
city and Ballymacarrett, District No. 6 in the east of the City. Also in the south
of the city, on the Ormeau Road, is Ballynafeigh, District No. 10, which has
seven private lodges. There is a large Orange hall on the Shankill in west
Belfast where No. 9 District meets. Districts 1, 2, 3, 4 and 7/8 meet at Clifton
Street Orange Hall in the north of the city.
    A District can also introduce its own bylaws as long as they do not
contradict the rules of the Orange Institution. District lodges, for instance,
can have differing attitudes towards the sale of alcohol on the premises. I am
aware of one district that only allows political meetings as long as both major
unionist political parties are represented and are supporting a common
interest. Just as private lodges maintain a sense of history and identity, so
too do District lodges. Many District lodges produce local histories, often to
coincide with major anniversaries such as the tercentenary of the Battle of
the Boyne in 1990, the bicentenary of the Orange Institution in 1995 or the
centenary of their particular District such as Ballymacarrett No. 6 District
or Ballynafeigh No. 10 District celebrated in 1996. In Belfast there is considerable friendly rivalry between Districts, particularly between the two

largest Districts of Sandy Row and Ballymacarrett. An Orangeman from one District will often make a little joke at the expense of the other and officials from each District pride themselves on the organisation and smart turnout of their District on the Twelfth. Certain local parades act as an expression of the prestige and reputation of a District and when the Belfast Districts march on the Twelfth they receive an especially loud reception in their own area.

Each District elects a set of officials every October: District Master, Deputy District Master, District Treasurer and District Chaplain being the most important. Depending upon its size each District lodge sends between seven and thirteen representatives to the County Grand Lodges. There are twelve County Grand Lodges in Ireland. Eight are in Northern Ireland: Antrim, Armagh, Belfast, City of Londonderry, Down, Fermanagh, Londonderry, and Tyrone. The other four are in the Republic of Ireland: Cavan, Donegal, Monaghan and Leitrim. A County Grand Lodge has a mainly coordinating and disciplinary role, not having major parades to organise. The Twelfth parades in each County are usually organised by the District hosting the parade. The venues are on a cycle of between four and eleven years depending upon the area, so that each District knows when it will next have a Twelfth to host. The exceptions to this are Belfast and Ballymena which both hold annual Twelfths. The Ballymena Twelfth is hosted by the local District but the Belfast Twelfth is organised by the Belfast County Grand Lodge with the County Grand Secretary chiefly in charge of arrangements. With the notable exception of the Twelfth in 1999, the parade follows the same route every year. Despite this, organising the Twelfth in Belfast is still quite a substantial task. The only other parade that a Belfast County Grand Lodge organises is the Orange Widows charity church parade, from the various Districts to the Ulster Hall, on the last Sunday in April. Most Counties have two meetings a year; County officials being elected in November.

The Grand Lodge of Ireland

Each County Grand Lodge sends a number of representatives, depending on the size of the County, to the Grand Lodge of Ireland, which has its Head-quarters at the House of Orange on the Dublin Road, in Belfast. It is the highest formal authority for Orangeism in Ireland and has a total membership of 373. A list of those in the Grand Lodge was recently published by the Irish Universities Shield of Refuge LOL 369 from a conference discussing the future of the Orange Order. The Grand Lodge in 1996 included: Grand Master, two Assistant Grand Masters (appointment in the gift of the Grand Master), fifty-two Deputy Grand Masters (some nominated by Counties, others appointed by the Grand Lodge, with six nominated by the Grand Master), Grand Secretary, Past Grand Secretary, Grand Treasurer, Deputy Grand Treasurer, Deputy Grand Secretary, Executive Officer (the only full-time, salaried official), four Assistant Grand Secretaries, four Assistant

Grand Treasurers, Grand Lecturer, Deputy Grand Lecturer, Grand Director of Ceremonies, Inside Tylor, Librarian, Assistant Librarian, Grand Committee (sixty members elected from the Counties) and two representatives from the *Orange Standard* (the monthly newspaper produced by the Grand Lodge). The Grand Lodge has twice-yearly meetings from which twice-yearly reports are produced. It has been noted by a number of Orangemen that the average attendance at a Grand Lodge meeting is only between 130 and 160. Recent divisions within the Orange Institution have produced a debate as to how democratic the Institution really is and changes are in the process of taking place. Information produced by the Grand Lodge to counter criticism from within the organisation suggests that 22 per cent of the Grand Lodge hold County office and 86 per cent also serve at District level.

Within the Grand Lodge there are a number of committees. The committee which now appears to be the most important is the Central Committee, though it is apparently a relatively recent development. This includes three members from each County Grand Lodge in Northern Ireland, two each from the Counties of Monaghan, Donegal and Cavan and one from Leitrim. The nineteen other members of this committee are drawn from senior positions within the Grand Lodge. The Central Committee controls the business for the full meeting of the Grand Lodge, oversees matters arising between Grand Lodge meetings and issues press statements. Other committees include the Grand Committee, sixty members elected from the Counties, which considers discipline and the application of the rules and regulations, the Finance Committee, the Education Committee, charged with educating both brethren and the general public in the principles of Orangeism, the Reformed faith and the Protestant historical heritage, the Press Committee (apparently inactive) and the Rules Revision Committee.

Since the mid-1990s there has been growing criticism of the structure of the Orange Order from within the Institution. The introduction to the *Twelfth Programme* of 1996 produced by the Belfast County Grand Lodge gives ample evidence of this:

The Orange Institution is in ferment. Talk of reform is in the air – some would say reform of some kind is inevitable. There are brethren who argue that the District lodge is the hub of Orangeism, the engine room: reform should be concentrated on improving the efficiency and impact of the District lodge on both the Private lodge at grassroots level and remote County and Grand Orange Lodges at higher levels of the Institution's structure.

Among the complaints are suggestions that Grand Lodge is undemocratic, and slow to act. It has been pointed out by members of the Spirit of Drumcree, a ginger group formed in 1995, that if an issue is raised in a private lodge and if the private lodge agrees that it should be taken forward, the issue must then be brought to the District lodge, which must give its approval for it to be brought to the County Grand Lodge, which then must agree that the issue should be raised at one of the Grand Lodge meetings, assuming that the

Central Committee of the Grand Lodge gives its approval. This ponderous system, they have argued, acts to protect the Grand Lodge from criticism. At a meeting in the Ulster Hall on 14 November 1995, organisers of the Spirit of Drumcree referred to the Grand Lodge as 'the old men', and criticised the fact that Deputy Grand Masters are not subject to annual elections. But perhaps one of the most important criticisms that many of the 'rank and file' have made concerns the relationship between the Grand Lodge and the Ulster Unionist Party.

THE ORANGE INSTITUTION AND THE ULSTER UNIONIST PARTY

In understanding the political workings of the Orange Institution, the relationship to be most aware of is that between the Ulster Unionist Party (UUP) and the Institution. The Orange Institution sends around 120 delegates to the Ulster Unionist Council, which has around 860 members; the Council being the body which elected David Trimble as leader of UUP in the Autumn of 1995. But of course many of the other members of the Ulster Unionist Council are also Orange brethren. In towns and villages throughout Northern Ireland UUP meetings still take place in Orange halls, although in some halls political meetings involving only one party are not allowed. To the best of my knowledge, of the ten Ulster Unionist Party MPs, eight are Orangemen. One of the two exceptions is Ken Maginnis, who is nevertheless in the Apprentice Boys. Interestingly, the Orange credentials of unionist MPs are not always obvious. Many of them speak on the Twelfth platforms, but not all of them. John Taylor, MP for the Strangford constituency in County Down is rarely pictured in his sash. But perhaps the most obvious public connection between Institution and the UUP was the Grand Master of the Orange Institution from 1972 to 1997, the Reverend Martin Smyth, an Ulster Unionist Party Westminster MP for the constituency of South Belfast from 1982. Some of the criticisms aimed at Martin Smyth by Orangemen during the crisis over the Drumcree march in 1995 and 1996 centred upon the idea that he tended to act in the interests of the UUP rather than in the interests of the Orange Order. Of course, since a significant number of Orangemen would be supporters of Ian Paisley's Democratic Unionist Party (DUP) such accusations are not surprising. It is interesting that Robert Saulters, Martin Smyth's successor as Grand Master, did not have overt political affiliations whilst high-profile potential candidates in the Ulster Unionist Party did not appear to want the job.

Even during the Stormont era the relationship between Orangeism and the Unionist Party was not without tension. But in recent years, with the implementation of direct rule and the success of the DUP, friction has become such that there is now significant support from both within the Ulster Unionist Party and the Orange Institution to break the link. The Democratic Unionist Party returned two MPs in the 1997 general election, gets around

30 per cent of the unionist vote and, at every European election, Ian Paisley
has come top of the poll within Northern Ireland. The DUP is popular in
working-class areas, particularly in east Belfast where Peter Robinson is MP,
and amongst fundamentalist Protestants. One Orangeman surprised me by
assuring me that Orangemen were not all 'unionists'. When I asked him to
explain, he pointed out that in the Districts in County Down that he was
familiar with there were DUP supporters, Popular Unionists (the now defunct
Ulster Popular Unionist Party led by the former North Down MP, the late
James Kilfedder), Conservatives, Alliance Party members and some Labour
supporters. What he meant, of course, was that many members were no
longer supporters of the Ulster Unionist Party, not unionism *per se*. To that
list of unionist political parties can now be added the Progressive Unionist
Party (PUP), Ulster Democratic Party (UDP), the UK Unionists (UKUP), the
Northern Ireland Unionist Party (NIUP) and the United Unionist Party, all
with seats in the Northern Ireland Assembly. The UUP, at a generous
estimate, represents not much over half of those who would support the
Union. Therefore, the relationship between the Institution, particularly the
Grand Lodge, and the UUP has caused widespread resentment. Significant
numbers of Orangemen felt that Martin Smyth tended to act more in the
interests of his position as an Ulster Unionist MP than he did as the Grand
Master of the Orange Institution. This was particularly strongly felt over the
issue of the right to parade when he failed to appear at Drumcree in 1995,
preferring to work from the Grand Lodge in Belfast. Nevertheless, in spite of
calls for him to resign his post in the Orange Institution, there was little
danger of him losing the annual election for the Grand Master taken in
December 1995 by the Grand Lodge. This simply increased the calls from
the Spirit of Drumcree Group for 'one man, one vote', the introduction of
greater democracy to the Institution, and the breaking of the hold of the
Central Committee which was, according to a Spirit of Drumcree leaflet,
'Official Unionist [UUP] to a man'.

The Orange Institution has a strong egalitarian ethos and a weak
authority structure. The Grand Master, although having a relatively secure
position, does not have enormous power within the Institution. The Grand
Lodge controls the rules of the Institution, and it is the final arbiter on
disputes and disciplinary measures. Importantly, it provides the main link
between the Institution and the media with Officials in the Grand Lodge, particularly the Grand Master and the Executive Officer answering for and
publicly defending Institution. Yet many parts of the Institution act with
great independence. County Grand Lodges, District lodges, and private lodges
organise the parades and make most of the decisions. In the disputes over
the right to parade the District and County Grand Lodges are the important
decision-making bodies. It has been particularly noticeable in the dispute
over the Drumcree church parade in Portadown that senior Orangemen
outside the District have had to act with care and not be seen to be overriding
the wishes of Portadown District. At times the relationship between

Portadown Orangemen and the Grand Lodge has been uneasy. Orangemen from outside the District could only take part in negotiations at the request of Portadown No. 1 District. Consequently, the Grand Master is often left to defend, in the name of Orange unity, actions that he has relatively little control over and it is also not uncommon for the media responses of the Grand Lodge to be criticised by others in the Institution. Taking into account the relative autonomy of the parts of the Orange Institution, the disparate nature of unionist politics and particularly the popularity of Paisley – a staunch unionist not in the Institution – we can better understand the tensions and political dynamics within parades.

BECOMING AN ORANGEMAN

The explicit ideological purpose of the Institution is to defend the 'Protestant Reformed Churches'. The Institution has a set of qualifications and rules that appear in the *Constitution, Laws and Ordinances of the Loyal Institution of Ireland* (Grand Lodge of Ireland 1967). Central to Orangeism are the 'qualifications' to which a member should adhere.

An Orangeman should have sincere love and veneration for his heavenly Father; a humble and steadfast faith in Jesus Christ, the saviour of mankind, believing in him as the only Mediator between God and man. He should cultivate truth and justice, brotherly kindness and charity, devotion and piety, concord and unity, and obedience to the laws; his deportment should be gentle and compassionate, kind and courteous, he should seek the society of the virtuous, and avoid that of evil; he should honour and diligently study the Holy Scriptures, and make them the rule of his faith and practice, he should love, uphold, and defend the Protestant religion, and sincerely desire and endeavour to propagate its doctrines and precepts, he should strenuously oppose the fatal errors and doctrines of the Church of Rome, and scrupulously avoid countenancing (by his presence or otherwise) any act of ceremony of Popish worship; he should, by all lawful means, resist the ascendancy of that church, its encroachments, and the extension of its power, ever abstaining from all uncharitable words, actions or sentiments, towards his Roman Catholic brethren; he should remember to keep the holy Sabbath day, and attend the public worship of God, and diligently train up his offspring, and all under his control, in the fear of God, and in the Protestant faith; he should never take the name of God in vain, but abstain from all cursing and profane language, and use every opportunity of discouraging these, and all other sinful practices, in others; his conduct should be guided by wisdom and prudence, and marked by honesty, temperance, and sobriety; the glory of God and the welfare of man, the honour of his Sovereign, and the good of his country should be the motive of his actions.

According to the *Constitution* when a man wishes to join the Institution he must be over 17 (or 16 if already a member of the Juniors), not a Papist and not have been rejected, expelled or suspended by the Institution in the past. An Orangeman must not betray the proceedings of his lodge; he must bear true allegiance to Her Majesty the Queen and to her successors as long as they remain Protestant; and must agree to 'assist the magistrates and civil authorities of these kingdoms in the lawful execution of their duties, when called upon to do so . . .' (Grand Lodge of Ireland 1967).

An individual wishing to become an Orangeman has to be proposed and seconded by members of a lodge and members are elected by a ballot. If there is more than one black bean in ten then a member will not be admitted. There are a series of rules, the breaking of which can lead to suspension or expulsion. A criminal conviction should, according to the *Constitution*, lead to expulsion although in practice this may well not happen. There are a series of laws governing the relationship an Orangeman should have with members of the Roman Catholic Church. Marriage to a Roman Catholic and attendance at a Roman Catholic service can both lead to a member being expelled. In practice the use of these rules tends to vary among lodges. On more than one occasion, debate has taken place throughout the Institution over a member who has attended the funeral of a Catholic. The situation can be particularly awkward when the Orangeman has an official capacity, such as mayor of a town and David Trimble, as First Minister (designate) of Northern Ireland, came under particular criticism in 1998 when he attended a Catholic funeral of victims of the Omagh bomb.

WHY BE AN ORANGEMAN?

The reasons most often given for membership of the Institution can probably be grouped into three overlapping discourses: 'religious', 'political' and 'cultural identity'. The most commonly expressed reason for being a member of the Orange Institution is for its religious significance, specifically, it is argued, because the principles of the Institution serve to defend the 'Protestant reformed faith'. A few Orangemen will go so far as to argue that Orangeism is not political at all, but simply religious. In some rural areas from the 1950s onwards there was a movement not to have overtly political speeches at the Field on the Twelfth, a position still maintained in part of County Antrim. Many Orangemen place great stress on the importance of biblical teaching within the Institution. The symbolism and ritual of the degrees within Orangeism, the Orange and the Purple, as well as that of the allied Institutions – the Royal Arch Purple and the Black – are based around biblical teaching. Some lodges particularly stress the religious aspects of Orangeism, demanding that their brethren give 'Christian testimony' in public. One Orangeman put it forcefully at a meeting I attended: 'If you don't understand Protestantism, you don't understand the Orange Order.' He went on to explain that 'Protestantism comes from the Latin word "*protestatio*" meaning "witness" "a stand for something".' A highly religious interpretation of Orangeism such as this, which stresses biblical authority and the relationship of man to God, would, I suggest, be a strong part of the discourse of 'respectable' Orangeism. It is often closely tied to ideas of temperance and abstinence, and the keeping of the Sabbath day. At its most extreme, the political is almost seen as polluting of the religious. Interestingly, as Bruce has pointed out, many fundamentalist, evangelical Protestants are ill at ease with Orangeism because it embraces more liberal strains of Protestant theology within the Church of Ireland, Presbyterianism and Methodism. Many fundamentalists, such as members of Ian Paisley's Free Presbyterian Church, remain unconvinced by 'respectable' Orangeism and remain outside the Order (Bruce 1986: 151–4).

In practice, very few Orangemen would deny that the Orange Institution in Ireland is political. The relationship between the 'religious' and the 'political' is not lost on members of the Orange Order; indeed that relationship is seen by many as fundamental. Their Protestantism, as they see it, can best be defended from Roman Catholicism by the relationship of Northern Ireland to the British crown, a Protestant monarchy. An Orangeman must be 'faithful and bear true allegiance to Her Majesty Queen Elizabeth II, and to her Protestant successors . . .' (Grand Orange Lodge of Ireland 1967: 3). With the notable exception of the commemoration of the Battle of the Somme, all those other apparently secular battles, the Boyne, Aughrim, the Siege of Derry, the Battle of the Diamond or Dolly's Brae, are understood as having been in defence of Protestantism. There may be arguments for remaining part of the United Kingdom that rely upon economic or cultural logic, but for Orangemen the central thesis remains being Protestant in a Protestant state. The Orange Institution is seen as important for providing a political unity for diverse Protestant denominations. At times there is almost an obsession with the call for unity within Orangeism. Given the fragmentation of political parties supporting the Union, the Orange Institution is still viewed by many as the uniting force for 'the Protestant people'. At a conference organised by the Irish Shield of Refuge LOL 369 into the future of Orangeism 'Orange solidarity' and 'the numbers of Orangemen' were consistently seen as expressions of the strength of the Institution. Apathy and 'signs of splits' were seen as weaknesses. Some Orangemen will argue that this is the reason that the Institution should break its links with the Ulster Unionist Party believing that by freeing itself from the UUP it might better be able to act as a pan-unionist force. Others would like to see the link broken so that the 'religious' elements within the Institution can be highlighted.

The third reason given for joining the Orange Order might broadly be described as the asserting of cultural identity. Put simply, the Institution is seen as part of the identity of both the Protestant community in general and the local communities in particular. Joining the Orange Institution is something that members of one's family do, or people from one's area, church or workplace do. It is understood as something that has bonded the community together. Members can trace their family roots through the lodge. On the Twelfth, all those that live in the area, and many who used to live in the area, come back together. It is claimed that the Twelfth is the day that the local Protestant community publicly asserts its identity. In other words, Orangeism is seen as a folk culture with its particular rituals and songs that are British and distinctive to Ulster. Orangemen will point out the peculiarities of their particular local lodges, that they march on particular days, that they visit particular memorials, that they always carry a particular flag, that they are always given tea by the same household at some point during a parade, or that the lodge always dresses in the same way. Every lodge, every District, will be able to describe one peculiarity or another.

In no way are these three very general discourses mutually exclusive. Clearly 'the religious', 'the political' and 'the cultural' reinforce each other. A half hour conversation with an Orangeman will reveal all these as aspects of being an Orangeman, but they exist in different measure amongst different individuals. And there are many contradictions and tensions. Many Orangemen, particularly in urban areas, are not regular church attendees. Indeed, Orangeism might be their one and only identification with 'Protestantism' in a religious sense. They will turn up for the parades around July and then not be seen for the rest of the year. It is not unusual for a religious minister taking the Boyne commemoration service on the Sunday before the Twelfth to chastise his Orange congregation because so many of them are only seen in church once a year. Even for those Orangemen who are regular church attendees, Orangeism clearly provides something that their church does not.

There is a fourth, less explicit, discourse. That discourse could be described as overtly sectarian or openly anti-Catholic, it is a discourse that reveals a distrust or hatred of Catholics. This is not the response of 'respectable' Orangeism and not the impression that most Orangemen want to give to an anthropologist, journalist or anyone else enquiring about their Orangeism. Most Orangemen do not see themselves as sectarian. Some Orangemen will explain at length that whilst the Institution opposes the false doctrines of the Roman Catholic church it is not sectarian. In other words, they claim it is anti-Catholic in terms of being 'Protestant' and therefore opposed the doctrines of the Church of Rome but is not anti-Catholic in terms of people who are Catholics. In fact it is common for Orangemen to go out of their way to tell stories that seem to prove the good relationships that they have with Catholics. Most have neighbours, friends, work mates, even occasionally relatives, who are Catholic. I have heard countless times the story about how 'once upon a time' Orange lodges in the country shared their banner poles with the Hibernians and the band shared their instruments with a nationalist band. I would not suggest that this is necessarily a myth, but it is interesting how often one is told the story. There is a clear disjuncture between the personal relationships an individual has with the 'other', and they way the 'other' is perceived as a group.

Much of what takes place in public on the parades appears to the outsider to be sectarian. In practice, for many involved in the parades, opposition to the doctrines of the Church of Rome is subsumed under a general distrust of

Irish Catholics – the 'other' community. This is sometimes revealed in the recounting of conspiracy theories such as the belief in the infiltration of Catholics into the media or in the influence of the Pope in the European Community. But the central reasoning is that Catholics are viewed as Irish nationalists and therefore a threat to Northern Ireland remaining in the United Kingdom. Opposition to a united Ireland is not in itself sectarian but the way it is expressed in the events that surround the Twelfth often is. The speeches at the field, the activities at the bonfires, the songs, the confrontations and the graffiti merge opposition to the doctrines of the Church of Rome as symbolised by the Pope, Irish nationalism and the activities of the Republic of Ireland, Catholics in Northern Ireland and the IRA into a generalised 'other'. It is interesting to note that whilst it used to be an effigy of the Pope that was most commonly burned on the Eleventh night bonfire, it is now the Irish Tricolour. A few Orangemen will explicitly explain that their Orangeism is about opposing the doctrines of Roman Catholicism and not Catholics *per se*. Orangemen frequently point out that the Orange Order stands for civil and religious liberties for all and that whilst their *Constitution* calls for an Orangeman to 'oppose the fatal errors and doctrines of the Church of Rome', the Orangemen must be 'ever abstaining from all uncharitable words, action or sentiments, towards his Roman Catholic Brethren'. Yet such subtleties are lost in popular Orangeism.

There have been some very practical reasons for being an Orangeman. As discussed in previous chapters, from the mid-nineteenth century onwards, belonging to the Orange Institution clearly had economic and political advantages. It was an institution of economic and political patronage. In what sense is this still the case? Orangemen have told me that in terms of getting a job or promotion, even in the security forces or civil services, membership of the Order is now a handicap. This argument is tied in to the belief, held by significant numbers of Protestants, that since fair employment legislation has been introduced in order to rectify religious discrimination, it has become harder for Protestants to get employment. This, they argue, is particularly true of firms whose work force was predominantly Protestant. Beyond all this they argue that being an Orangeman is now frowned upon by the establishment and is thus a handicap to achievement. In addition, the collapse of local manufacturing and its replacement by international businesses has meant that economic patronage that did exist has now been severely reduced. It has not, however, disappeared. At the very least, one might describe the Institution in the same terms as a golf club. Especially in rural areas, membership may well provide business connections.

The position of Orangemen in the police also seems to be changing. It is difficult to estimate the numbers of police officers that have been or are Orangemen. In the past, however, there was a clear close relationship between the Orange Order and the B-Specials, disbanded in 1970, and there is evidence to suggest that maybe up to a fifth of members of the Ulster

Defence Regiment were Orangemen (Pat Finucane Centre 1997: 42). By comparing those members of the Orange Order on the Orange Insitution's Roll of Honour of those killed in the troubles who were RUC officers the Pat Finucane Centre estimates 13 per cent of RUC officers to have been Orangemen (Pat Finucane Centre 1997: 42). I suspect the figure has become much lower in recent years. It is certainly true that senior policemen would not now be allowed to hold a prominent public post in the Institution. There have been recent well-publicised cases of policemen being reprimanded for taking part in an Orange parade. As such, while the overlap between membership of the security forces and membership of the Orange Order is still significant, probably more so in rural areas, an overt relationship is no longer present. Crucially, disputes over parades in the 1980s and 1990s have regularly brought the Orange Order directly, and sometimes violently, into conflict with the RUC. It would be ridiculous to suggest that the relationship which the Orange Institution, and Protestants in general, have with the police or army is now similar to that of nationalists and the Catholic community, or that the police force is seen as 'neutral'. There is continued evidence of an overlap between the local, particularly part-time, elements of the British army, the Royal Irish Regiment, and support for the Orange Order. Most Protestants remain very supportive of the police force and I am aware of incidents when an overlap between membership of the Orange Order and the police may have made a direct difference to a dispute. Nevertheless, the relationship has changed quite dramatically over the last thirty years (Bryan *et al.* 1995: 60–1; Hamilton *et al.* 1995; Weitzer 1995; Jarman and Bryan 1998).

The situation regarding political patronage is less complicated. It is certainly possible to achieve some seniority within the Ulster Unionist Party without being in the Orange Institution or any of the other loyal orders. Nevertheless, the relationship is still close and, in terms of political perceptions, non-membership of the Institution could still be used to raise questions about the loyalty of a particular individual. The most senior member of the Ulster Unionist Party not in the Institution is Ken Maginnis, MP for Fermanagh and South Tyrone. He also has a reputation as a moderate within unionist-circles and probably enjoys a higher standing amongst Catholics. However, he served with the Ulster Defence Regiment (UDR) and can therefore be seen as having defended Ulster. The most significant change in the relationship between Orangeism and political power was the 'collapse' of Stormont in 1972 and the consequent introduction of direct rule, since which, the Institution has had significantly less influence. Whether this will change if a local assembly, provided for under the Good Friday Agreement, is sustained, will be interesting to follow. While membership of the Orange Institution can certainly facilitate the organisation of both economic and political influence, I think that it is unlikely that this now forms a significant reason for individuals to join. Being an Orangeman may still have its advantages, but many brethren would certainly feel that it now carries disadvantages with it.

THE DECLINE OF THE INSTITUTION?

The Orange Order developed from a largely rural or proto-industrial organisation, growing in specific areas of Ulster, attracting labourers, small farmers and particular, predominantly Anglican, landowners. It expanded into a much broader-based organisation, in terms of class and Protestant denomination, with particular growth amongst the Protestant population of a rapidly growing and industrialising Belfast. It was adopted by nearly all liberal and conservative unionist politicians, and it has evolved into an institution of significant economic and political patronage playing an important role in the development of a Protestant ethnic identity in the north of Ireland. Yet just as political and economic conditions, from the middle of the last century until the second half of this century, allowed the Institution to prosper, political and economic conditions since the 1960s appear to have been detrimental. The number of Orangemen appears to have been in decline. Estimating numbers in the Institution is always difficult, not least because claims by the Institution itself always appear exaggerated. Exact figures for membership are not published. Nevertheless, because each lodge makes an annual return to the District of its membership, figures do exist within the organisation. The figure regularly expressed in the press from the end of the last century up until very recently was 100,000. However, recent internal criticism of the Institution coming from the Spirit of Drumcree group, when questioning the leadership given by Grand Lodge, discussed membership reducing to under 50,000. Whilst this has not been publicly acknowledged by the Institution, privately Orangemen accept that numbers have declined.

This decline needs to be explained as it has taken place at a time when many Protestants viewed Northern Ireland as under great threat. While the Orange Institution seems to have lost members from all social strata it has been clear that the middle classes, particularly those from a professional background in urban areas, have tended to leave the Institution. This is a problem of which members of the Institution are aware and it has regularly come up in discussions I have had with Orangemen. One County Grand Master compared his own work in the building trade with illustrious, often aristocratic, positions his predecessors had all had. Certainly a look at the senior members of the Institution reveals a lower class background than might have been true up until the 1950s (Haddick-Flynn 1999: 413). Both of the last two Grand Masters, Martin Smyth and Robert Saulters, come from 'ordinary' working-class communities in Belfast. This argument is strengthened by the general thesis that middle-class Protestants have left active politics altogether (Coulter 1994). Whilst much is speculation, it is possible to identify reasons why the middle classes might not find membership of the Institution so attractive. Most obviously, the decreased role of the Institution in offering significant political or economic patronage could be significant. However, of perhaps more importance is the connection of Orange parades to civil unrest in the late 1960s and early 1970s. As the parades increasingly became the catalyst for destabilisation, and even led to confrontations with the RUC and British army, one would expect certain sections of the Orange Order to become disillusioned. The Orange Institution may have been perceived as too loyalist, and had the nasty whiff of sectarianism surrounding it. Street politics, with sectarian clashes in fractured urban areas, was not the place for the budding solicitor or accountant. Orange parades, particularly in urban areas, had started to be in direct confrontation with the forces of the state: Orangeism was struggling to remain 'respectable'.

However, the middle class abandoning the Institution cannot in itself explain the decline in numbers. There also seems to have been a shift in working-class areas from the Orange Institution into other expressions of loyalism, particularly the marching bands, which I will discuss in the next chapter. Reports and political speeches from the time, and particularly material that appeared in news-sheets supporting the paramilitaries such as the UVF's *Combat*, suggest that the Orange Order had become widely perceived as being politically impotent. It is significant that from 1972 the UDA organised large groups of men marching in Protestant working-class areas like the Shankill. This is a continuation of the critique that developed in the 1960s and crystallised in the fundamentalist politics of Paisley and the loyalism of the paramilitary groups. Neither would be directly critical of Orangeism, but the Paisleyites would tend to criticise the Institution for its 'Romeward trend' and connections with the Ulster Unionist Party, and the loyalists would criticise its moderate views and its lack of leadership and practical activity. The Orange Institution, particularly its formal leadership, was no longer seen as representing the heart of unionism and its authority, its ability to offer leadership, thereby significantly declined. There were, and are, links between Orange lodges and loyalist paramilitary groups, both symbolic and in terms of personnel, particularly in specific areas. But I would suggest that they have reduced in number and that those with allegiances to the paramilitaries who have stayed in the Order have become disenchanted with the Grand Lodge. This political matrix has been further complicated by some within the political groupings connected to the paramilitaries (the PUP, associated with the UVF, and the UDP, associated with the UDA) trying to distance themselves from Orangeism and to articulate a left-wing, non-sectarian form of unionism. The fractures within unionist politics have made some loyalists doubt the relevance of the Orange Institution to the loyalist cause. Put simply, the middle class have left because the Institution is too loyal and some of the working class have left because it is not loyal enough. The working class tend to leave because they do not trust the leadership of the Institution to wield its influence properly whilst the middle class tend to leave because they believe the Institution has no influence. Consequently, caught between the need to satisfy hard-liners and yet retain respectability, with widespread political divisions within unionism and no local assembly, the Orange Institution has become relatively politically ineffectual.

This complex network of political relations within unionism, in which the Orange Order played a central role, has continued to reveal itself during the parade disputes in both the mid-1980s and the 1990s. For instance, in 1985 and 1986 the disputes of parades in the Tunnel area of Portadown led to a struggle between the Grand Lodge, Ian Paisley and the UDA in an attempt to portray themselves as leaders of unionism through a defence of the right to parade. Attempts were made to provide organisations that all unionists could support, such as the United Ulster Loyalist Front which became the Ulster Clubs, but their influence was short lived (Bryan *et al.* 1995; Bryan 1998b). Similarly, the Drumcree disputes in 1995 and 1996 were characterised not only by competition between UUP and DUP politicians but also were in part responsible for the Loyalist Volunteer Force (LVF) breaking away from the UVF. The Orange Insitution has failed to be a unifying body for unionism.

THE LOYAL ORDERS

Before moving on to examine ritual expressions of Orangeism more closely, it is important to discuss other organisations involved in the parades. The generic term 'Orange parade' is frequently used to cover parades that are held by other loyalist organisations, commonly termed the loyal orders, and bands. However, whilst many individuals are in more than one of the loyal orders there are some substantial differences in the ethos and political role of the various organisations which reflect on the range of events that go to make up the 'marching season'.

Two of the loyal orders related to the Orange Institution, the Royal Black Institution and the Royal Arch Purple, have developed from being Orange 'degrees'. The 'degrees', which are associated with Old Testament texts, are similar to divisions used by the Freemasons and are part of the internal structuring of Orangeism which I do not consider here (see Buckley 1985; Buckley and Anderson 1988; Haddick-Flynn 1999). The relationship between the Royal Black Institution and the Orange Institution is so close that it is debatable whether one can see them as separate organisations. The early Orange Institution developed a series of 'degrees' through which members passed, some of which were sanctioned by the Grand Lodge, such as the 'Arch Purple', and some of which were not and were banned. Nevertheless, these alternative degrees continued to exist and one of these 'the Black' had become particularly widespread by the 1850s. Eventually, the Royal Black Institution was officially constituted as a separate organisation from the Orange (McClelland 1990: 22). Individual members of the Black

Institution are grouped into Preceptories and the organisational structure in many respects mirrors that of the Orange. One can only become a member, and acquire the title 'Sir Knight', by proceeding through certain Orange degrees. The Black Institution is best described as more religious and less overtly political than the Orange. Its banners and regalia reflect this religious bias, particularly in the form of Old Testament imagery (Buckley 1985; Jarman 1997a: 184–7, 1999b). It is strongest in the rural areas of Counties Down and Armagh and has its headquarters at Brownlow House in Lurgan, County Armagh. The Black Institution is more middle class, rural, elderly and religious. It is the more conservative face of Orangeism, the more conservative face of unionism. Nevertheless, while it displays many more of the attributes of 'respectable' Orangeism it has similarly lost middle-class membership and most Black parades do have blood and thunder bands taking part. Major Black parades take place in 13 July at Scarva, County Down and on the Last Saturday of August and, like the Orange, Black preceptories would organise parades to church services. To join the Black you first have to join the Royal Arch Purple. The Royal Arch Purple is even more closely tied to the Orange Institution than is the Black. The first meeting of the Grand Royal Arch Purple Chapter of Ireland was in 1911, the Royal Arch Purple developing out of an Orange degree (Royal Arch Purple Research Group n.d.). The Royal Arch Purple has very few parades.

There is also a youth section of the Orange Order. Junior Orange lodges first appeared in the last century but did not come under the control of the Grand Orange Lodge until 1925. It is probably at its strongest in Belfast, catering for boys under 16. In 1974 the running of the organisation was handed over to the Junior Grand Lodge of Ireland. The 'Juniors', or 'Juveniles' as it is sometimes referred to, organise parades but also tries to involve the youngsters in other recreations and holiday trips. There are also Women's Orange lodges that parade. They are structured into a separate organisation known as the Association of Loyal Orangewomen of Ireland. Their profile has risen in recent years particularly around support of the Drumcree dispute.

Smaller than the Black or the Orange Institution, with around 12,000 members, the Apprentice Boys of Derry was founded in its present form in 1814. If the Orange Institution has the Battle of the Boyne as its main commemorative event, the Apprentice Boys have the Siege of Derry from 1688 to 1689. Whilst the Apprentice Boys share the Protestant religious ethos of the Orange Order the central purpose of the organisation is to commemorate the Siege. Apprentice Boys wear a distinctive crimson collarette and usually carry bannerettes rather than large banners. The City of Londonderry is seen as so important that anyone wishing to become an Apprentice Boy must be initiated within the city walls. The organisation is divided into eight 'Parent clubs': Baker, Browning, Campsie, Mitchelbourne, Murray, Walker, the Apprentice Boys of Derry Club and the No Surrender Club. Affiliated to one of these clubs are a series of branch clubs organised through Ireland, Scotland, England and beyond. The clubs in a particular area combine to form an Amalgamated Committee (Jarman and Bryan 1996: 11–12).

The Apprentice Boys of Derry is a quite separate organisation from either the Orange or the Black Institution. It is impossible to know exactly how many of its members are in the Orange as well but I would estimate it as certainly over 50 per cent. It is more regional than the Orange, with its greatest strength being in the Londonderry area, and it has fewer major parades. Significantly, although the Apprentice Boys used to have formal connections with the Ulster Unionist Council they parted company in 1974. There are also fewer occasions at Apprentice Boys events at which politicians speak or get directly involved. Senior Apprentice Boys stress that their organisation exists to commemorate the siege of Derry. This appears to have left the organisation better able to cope with diversities within unionist politics. Ian Paisley is a member, although his relationship with the Apprentice Boys has not been without its ups and downs. In some areas the political position of the Apprentice Boys might be more closely allied to the politics of the DUP but there is no direct relationship and on some issues there are significant differences (Bryan *et al.* 1995; Jarman and Bryan 1996). For instance, in contrast to the Orange and to many DUP supporters, the Apprentice Boys are more relaxed in their attitude to the consumption of alcohol on its premises. The Apprentice Boys are also less strict on controlling the types of flags that are flown at its parades. I have seen flags supporting the Ulster Independence movement carried at a number of Apprentice Boys parades.

The symbolic importance of the City of Derry to the Apprentice Boys is reflected in power relations within their Institution. The Governor of the Apprentice Boys is always from the city and the views of Apprentice Boys in the city carry great weight in the organisation. This greater centralisation has made the organisation better able to develop a strategy for dealing with opposition to their parades in the City of Derry from the Bogside Residence Group (Jarman and Bryan 1996; Kelly 1998). Whilst the Orange Order's Grand Lodge has failed to give an authoritative lead on the parading issue, Derry Apprentice Boys have entered into talks with residents and the Parades Commission on a number of occasions. They have attempted to make significant changes to their parades held in the city on the nearest Saturday to 12 August, including developing one part of it as a pageant. The Apprentice Boys and the Orange Order share many members in common as well as the use of many lodge buildings and a broad Protestant and unionist perspective. However, there is relatively little communication between the two organisations at a senior level and the Apprentice Boys have taken significantly different approaches on a number of issues in recent years.

There is also a relatively small organisation, the Independent Orange Order, the origins of which were explained in Chapter 4. It is numerically strongest in the north Antrim area where the Orange Institution is sometimes referred to as the 'old Order'. There are two distinctions between the Independent Orange Order and the 'old Order'. First, the Independents place great stress upon certain religious issues, particularly the protection of the Sabbath day, and they have a more overtly strict attitude to alcohol. Second, the Independents pride themselves on not being affiliated to a political party. It was due to disagreements with senior Ulster Unionists that the Independent Institution was founded. There is also some evidence in recent years to suggest that disenchanted members of the 'old Order' join the Independents as an alternative. After an incident at the Scarva Black parade in 1976 involving the heckling of Martin Smyth, some Portadown Orangemen were suspended and went on to form an Independent Orange lodge in the area, which held its first parade in 1979 (Bryan *et al.* 1995: 20).

The perception amongst many outsiders is that they are connected to the DUP. It is easy to see why this misconception comes about. North Antrim is Ian Paisley's Westminster constituency and he gives a speech wearing a sash at the Independent's Twelfth demonstration (usually held in Ballycastle, Ballymena or Ballymoney) and is consequently always depicted on local and national television as if he were an Orangeman. This gives Paisley an ideal opportunity to demonstrate broader Orange credentials. In fact the sash is white, with red and blue trim which, I think, belongs to an organisation called the Ulster Protestant Volunteers with which Paisley was involved in the mid-1960s.

To many outside the loyal orders, members of all these various organisations are just 'Orangemen', parades being consistently referred to as 'Orange parades' regardless of who actually organises them. Indeed, parades are frequently used by the media as an image of the whole Protestant community in Northern Ireland. Certainly, there is a sense of common purpose amongst all those in the loyal orders. Nearly all of them are unionist, that is, if we ignore the small number with Ulster Independence leanings. Also there are many who are members of more than one of the Institutions. All of the institutions draw upon a similar set of symbolic references and upon a discourse of loyalty and the defence of the Reformed faith, and they all have similar ritual practices. However, in this chapter I have set out the more specific and localised sense of identity that exists within the Orange Institution, and have argued that not all Orangemen share the same understanding of what it is to be an Orangeman, that the particular form of the Orange Institution and present political divisions within unionism give the Orange Institution a relatively decentralised authority structure, and that there are significant differences between the different loyal orders. They have different organisational structures, different leaders, and have their own particular political and regional profiles. All this is important when we examine the large number of parades in Northern Ireland. I have also begun to explore the changes that have taken place to the Orange Order since the 1960s. Most significantly, the reduction of membership has left the Orange Order struggling to depict itself as representative of Protestantism in Ireland. Further, the fragmentation of unionist party politics has inevitably led to increased political tensions within the Institution. The events in Portadown since 1995 have started to make these changes much more obvious.

8 THE MARCHING SEASON

In this chapter the Twelfth parades are placed within the context of a cycle of parades commonly referred to as 'the marching season' and the way participants prepare for the forthcoming 'big day' of the Twelfth is examined. Key players in all loyalist parades are the marching bands and I will elaborate on the role of the bands and suggest that they have their own regional, class and political profile. Locality is also of importance in the events. As has already been stressed, the Orange Institution is geographically divided and this is reflected in many of the events leading to the Twelfth. Rural Orangeism can be distinguished from Orangeism in Belfast and in Belfast itself local identities can be clearly distinguished. I therefore discuss the way particular parts of Belfast hold their local parades and how the class and ethnic make-up of the local affects the parades. One Orange parade is not just like any other (see for instance Cecil 1993).

In 1997 there were 3,314 parades in Northern Ireland according to figures produced by the RUC (see Appendix 1). The vast majority of these, 2,582, are classified as 'loyalist' (230 'republican', 502 'other'). Northern Ireland now has specific, unique, provisions for the control of parades. Under the Public Processions Act (Northern Ireland) 1998, an organisation wishing to have a parade must submit a 'Notice of Intention to Organise a Procession' – known as the '11/1' – to the police twenty-eight days in advance. The only sorts of procession not requiring an application are funeral processions and those held by the Salvation Army 'along a route customarily followed by them'. Surprisingly, legislation does not define what is meant by a procession. Those organisations applying for permission must indicate the date and time of procession, the route, the numbers likely to take part where practicable, the number and names of bands likely to take part, the arrangements made for controlling the procession and the name of a person representing the organisation. Previously, under the Public Order (NI) Order 1987, senior RUC officers were empowered to place conditions upon such an event so as to 'prevent disorder, damage, disruption, or intimidation'. Under the new legislation, brought about by the parades disputes, a Parades Commission makes determinations on a disputed parade or lays down various conditions for a parade to take place. The '11/1' also asks for information such as the uniforms and regalia to be worn, the banners and flags to be carried, the names of the speakers if there is to be a meeting, and the methods of transport if participants are moving to another parade. Guidelines from the Parades Commission are now given to procession organisers about how to control the procession, where it should position itself on the public road and the role of stewards. Guidelines also ask that bands should cease playing when approaching a place of worship if a service is in progress.

The legislative changes came about because of the escalating number of disputes after 1995 and calls from certain politicians, from inside the RUC and from some nationalist groups, for even tighter controls. In the pages that follow I will explain some of the reasons for all these requirements and the push for greater control. The sheer number and nature of loyalist parades is bewildering, so to begin with I suggest the following typology for parades which Neil Jarman and myself developed (Jarman and Bryan 1996:15–24), and discuss the annual cycle of events.

(1) *Main Annual Commemorative Parades*. These parades are the focal events for the loyal orders. For the Orange Institution – the Boyne Parades on 12 July, for the Black – the demonstration at Scarva on 13 July, the commemoration of the Battle of Newtownbutler held in County Fermanagh early in August, and 'Last Saturday' parades held at six venues on the last Saturday in August, and for the Apprentice Boys of Derry – the 'Relief of Derry' parade held on or around 12 August, and the closing of the Gates of Derry on or around 18 August. These parades are seen as the most important commemorative dates by members of the loyal orders and are the occasions that attract the biggest crowds. There are nineteen major parades on 12 July, organised by various Orange Districts. Most areas have the Twelfth organised according to a cycle so that a particular District will hold a main parade every so many years. The main commemorative Last Saturday Black parades do not strictly commemorate anything but appear to mark the end of the marching season. The two major Apprentice Boys commemorative parades are always held in the City of Londonderry.

(2) *Local Parades*. Within this category are 'mini-Twelfths', 'little Twelfths' or 'pre-Twelfths' held by the Orange Institution from the middle of June until a few days before July. They take place within particular Districts and involve a full display of regalia and banners. Some invited lodges from outside the District might take part, but they are essentially a local event. The parade in some senses marks the boundary of the District since it stays within a certain area, although there are no rigorous District boundaries. The mini-Twelfth parades of No. 5 and No. 6 District in Belfast, that commemorate the Battle of the Somme, always take place on 1 July (unless 1 July is a Sunday). There has been a great increase in the number of mini-Twelfth parades since the mid-1960s. Prior to the Troubles local lodges paraded the banner to the lodge Master's house. As the security problems increased, this practice became awkward for the police and it was replaced by a single District parade. New mini-Twelfths have continued to appear during the 1980s and 1990s,

including one in Portadown in 1990 which has a different theme every year (Jones *et al.* 1996: 57). For many Districts the mini-Twelfth may be the biggest parade they have that year, since the Twelfth itself will involve them travelling to another District in the County. Some Blackmen will also have local parades prior to the Last Saturday parade.

(3) *Feeder Parades.* Many lodges, and most Districts have small parades in their own area before leaving to travel to a main commemorative parade, and have another parade on their return. There may be only nineteen main commemorative parades on the Twelfth, but the RUC recorded 547 processions in total on the Twelfth of 1995. In Belfast the feeder parade leads directly onto the main commemorative parade. Many of the Private lodges would have assembled away from the District lodge and marched to the District hall before that. However, in country areas the feeder parade will start at a lodge hall and take a route through the village to the buses that will transport the lodges and bands to the main parade. Most Apprentice Boys Clubs will also have feeder parades in their area before proceeding to Londonderry on buses for the August Relief of Derry commemoration. Similar parades also take place on the return home from the main commemorative event.

(4) *Church Parades.* Parades take place prior to the church services that are arranged by all the loyal orders. They meet at the hall and parade to the church and they parade back, possibly by a different route, after the service. Private lodges, Districts and occasionally Counties may organise church services. There will be services on St Patrick's Day, for the Loyal Orange Widows Fund late in April, to commemorate the Battle of the Somme on the Sunday before 1 July, on the Sunday before the Twelfth for the Boyne Service, on the Sunday before the Last Saturday, and on Reformation Sunday late in October. Many private lodges will have their own particular Sunday service and the Apprentice Boys have services in different areas throughout the year. Some new church parades have developed in the last few years, for instance, lodges in east Belfast have had a church parade on St Patrick's day only since 1985.

While bands do accompany lodges on church parades they are asked not to play party tunes and it is often the accordion and more respectable bands that are arranged for these occasions. Nevertheless, even on some church parades there are blood and thunder bands playing 'The Sash'.

(5) *Arch, Banner and Hall Parades.* These parades are held at the opening of an Orange Arch, which may well take place annually and could be part of a mini-Twelfth parade, and at the unfurling of a new banner or the opening of a new Orange Hall. Prominent politicians often make speeches at these events and it is also common to have a religious service at some point in the proceedings. These events are usually relatively small, involving just local lodges and bands.

(6) *Social Parades.* Parades organised by the Junior Orange Institution on Easter Tuesday, in May and June, a number of parades organised by the

Women's Orange Institution, the Apprentice Boys parade on Easter Monday are not related to any particular anniversaries.

(7) *Occasional Parades*. In recent years there have been a number of notable, sometimes large, one-off parades. On 15 May 1982 Belfast Orangemen organised a parade to point out the serious problem of unemployment.[1] In 1990 there were numerous events to mark the tercentenary of the Battle of the Boyne, including a large parade through the centre of Belfast. In 1994 the Institution held a rally in Belfast on the theme of 'British citizens demand British rights'. In September 1995, possibly the largest Orange demonstration ever took place in Loughgall, County Armagh, to mark the bicentenary of the Institution. And during the dispute at Drumcree in 1996 and 1998 there were a whole series of protest parades in Districts all over Northern Ireland. Many parades of this class may well be preceded and followed by feeder parades.

(8) *Competitive Band Parades*. The most obvious development in parades since the 1960s has been the enormous increase in what are known as 'blood and thunder' or 'kick the pope' flute bands. As well as playing a large part in other parades, many of these bands have started their own competitive parades. These parades are held in the area a particular band comes from and the host band judges and presents a number of trophies in different categories covering style, music and the different types of band. At these parades a street collection is often made to raise money for the host band. There are competitive band parades taking place on most Friday and Saturday evenings and afternoons on almost every weekend from March right the way through to September. The largest of these, such as the ones held in Markethill, County Armagh or Ballymena, County Antrim, can attract over fifty bands from all over the countryside. Bands advertise their own event by going to other bands' events and issuing an invitation. The more events a band visits, the more visitors they should have at their own band parade. If a town has more than one band, it may well have a number of band parades in the year. Portadown has three band parades a year and there are over a dozen in the Belfast area throughout the summer. When one considers that some bands also parade in their local area, when returning from a band parade, then it is clear that band parades partly explain the increase in the total number of parades in recent years.

(9) *Commemorative Band Parades*. These parades chiefly involve bands but are usually organised by loyalist paramilitary groups to mark the Somme in July, or Armistice Day in November, and also on occasions to commemorate the loyalist paramilitary dead. Wreaths are often laid, in the first case at official memorials and in the second at paramilitary wall murals or commemorative plaques (see Jarman 1993, 1997a).

The above typology gives some idea of the diversity and extensive range of events that make up 'the marching season' (see Appendix 2). The Black Last Saturday parades appear to have developed as major events after the First

World War. The Apprentice Boys and Junior parades that take place on Easter Monday and Tuesday respectively were started in the 1930s, apparently as a deliberate attempt to counter republican Easter Sunday parades. A few mini-Twelfths started after the Second World War, but most have appeared since the mid-1960s. Irregular band parades have taken place since the last century, but the more highly developed and organised competitive band parade events have increased in number throughout the 1970s and 1980s. The marching season used to be understood as starting in late June and finishing at the end of August. Now it is commonly seen as starting at Easter and continuing into September.

There are a number of parades which take place before Easter. In a number of areas there are church parades on the nearest Sunday to St Patrick's Day. On Easter Monday the Amalgamated Committee of the Apprentice Boys hold a parade at a rotating venue away from Londonderry. Easter Tuesday sees the Junior Orangemen from Belfast and South Antrim march, normally at a seaside resort in Antrim or Down. The Orange Widows service at the Ulster Hall takes place at the end of April. In May, a relatively quiet month, there are a number of church parades, Orange and Apprentice Boys, from particular lodges and clubs and the Juniors of Armagh, south Tyrone and Fermanagh parade at a seaside resort. There are a number of band parades every Friday and Saturday on every weekend from May until September unless there is a main commemorative parade taking place. On the first Saturday in June the Belfast Amalgamated Committee of the Apprentice Boys hold a parade in north, south, east or west Belfast on rotation. The following Saturday sees the first mini-Twelfth of the season, in Portadown, and the landing of William at Carrickfergus is commemorated in the town with a re-enactment and a parade. From mid-June on there are mini-Twelfth parades on most Fridays and Saturdays somewhere in Northern Ireland up until the Twelfth. On the final two weekends of June there are large mini-Twelfths that take place in north and west Belfast respectively. There are church parades on every Sunday in June with the Somme commemoration services taking place on the last Sunday in June, or 1 July if it is a Sunday. This is the date for a number of Somme anniversary mini-Twelfths, most notably in south Belfast, Sandy Row No. 5 District and in east Belfast, Ballymacarrett No. 6 District. Between 1 July and the Twelfth, mini-Twelfths take place on weekdays as well as over the weekend in Belfast and towns all over the north. On the Saturday before the Twelfth many bandsmen and some Orangemen go to the Boyne commemoration parades held in Scotland, and by the Donegal County Lodge at Rossnowlagh in the Republic of Ireland. The Sunday before the Twelfth, or 12 July itself if it falls on a Sunday, Orange lodges attend a Boyne commemoration service at a church with a consequent parade to and from the service. On 12 July, or 13 July if the Twelfth falls on a Sunday, the major Twelfth Boyne commemoration Orange parades take place. On the following day, or on the Monday if the following day is a Sunday, the Black Preceptories of Counties Armagh and Down hold a parade and a Sham Fight at Scarva in County Down to which Blackmen from all over the north travel, with associated feeder parades beforehand. There is also a smaller Black parade held in Bangor, County Down. Both 12 July and 13 July are public holidays in Northern Ireland. On the weeks following the Twelfth there are a number of band parades, including a couple on Saturday afternoons in parts of Belfast. There are also some church parades late in July. Early in August, east Belfast Junior Orange Lodges parade in east Belfast, then travel to a parade at a seaside resort and some Black Preceptories hold Sunday church parades. On the Saturday nearest to 12 August the Apprentice Boys hold their main commemorative parade in Londonderry with many amalgamated clubs holding feeder parades before and after their journey to the Londonderry parade. Also on the Saturday nearest 12 August the Blackmen of County Fermanagh parade to commemorate the Battle of Newtownbutler. As the end of August approaches Black Preceptories hold local parades and church parades and on the Last Saturday of August there are six main Black parades and a large number of feeder parades before and after the main parades. There are some band parades right into October, with the last major Orange church parade taking place on the last Sunday of October, Reformation Day. There are a variety of loyalist parades in November to mark Armistice Day and there are a few Orange lodges that hold church services to mark Guy Fawkes Day. Finally, on the Saturday nearest 18 December the Apprentice Boys in Derry mark the Closing of the Gates of Derry in 1688 by burning an 18-foot-high effigy of the traitor Lundy. The burning is preceded by a parade.

There are bound to be smaller parades that I am unaware of, but the above description of the parading calendar gives some idea of the plethora of events that go to make up the 2,500 plus loyalist parades (for further details see Jarman and Bryan 1996: 25–34). To many outsiders, particularly to nationalists, they are all just 'Orange' parades; to loyalists they have their own particular meanings and their own particular importance.

PREPARING FOR THE BELFAST TWELFTH

The most important and most popular of the parading dates is 12 July. It was made a public holiday in 1926 and the nearest weekend to the Twelfth still marks the date when factories close for two weeks and large numbers of the population prepare to take their holidays. The schools in Northern Ireland close for the summer three weeks earlier than in England because of the Twelfth. A particular band may or may not take part in various other parades during the year, but all bands will try to be booked by a lodge to march on the Twelfth. Preparation for the Twelfth starts well before July. The Secretary of the County Grand Lodge of Belfast will have a meeting the previous August with the marshals of the parade to see if any problems arose at the previous July demonstration. In November the Secretary will meet with District marshals to discuss the problems. In February the Twelfth committee, made up of the District Master, Deputy District Master and District Secretaries of all the Belfast Districts meet to make decisions on the forthcoming Twelfth. Sometimes some of the rules need to be adjusted, for instance, recently the rule that forbids members wearing insignia from going into pubs was tightened to include private 'clubs'. The speakers for that year's Twelfth platform also have to be arranged. Arrangements have to be made for toilets, first aid and litter disposal at the field venue, Edenderry. It is the job of the County Grand Secretary to coordinate all the arrangements for the Belfast parade whereas in areas outside Belfast it would more often fall to the Secretary of the District organising that year's main Twelfth parade. In Belfast the arrangements for the District to meet in the morning, which often involves private lodges and their bands marching to the District lodge, must also be done at a District level. As July approaches, the Secretary of the Belfast County Grand Lodge will have prepared the route maps and timings, the order of the day, the platform order, the hymns to be sung at the platform, the letter to the Queen, permits to those traders who will be at the field at Edenderry, official passes for lodges either taking a car into the Field or erecting a marquee, and the list of bands arriving from outside Northern Ireland.

The main concern of most private lodges will be to book a band for the forthcoming events. Yet a significant number of lodges fail to get a band or choose not to hire one. In 1996 there were about 130 lodges marching in Belfast and only seventy-six bands. Often a lodge uses a band that it has marched with for a number of years. Belfast lodges do not necessarily hire Belfast bands. Some lodges may well have built up a relationship with a particular country band. The band might well be Scottish with up to twenty or thirty bands coming over from Scotland to march in the Belfast Twelfth each year. Scottish bands planning to march need the permission of the Orange Institution in Scotland, and the Orange Institution in Belfast also has to be notified so that it, in turn, can notify the police of which bands are coming over. If the County has not been notified, then the band will not be allowed to parade. The same is true of the smaller number of bands that come over from England. The band booked by a lodge for the Twelfth may well not be the same band as that for the District's mini-Twelfth. The monthly newspaper produced by the Grand Lodge, the *Orange Standard*, contains advertisements by lodges requiring bands for forthcoming events and by bands that are looking for lodges to march with. Bands can be in short supply, particularly so for the Twelfth. It is not unheard of for one lodge to poach a band from another lodge. Due to lodge demand outstripping the supply of bands, some of the fees paid to bands have risen. I believe the range in Belfast is between £300 and £800, although prices up to £1,000 have also been mentioned.

There have been forms of contractual agreement between lodges and bands for a long time, but in 1986, after two summers of major disturbances at parades the Grand Lodge decided to introduce a specific band contract (Bryan *et al.* 1995: 52–3). It is worth reproducing it in full:

Grand Lodge of Ireland
CONDITIONS OF ENGAGEMENT
Clause 1. All bands shall come under the jurisdiction of the Private, District, or Grand Lodge with whom they are parading and shall obey the Instructions of the Parade Marshals.
Clause 2. No band shall have on parade a member of the Orange Institution who has been suspended or expelled for any offence other than non-payment of dues. Neither will a Band have on parade members or ex-members of a Band which has been debarred from participating in parades by a District Lodge, County Grand Lodge, or Grand Orange Lodge of Ireland. A County Grand Lodge or its Band Committee shall have the power to adjudicate on transferred ex-members of a debarred Band.
Clause 3. All members of a Band must maintain uniformity of dress to a standard reflecting on the dignity and decorum of the Institution with whom they are on parade.
Clause 4. Shouting in an unseemly manner for the emphasis of certain tunes is strictly forbidden.
Clause 5. Bands will employ Regulation Step only while on parade. Double or Twin Drumming, (i.e. two people beating one bass drum simultaneously) Dancing, or Jig Time Step by any member of the Band is prohibited.
Clause 6. On the occasion of Church Parades (under all jurisdictions) – RECOGNIS-ABLE HYMN TUNES & SACRED MARCHING ARRANGEMENTS ONLY SHALL BE PLAYED.
Clause 7 Bands taking part in Church Parades must also attend the Church Service.
Clause 8. No bands will play any music or indulge in drumming in the field during the public meeting at a Demonstration or Rally.
Clause 9. No intoxicating liquor shall be conveyed into a Demonstration Field under the auspices of a band or its individual members. Under no circumstances should liquor be consumed in the ranks while on parade, or taken aboard Coaches or other Public Transport. (It is expected that lodges will lead by example).
Clause 10. Flags which may be carried by bands are approved at the discretion of Parade Marshals, or the Senior Officers of a District Lodge under whose jurisdiction the Parade is taking place.
Clause 11. The conditions of agreement will be applicable until revoked by either party.

The reasons for many of these rules, particularly clauses 3, 4 and 5 referring to behaviour on the parade, clause 6 referring to alcohol and clause 10 referring to the flags, will become clear when I discuss the parades themselves. It is significant, however, that the Grand Lodge introduced, and has made some attempt to enforce, the conditions of engagement. These are the rules of 'respectable' Orangeism.

The most obvious feature that all the loyalist parades in Northern Ireland have in common is musical accompaniment. Different forms of musical accompaniment have played a role in parades organised by the Orange Institution since 1795. In previous chapters I outlined the early role of the drumming parties, made up of a large drum and 'fife', the development of the use of lambeg drums in Belfast, the consequent disapproval of the rougher groups and the encouragement given to more respectable pipe and silver bands, the role played by some of the rougher bands from Scotland and the rough accordion bands in Belfast in the 1920s and 1930s, and the development of blood and thunder bands in urban areas from the mid-1960s. Especially since the 1880s there has been an ever present friction within the parades between the orderliness of the 'respectable' Orange parade and the 'rougher', 'undisciplined', raucous, more overtly carnivalesque, yet threatening performances, by the predominantly working-class bands.

Broadly speaking, there are five types of bands. The least common type is the silver band. Silver bands require members to have considerable musical ability, and the upkeep of such a band, particularly given the instruments involved, is enormous. Some bands used to be connected to factories, but with the decline in local industry such patronage is long gone. Many of the remaining silver bands take part in major Irish and British competitions and draw their membership from both Protestant and Catholic communities. Orange lodges find it difficult to afford silver bands and, given the nature of their instruments, they are less inclined to take part in the long trudge of a Belfast parade. Silver bands can be found on country parades, particularly Black parades in Counties Down, Armagh and Fermanagh, but they are now a rarity in Belfast. More common are 'kilty' or bagpipe bands. These are very popular in Ireland and again take part in competitions all over the British Isles. A little cheaper than a silver band, there are quite a lot of kilty bands to be found in country parades and usually a few in the Belfast Twelfth, although there were none in 1996.

The third type, that is more common still, is the accordion band. Earlier in the century they had a reputation for being one of the more rebellious types of band, but the accordion is not an instrument that lends itself to being heard against the banging of a big drum. The accordion bands presently found in parades have a high female membership and by their nature do not evoke much of an animated atmosphere at parades. Their actions tend to be less animated than the flute bands, the music is quieter, and they have fewer followers walking alongside. There are one or two more boisterous accordion bands still to be found which have been involved in a number of confrontations during the parade disputes.

By far the most common form of band is the flute band. Three types can be distinguished. A full music flute band uses a five-key instrument and its members may be able to sight-read music. Members of a melody or 'part music' band are slightly less skilled, use a simpler single-key flute but can, nevertheless, play some harmonies. The 'blood and thunder' or 'kick the pope' flute bands play a single-keyed flute and may well have members with almost no musical knowledge whatsoever. Indeed, some members will not know all of the tunes being played and on parade they periodically 'dummy flute', that is, pretend to be playing, while others in the band actually play.

The centrepiece of all of the above bands is usually a large bass drum and some side drums, with flute bands tending to have a particularly large bass drum. It is, in the main, melody and blood and thunder bands that take part in band competitions and it is the blood and thunder bands that dominate.

With the notable exception of Bell's (1990) examination of loyalist bands within the context of youth culture in Londonderry, Jarman's (2000) general look at the development of blood and thunder bands, and sections of Jenkins' (1983) examination of working-class youth in north Belfast, there has been remarkably little research on such a vibrant cultural development. Setting up a blood and thunder band is relatively cheap and easy. Often a few members break away from another band and to begin with all that is needed is a second-hand set of instruments, a rudimentary uniform and somewhere to practice. Senior band members will be given charge of teaching younger members at band practices. Splits in bands are not uncommon and bands come in and out of existence as the number and compatibility of the membership dictate. Many bands develop quite a sophisticated personnel structure with a band 'Master' or 'Captain', a secretary and treasurer, drum major who heads the band and a number of marshals. These members plus others form a committee that makes decisions for the band. Some bands draw up written rules that cover such matters as failure to turn up at band practices, failure to attend band parades, poor discipline in terms of punctuality, shouting in the ranks, disobeying a marshal's instructions on parade, excessive drinking, the inappropriate use or loss of band uniforms and inappropriate use of band instruments. There may well be a disciplinary committee that can impose fines or exclude a member from the band if the infringement is serious enough. As the running of the band begins to demand considerable organisational skills and control of financial resources, authority and bureaucracy become inevitable. Yet many of the bands are highly democratic, putting many decisions to the vote. For instance, bands can be approached by paramilitary groups and asked if they wish to carry their flag on parade. There may be some financial inducement involved. With bands strapped for cash this sort of assistance may be attractive over and above the support some members of the band might have for that paramilitary group. The standards can be handed over at a 'colours' ceremony. Certain bands are born right out of the paramilitary organisations and may even be used as a means of recruitment. However, there are also blood and thunder bands that show a good deal of antipathy towards paramilitary groups. I am aware of at least one band in Belfast voting against carrying such a standard. It is therefore not easy to produce a typical model for the politics of blood and thunder bands (Bell 1990: 115–16). The one feature that nearly all of them have in common is their social setting. They are nearly always based in working-class urban areas or on housing estates in rural areas.

The blood and thunder band has been, without question, the most distinctive development in loyalist political culture since the 1960s. Bell described their role in parades as youths attempting 'to breathe life into an established tradition' (Bell 1990: 124–5). The bands 'with their own regimental style, seem to mediate youthful style and "traditional" Loyalist culture' (Bell 1990:123). There are a number of characteristics that make them quite visibly distinct from other bands, including the development of distinctive uniform styles and the carrying of flags. In the 1970s most of them appeared on the streets wearing simple V-neck jumpers, white shirts and grey flannel trousers with perhaps a coloured cap. Some bands quickly advanced to wearing blazers and further developing the uniforms. The name of the band, along with a variety of loyalist symbols, were painted on the drum. Names such as 'Defenders', 'True Blue', 'Volunteers', 'Young Conquerors' and 'Young Citizen Volunteers' invoke a popular loyalist history as well as a sense of being protectors of their community. Some of the names and regalia make direct reference to loyalist paramilitary groups. This is particularly true of the UVF because that organisation itself claims inheritance from the organisation formed out of Orange lodges in 1912. UDA insignia, and the insignia of a particular military wing, the Ulster Freedom Fighters (UFF), also appear on some band regalia. During the 1970s and through the 1980s more blood and thunder bands started carrying flags, prior to this only lodges carried flags on parades. Through uniforms, through the display of insignia on the bass drum and through the carrying of flags, blood and thunder bands have imposed their own symbolic expressions on parades organised by the loyal orders. Since many of the symbols are drawn from the lexicon of loyalism and unionism, significant numbers of Orangemen are supportive of these expressions, but the association of some of the bands and their symbols with paramilitary groups is also highly problematic for 'respectable' Orangeism. Concern over blood and thunder bands, some of the flags they have begun to carry, and their 'rowdy' supporters are not uncommon in the *Orange Standard*.[2] Stricter rules have been introduced to control the situation in the form of the band contract and an official list of flags approved by the Grand Lodge for carrying on parade. Those officially permitted flags are: the Union flag, the flags of the four countries comprising the UK, the Cross of St Patrick, flags of overseas Orange jurisdictions, lodge flags, banners and bannerettes, the Orange Standard, band flags and bannerettes, and flags issued for approved anniversaries such as the Boyne tercentenary. In spite of this attempt at regulation, UVF flags are commonly carried by blood and thunder bands and I have seen both Red Hand Commando (a wing of the UVF) and UDA and Ulster Freedom Fighters (UFF) flags carried during Orange parades. The carrying of UVF flags is legitimised by some Orangemen by reference to the UVF of 1912 which went on to form a large part of the 36th Ulster Division in the British army. Indeed, some of the flags show battle honours from the First World War. However, the UVF of 1912 was a paramilitary organisation preparing, if necessary, to fight the state and was clearly quite separate from the 36th Ulster Division. The carrying of other flags, such as those of the Red Hand Commando and UDA, is clearly against the rules of the Orange Institution.

I will discuss the blood and thunder bands further in the context of describing the parades themselves, but it is important to stress a number of points at this stage. Generally, bands have no direct connection to the Orange Institution, although there are a few rural bands that are drawn directly from an Orange lodge. The economics of parades are such that lodges cannot afford to hire very expensive bands. While bands that do take part in the parades accept that they have a contractual obligation to the lodge that hired them, and therefore that they are technically under the authority of the Institution during Orange parades, members of bands feel that they are as much part of the Twelfth as the Orangemen. Some bands and band members have a distinct political agenda of their own, linked as they are to loyalist paramilitary organisations and therefore to their political parties the Progressive Unionist Party (PUP) and the Ulster Democratic Party (UDP). Also, many bandsmen have clear ideas of what the Twelfth is all about, and some of their ideas do not coincide with those of 'respectable' Orangeism. This is particularly revealed in their attitude to drink and their decorum during parts of the event. The *Conditions of Engagement* codify some of the rules and tie the bands closer to the parade authorities, making them answerable to the lodge hiring them. The way these new restrictions were introduced was criticised in the UDA magazine *Combat* and there were some attempts to set up a permanent United Bands committee. As the UVF's magazine *Ulster* put it, 'the bands are the backbone of any parade or rally'.[3] The same publications expressed quite a degree of disgust over some of the 'Orange leadership' and the contracts went on to cause a good deal of controversy.[4] In many ways it is the bands that put in the most preparation for the Twelfth, they start practising for a new marching season in January. They will be on all parades organised by all the loyal orders from Easter onwards and attend band parades on many weekends. They are at least as important to loyalist parading scene as the loyal orders.

AROUND BELFAST

The first physical sign that 12 July is approaching is the piles of wooden pallets on spare bits of waste ground and street corners in Protestant working-class areas. They will go to make the bonfires to burn at midnight on the 11 July. Locals generally do the organising of such events, not the loyal institutions, and it is younger children and teenagers that take the most interest. There is competition between different areas, and different streets, to make the best bonfire and it is quite common for material to be stolen from one site, only to reappear at another, and also for a bonfire in preparation to be mischievously, prematurely burnt. Accordingly, the local children will stand guard over their bonfire for weeks beforehand, even building shelters in which to sleep overnight.

As well as the collection of wood for the bonfire, street decorations are prepared in Protestant working-class areas, political murals are brushed up or re-painted (Loftus 1990, 1994; Rolston 1991; Jarman 1992, 1993, 1997a), kerbstones, lamp-posts, bus-stops, bollards, and anything else that might take a lick of paint, are painted red, white and blue, bunting is strung between the houses on many streets and the Orange Standard, Union, Northern Ireland, Scottish and other flags are placed outside houses. Many houses in Protestant working-class area have metal fitments on the wall into which a flagpole can be placed. As the Twelfth approaches, Orange Arches go up in many areas. These are now usually metal constructions spanning the road, and have numerous Orange and unionist symbols on them. Their annual opening may well be combined with a mini-Twelfth and undertaken by a senior Orangeman or unionist politician, who makes a speech. Although there are very few arches now to be found in Belfast they are still common in country areas (Loftus 1994; Jarman 1997a).

On the second or third Saturday in June, Carrickfergus District Lodge, Antrim No. 10 District, hold a re-enactment of the landing of William at Carrickfergus harbour, about 12 miles outside Belfast. Orangemen, some dressed as Williamite soldiers, parade with bands through the town to the harbour. William of Orange enters the harbour in a small boat and is greeted by Orangemen dressed as the dignitaries who were apparently present in 1690. In 1993 some set-piece political speeches were made from a platform at the harbour including some words from the then Grand Master, Reverend Martin Smyth. The following year these formalities were dispensed with. At the re-enactment there is a commentary reminding the audience of 'King Billy's' achievements. William then mounts a white horse next to a statue of the Prince of Orange, erected in 1990 for the tercentenary, and leads a parade of the Williamite soldiers, local Orangemen and about half a dozen bands, through the town. In 1994 William took so long to get going that one irate bandsman shouted at the king 'Come on Billy we've got a pub to go to'.

North Belfast

The following weekend in north Belfast there is a parade organised by Districts 1–4 called the Tour of the North. This parade takes two different routes on alternate years. One route takes in the more northern area of Belfast around the Antrim Road, Tiger Bay and York Road, the other route takes in a more northwest area encompassing the Crumlin Road and Woodvale areas. Given the chequer-board like ethnic geography of north Belfast (Doherty and Poole 1995), both parades inevitably go near or through nationalist areas. In 1996 there were serious disturbances between police and members of residents' groups trying to halt the parade on the

Antrim Road route (Jarman 1997b), and in 1998 the Parades Commission re-routed the parade. On the Saturday there is also a small parade at Legoniel in the north of the city.

West Belfast

The last weekend of June has a number of mini-Twelfths on the Friday and Saturday and the Somme commemoration church parades on the Sunday. The most significant mini-Twelfth for the Belfast area that weekend is the Whiterock parade in west Belfast. This parade, possibly first held in the late 1950s, essentially links the small Whiterock Orange Hall on the Springfield Road with the larger lodge on the Shankill used by No. 9 District. It has regularly sparked disturbances and, since the late 1960s, has had its route changed on a number of occasions. The area leading from the Shankill to the Springfield Road is largely loyalist and has nearby areas of industrial parks and wasteland. The parade used to take in a larger section of the Springfield Road in the Falls area of Belfast, and, in spite of a number of routes changes, it still crosses onto a section of the Springfield Road perceived as nationalist. Relatively few houses are passed by the parade in a largely industrial area but a community group opposed to the parade has demon-strated against it.

This parade is dominated by blood and thunder bands. In the 1996 parade there were nineteen bands, all of which were flute bands and, at most, no more than two were melody flute bands. A large amount of UVF regalia was carried and worn. Old Boyne Island Heroes LOL 633 carried a bannerette depicting a UVF man, and a large number of the bands carried UVF flags and had bass drums painted with references to the UVF or Young Citizens Volunteers (YCV), the youth wing of the UVF. Numerous young people watched the parade, many of them drinking, and yet it is quite clearly a day for the community with families and old people also out for the event. All the Orangemen in the District No. 9 colour party were in suits and bowler hats. The parade weaved through the streets around the Shankill, which were bedecked in red, white and blue bunting and Union, Northern Ireland, Scottish and Orange flags. Despite the intimidating appearance to an outsider, it is difficult not to get caught up in the sounds, colours and excitement. Some of the bands lay wreaths at the plaques and murals that are in memory of those from loyalist paramilitary groups who have lost their lives (Jarman 1993).

The tension rises as the Whiterock parade reaches Ainsworth Avenue, from where it moves onto Workman Avenue. Since a high 'peace wall', punctuated by gates, separates the Protestant and Catholic areas, it is quite clear when the parade is moving into the Springfield Road area. In 1994 I watched as the police allowed the parade through but stopped the spectators from following. The parade went over to the other side of the peace wall and the crowd was left standing in front of the police. Bottles and stones were thrown. There was a large explosion in the crowd and a full-scale riot erupted, with the police firing baton rounds. It later transpired that a member of the UVF had tried to throw a grenade at the police, but it went off in his hand, killing him and injuring over a dozen others. There is now a memorial plaque on the wall to the UVF man beside which flowers were placed during the parades in 1995 and 1996. Because of the loyalist ceasefire late in 1994 and the increased political activity of those groups in the form of the PUP and UDP, it was in their interests to be seen to be controlling the situation. Members of the UVF on both the 1995 and 1996 parades acted to stop the crowd getting near the police lines. Indeed, it is significant that it was members of these organisations, not the Orange Institution, which was able to control the crowd.

East Belfast

On the afternoon of the Sunday on or before 1 July, Orangemen attend services to commemorate the Battle of the Somme. In particular the 36th Ulster Division LOL 977 holds a service at the Ulster Hall in the centre of Belfast to which many Districts parade. The routes of these smaller church parades are unproblematic except in south Belfast, on the lower part of the Ormeau Road, where residents of a predominantly nationalist area have protested. This particular Somme commemoration church parade has been banned since 1995.

On 1 July a number of Somme anniversary parades are held by the Orange Institution around Northern Ireland. Probably the two longest-standing are those in east Belfast, held by Ballymacarrett No. 6 District, and one in Sandy Row, organised by Queen Victoria Temperance LOL 760. Both of these parades not only involve the respective Districts but also attract Orangemen and bands from other areas and draw a significant number of spectators. The Ballymacarrett parade in east Belfast has a distinctive friendly and relaxed atmosphere. Many who have moved away from east Belfast make sure they return for this occasion. A number of Orangemen suggested to me that they prefer this day to the Twelfth. Members of the District are quick to point out that this is not a mini-Twelfth parade, such as many other Orange Districts hold around these weeks, but the Somme anniversary parade. They go up to lay a wreath at a small memorial set into the wall at the bottom of the Belmont Road, but the circular route takes them on a 3–4 mile circuit of east Belfast. East Belfast only has a small Catholic area, called the Short Strand, which the parade passes a dual carriageway's width away from at its start. In that regard this parade does not manifest quite the same tensions that might be found on parades in north or west Belfast. Nevertheless, a large number of police are required to fill the space between the road and the houses of the Short Strand, and, in 1996, with tensions over parades running high, I watched as some shouting was exchanged between spectators and youngsters on the Short Strand.

At the east Belfast parades I have witnessed in 1993, 1994 and 1996 the spectators at the side of the road were most numerous in the more working-class areas around Ballymacarrett and the Ravenhill Road but thinned in the more middle-class areas. The laying of the wreath took place towards the end of the parades with the main body of the procession halting while the colour party surrounded the plaque and a small service was held. As so often happens at Orange events around war memorials, bands and spectators caught up in the excitement of the parades seemed oblivious to the more sombre moments. Nearby bands keep playing away, and, at one point in 1994, a couple of men carrying blue plastic bags of beer staggered right through the ceremony. A few yards down from the plaque, on the other side of the Belmont Road, is the Stormont Inn where crowds gather, with women providing much of the singing and dancing. As the parades restarted the blood and thunder bands received an especially warm welcome, the local bands getting the biggest cheers of all. The women on the street corner and the men in the band perform for each other, encouraging the music and the singing to get louder. The parades continued back down to the District hall where the colour party and District officers line the side of the road for a march past. These events, as with all Orange parades, were concluded with the playing of the British national anthem.

Looking from the war memorial to the Stormont Inn a few yards away, one sees many of the apparent contradictions within Orange parades. They seem to be both a religious, sombre, commemorative ceremony and a secular, drunken, carnival at one and the same time. When passing the nationalist area of the Short Strand, some of whose residents would view the parade as threatening, the parade is flanked by dozens of armoured RUC Land Rovers and the atmosphere feels tense. When passing through the streets of east Belfast, with old friends and family members meeting each other, the atmosphere is welcoming. Bands mix sectarian tunes with numerous popular songs, and their young female supporters, in short skirts and high heels, mix sexual innuendo with sectarian chants.

South Belfast

The two Districts that encompass the area of south Belfast are Sandy Row No. 5 District and Ballynafeigh No. 10 District. Sandy Row is a large District with over thirty lodges, taking in the loyalist working-class areas of Donegall Pass, Sandy Row, the Village and Windsor Park, although much of south Belfast is middle class and affected by a transitory university population. No. 5 District holds a large Somme anniversary parade on the same day as that of east Belfast.

On the other hand, Ballynafeigh No. 10 District, which is centred at the top of the Ormeau Road, has only seven lodges and is an area with a less working-class population. Indeed, the area of Ballynafeigh itself probably has a higher proportion of Catholics than Protestants and is 'mixed' (Hanlon 1994; Doherty and Poole 1995). Nevertheless, over the past few years the public profile of this District has changed dramatically. In February 1992 five people were murdered by the UFF in a bookmaker's shop in the lower part of the Ormeau Road below the bridge. Shortly afterwards the Lower Ormeau Concerned Community (LOCC) started a campaign to have parades by the loyal orders re-routed away from the lower Ormeau Road, which has a largely nationalist community along part of it, and a transient student population along another. The campaign received national prominence when, during the mini-Twelfth of 1992, some bandsmen and Orangemen waved five fingers (indicating the five dead) at those residents protesting by the side of the road. Northern Ireland Secretary, Sir Patrick Mayhew, stated that the behaviour would have 'disgraced a tribe of cannibals'.[5] Consequently, although the District continued to have other parades down the road they agreed under some pressure to take the mini-Twelfth on a route that did not involve crossing the Ormeau Bridge onto the lower part of the Ormeau Road. This decision was unpopular with other Orange Districts, some of whom refused to join the 1993 mini-Twelfth. Since 1995 the police have blocked all Orange Institution parades other than the Twelfth. The Twelfth was voluntarily re-routed by the Orange Order in 1997, and re-routed by the Parades Commission in 1999. In 1995, as the mini-Twelfth parade reached the junction at the Ormeau Bridge, some bandsmen and spectators clashed with the RUC blocking the bridge. The following year, it appeared to me that the bridge was marshalled better by the Institution and the parade maintained great discipline, despite efforts by loyalist spectators to encourage a confrontation. Therefore, since 1992 the parades organised by this small Orange District have not only become a focus for political discussions within Northern Ireland but also have received the attentions of the world press (Jarman and Bryan 1996).

THE BOYNE ANNIVERSARY SERVICE

The Sunday afternoon before the Twelfth, or 12 July if it falls on a Sunday, all Orange Districts have Boyne commemoration services that involve a parade from the lodge hall to a church and a return parade. The service may circulate between a number of different Protestant churches in an area over a number of years, or it may visit one specific church as with the Portadown Drumcree parade (Bryan *et al.* 1995). Although these parades are small scale and usually involve hiring a couple of accordion bands to play hymns, sometimes blood and thunder bands are hired. The band is expected to join the lodge in the church service but this does not always happen. It must also be noted that the numbers in a District that take part in a 'religious parade' and attend a church service do not usually compare well with the numbers that turn out for the Twelfth parade itself.

While clearly the Boyne anniversary service is an occasion when the religious aspects of Orangeism are highlighted, sermons often have a more overtly political content. The Orange Institution, of course, has many ministers as chaplains, but there is nevertheless a tension between the liberal, more ecumenical, wings of the Anglican, Presbyterian and Methodist churches and Orangeism. This has become more acute in recent years as the parade disputes, particularly at Drumcree, have engaged members of all three churches north and south of the border. It is not unheard of for church ministers to refuse to take an Orange church service, or even for members of the church to refuse to give permission for the use of their church, but in general the use of churches by the Orange Institution is not problematic. It is my impression that church authorities ignore these tensions for fear of the divisions they might cause.

THE BIG DAY DRAWS CLOSER

Loyalist parading culture in Northern Ireland is about much more than just the Twelfth. There is a whole complex of events before and after which reflect the diversities within unionism and the particularities of local identity. I have concentrated on Belfast where preparations are quite different from many rural areas, but even within Belfast there are distinct localities with their own parading 'traditions' expressing particular senses of identity. This sense of local identity has been most vividly articulated by the work of Holloway on the loyalist Donegall Pass area, at the city centre end of the Ormeau Road, in south Belfast. He argues that it is wrong to overestimate the strength of the relationship of the population of the Donegall Pass area to the neighbouring loyalist area of Sandy Row.

It may be possible to cross to Protestant Sandy Row in seconds but Shaftesbury Square marks a deep gulf between these communities. Neighbours are not united in their Protestantism but divided by strong tribal loyalties based on shared experience within defined territories. The Pass, Sandy Row, the Village, all Protestant communities neighbouring each other, define their relations in terms of rivalry. They fight each other at school; their bands clash in the marching season, they are expelled from city clubs for the same mutual aggression. Cooperation is only likely in a fight against Catholics. (Holloway 1994: 9)

Even if quite such strong feelings of locality are not repeated in other parts of Belfast, my own experience when talking to Orangemen and bandsmen about the parades is also of a sense of local identity. Their local parades are of special importance to them and each parade is believed to have its own atmosphere and peculiarities. As will be seen with the Twelfth, parades that bring areas together nevertheless serve to point up the differences in locality. One Orange lodge is not exactly like another, one Orange District is not completely like another and one Orange parade is not totally like another. It is understandable that to outsiders, particularly those in the Catholic, nationalist community, all parades are just Orange parades; but in attempting to understand the parades it is important to be aware of the local character of specific events, and the local and internal politics that influence the control and development of those events.

9   THE TWELFTH

Despite the construction of a discourse around 'tradition' and the unchanging, 'familiar', nature of the parades, all are unique social events allowing a degree of creativity from the participants. My generalised description of the Twelfth in this chapter will provide an understanding of the event itself – its apparent contradictions, its nuances, its moments of conflict and, above all, its political dynamics. I will contrast an understanding of the Twelfth as 'traditional' and 'respectable' with some of the contemporary and carnivalesque developments in the parades. The Twelfth of July is a public holiday in Northern Ireland. Many people, Catholics and Protestants, who do not want to take part in the events, or indeed want to avoid them, take the opportunity and leave Northern Ireland for holiday elsewhere. County Donegal, for instance, is inundated with visitors from across the border. Orangemen sometimes claim that the Twelfth is good for tourism; ironically, the tourist board in County Donegal would probably agree.

THE ELEVENTH NIGHT

For the participants the Twelfth requires great stamina. For many, it starts early on the evening before, the focus being the Eleventh night bonfire. In some country areas local Orange lodges have more organised Eleventh night festivities, but young lads in the area prepare most of the Belfast bonfires. By any standards some of the bonfires are huge. The bulk of the construction is made from wooden transport pallets liberally interlaced with tyres, the size of the bonfire depending to a large extent upon the area in which it is built. Sandy Row, for instance, has a reputation for having one of the biggest bonfires although there are a number of smaller fires around the same area. Prior to the Eleventh night a Union flag or a Northern Ireland flag may well sit on top. As the evening progresses the local bars fill up, barbecues are lit, and impromptu street parties begin. The atmosphere in my experience is relaxed and friendly. Some people might return to bonfires in areas they lived in as children. Parents park their cars and take their kids to see the fire. Local fish and chip shops do a particularly good trade and in some areas the local band will parade, providing entertainment. A disco may also be set up near a large bonfire. As midnight approaches the crowd gravitates towards the largest fire. It is not uncommon for smaller local fires to be burnt first so that people can move to the large fire. People move from one bonfire to the next, many carrying their tins of beer or bottles of cider in the blue plastic bags that so many of the local off licences in Belfast use. Young teenagers are particularly in evidence. The girls wear the latest fashions that so often seem to be quite unsuitable for walking around on what may well be a cool and wet Belfast night. Most of the lads wear various types of sports gear, almost inevitably connected to Glasgow Rangers Football Club in some way. And in the 'infamous' areas like Sandy Row one or two camera crews wander about getting their shots for tomorrow's news or their next documentary on Northern Ireland.

Part of the significance of the event is in what is burnt (Kertzer 1988: 122). At some point during the evening someone scales the bonfire to take down the Union flag, and replaces it with the symbol to be burnt. In the last century it could well have been an effigy of the Pope, O'Connell, the traitor Lundy or even a local unpopular magistrate, but in recent years one item above all goes to the flame – the Irish Tricolour. That is not to say that the Pope or a Papal flag is never seen, and Lundy is certainly burnt on 1 July in Portadown and in Derry in August, but the Tricolour is by far the most popular target. At midnight the bonfire is lit. On a wet night, large amounts of flammable liquid need to be applied to the foot of the fire to ensure successful combustion. Often it takes 10 or 15 minutes before the fire really takes hold, but when it does the heat is incredible, and the crowds surrounding the fire back away. Excitement rises as the flames climb the construction. The biggest cheer goes up as the Tricolour bursts into flames and is quickly reduced to a charred flagpole and then to cinders. As the flames become more intense anything within 50 or 60 yards or so is in danger. Advertising hoardings start to peel, telegraph poles catch fire and in some cases nearby properties are quite clearly at some risk. The larger bonfires often come crashing down after burning for 20 minutes or so, scattering the crowd. The fire brigade will spend most of the night rushing from bonfire to bonfire. The atmosphere smells of burning rubber, the air above Belfast becomes thick with smoke and the clouds are tinted orange. After about half an hour the families that have come by car head away and leave the locals and the teenagers to the disco. The revelry continues into the not so small hours of the morning.

THE TWELFTH

The day's events start early despite the late celebrations of the night before. The sound of flute bands can be heard around Belfast well before eight o'clock. The roads around the city have few cars on them and on the Lisburn Road, along which the main commemorative parade travels, people will already be setting out their garden chairs to get the best spot on the route. Stalls are erected on the route and are soon selling Union or Northern Ireland flags, red, white and blue hats or plastic marching batons for the kids to play with. The vans that sell burgers and chips also position themselves. Tables are set up outside some of the churches along the route to sell tea and sandwiches to the passers by. Policemen organise parking restrictions and contractors deliver crowd-control barriers for certain parts of the route.

More than one Orangeman has described to me the expectation and excitement they feel before the Twelfth as being greater than before Christmas. The Twelfth Committee does most of the organising for the day in Belfast, but the bulk of the responsibility falls upon the County Grand Secretary. He starts very early in the morning. Two limousines are booked, one which picks up the Secretary as well as refreshments for guests, and the other which picks up the County Grand Master, County Grand Chaplain and County Grand Secretary. There is also a taxi organised for the elderly marshals who work at the pedestrian crossing points on the parade route. A wreath is also arranged to be laid at the cenotaph. The District Officers and the lodges that use Clifton Street Orange Hall all meet at the hall. Some of the lodges and bands might make a small parade to the hall, starting from the lodge Master's house if that is convenient.

At District halls in other parts of the city, preparations are also being made. At Sandy Row, lodges from No. 5 District and their bands march to the hall and prepare to form up to parade up to the Clifton Street Orange hall to join the main parade. The same goes for the District meeting on the Shankill. Districts No. 6, No. 9 and No. 10 at Ballymacarrett Orange hall, West Belfast Orange hall and Ballynafeigh Orange hall prepare to march to two points near the centre of the city where they will take their place in the main parade as it comes through. In all areas there is a well-used routine for preparing to march. Permission for each of these parades must be applied for by submitting an 11/1 form to the police.

In Ballymacarrett, when bands and lodges arrive they form up in the side streets off Templemore Avenue. Each lodge has its banner unfurled, some leaning up against the wall as the lodge awaits its turn to join the feeder parade. Some banners have black ribbons attached indicating a recent death in the lodge and many have bunches of Orange lilies hanging from the banner poles. In 1993 the words 'No Dublin Interference' hung from the top of some banners. Certain lodge members will take it in turn to carry the banner and some young lads might well be paid to hold the rope that keeps the banner steady. On a windy day carrying the banner can be difficult and a few lodges, with insufficient young men, have resorted to attaching it to the back of a car.

Most Orangemen are in suits with their collarettes displaying their lodge number and any present and past position they have held within the Institution (e.g. PDM = Past District Master). Some collarettes are plain, but others display a variety of badges. The lodge Secretary and lodge Master will check that the band knows what is expected. The wearing of bowler hats and white gloves is not quite as common as the stereotype of Orangemen, found in the newspapers, might lead one to believe, but most officials are attired in that way and some lodges are particularly smart. Often Orangemen carry umbrellas.

Each lodge has a couple of Marshals who should have received instructions from the District Marshals who have in turn received instructions from the County Marshals at a meeting the previous month. At the front of the lodge the banner is held, followed by lodge officials if they wish to go towards the front. Quite a number of lodges carry flags such as the Union flag or the Orange standard. Also towards the front of the lodge, flanking the colour party, are the 'Tylors' who carry 'symbolic' weapons, usually a sword or pike. I put symbolic in inverted commas since there have been odd occasions when these weapons have become something less than ornamental. I have spoken to one policeman who was attacked by one of the 'symbolic' swords during an incident in the early 1970s.

There are no rigid rules as to what order the elements of the parade march in but generally the band is first, then the banner, officials and flags, flanked by sword-carriers, then usually two, sometimes three, files of Orangemen with pike-bearers to the rear. The two files are little more than the width of the banner apart, taking up about half the width of the road. Alternatively some lodges have the banner taking the lead followed by the band and then lodge members, and I have also seen the band to the rear of the lodge. Some lodges, short on numbers, can appear rather pitiful groups, but others, with a large number of members smartly dressed and walking in good files, certainly give a military impression. If really elderly brethren need to be transported, then a car drives with the lodge. The car number plate is usually blotted out and replaced by the lodge number for security reasons.

The feeder parade from east Belfast must have enough time to get to Donegall Street to join the main parade. Sometime around 9.30, the District officers, headed by the District bannerette with No. 6 and a crown and open Bible depicted on it, form up in Templemore Avenue and head down the Newtownards Road and into town. Each lodge and band follows on in turn. By now the crowds in east Belfast will be three and four deep on the side of the road. Some of the local bands receive particularly popular attention from spectators. The Gertrude Star Flute band are a large blood and thunder band that come from around the lower end of the Newtownards Road and were formed in the early 1960s. As with so many of the flute bands they have a large following, mainly of teenage girls dressed up as if for a party, who will stay with them for the whole day.

All the lodges from the Clifton Street hall, plus Sandy Row and Shankill Districts, form up in the streets beside the Crumlin Road above Carlisle Circus. The order in which the Districts will march is taken on rotation. Up until 1960 No. 1 District went first down through to No. 10. From 1960, whilst different Districts took turns to be the lead District, the following District was always No. 1, then No. 2 and so on. This meant that except when it led the parade, No. 10 District was always last. This changed in 1972 when it started in rotation so that if No. 9 led, No. 10 would follow then No. 1 down to No. 8, who would in turn lead the parade the following year. Every lodge had a turn at the back. This change apparently took place because some of the lodges consistently were getting home late and this worried them in the deteriorating security situation of the early 1970s.

The honour of leading the parade is taken with competitive banter, the annual *Twelfth Programme* containing reasons why that year's District deserves to be out in front. District No. 4 might claim to be 'the leading District', or No. 1 District 'the premier' and 'democratic' District, while No. 10 might conclude that 'the last shall be first, and the first shall be last'. Sandy Row District, 'the pride of Belfast', and Ballymacarrett District, 'the wise men from the east', are particularly competitive.[1] Each year a different lodge from the leading District takes its turn to be the first lodge on parade.

The main parade leaves Carlisle Circus at 10.00 a.m. Officially, it is under the direction of the Chief County Grand Marshal, and two County Grand Marshals, with the District Marshals – two or three to a District – being answerable to them. On at least one occasion walkie-talkies have been used to keep the Marshals in touch with one another, but given the length of the parade, this apparently became impractical. Orangemen frown upon large gaps in the parade, and Marshals attempt to ensure that this does not happen. There are also designated crossing points along the route at which elderly Marshals are in attendance. While this may seem unnecessary since there often obvious gaps between one lodge and the next it is actually an issue that is treated as one of some importance. Since the parade could take over an hour and a half to pass one point it causes significant inconvenience for passers-by as well as spectators. Perhaps understandably, anyone moving through the ranks of a lodge or band would be stopped. Attempts by spectators or passers-by to cross without permission often cause problems. At almost every large parade I have ever watched I have seen at least one incident of a pedestrian attempting to get across the road and being manhandled, often roughly, back to the side of the road he or she started from. If one asks senior Orangemen about this behaviour they will always tell you that sometimes their members overreact a little and that people are worried about the security of the parade. It is true that if a spectator or pedestrian approaches a Marshal or any Orangeman and asks permission, they will usually be shown across, but the number of times I have seen an apparent overreaction does seem significant. It seems to reflect a strong attempt on the part of members of the parade to control the physical integrity of the event. I will discuss some of the ways this integrity later breaks down, but certainly during the first half of the day there is a more 'military' bearing to the parade.

In front of the official Orange parade is always a Christian group carrying their own simple 'Jesus Saves' type banners. Preachers with megaphones proclaim 'the good news' and on occasions I have heard them warning of the false doctrines of the Roman Catholic Church. Leaflets explaining how one might be 'saved' are handed out through the crowd. They are not officially part of the parade, but, as long as they keep their distance up front, no one seems to object. In both 1995 and 1996 the loyalist political parties, the PUP and UDP, also organised demonstrations that marched in front of the main parade calling for the release of loyalist prisoners. Members walked with banners stretched across the road, to a mute reception from the crowd in some areas but, not surprisingly, they received a better reception around Sandy Row.

At the front of the Belfast Twelfth parade are the Burdge Memorial Standards, a colour party comprising the Union flag in the centre with the Belfast County Orange Standard to the right and a Belfast County Purple flag to the left. The colour party is followed by the first band, often the Millar Memorial melody flute band, then the County bannerette, County officers, guests, limousines, and some boys from the Junior Orange Order with the national flags of the nations with Orange Associations, except the Republic of Ireland. Then follows the lead District, with its colour party, band and first lodge. Which lodge takes the lead is sometimes decided by which lodge has the best band. In recent years some women from the Association of Loyal Orange Women of Ireland have also taken part in the parade. This seems to have started in Belfast in 1990 although I have been led to believe that it always happened in some country areas. Scotland is also well represented, not only in the form of the many Scottish flags carried, but by up to twenty Scottish bands that make the trip over. Scottish bands have a reputation for being boisterous and are sometimes blamed for introducing the more rowdy elements to the Twelfth. The front of the parade may be nearly a couple of miles down the road before the end of the parade starts to walk. Despite claims throughout the local press that there were 250 lodges and 150 bands in 1996, I estimated between 130 and 150 lodges and there were exactly 76 bands. Nevertheless it is still an impressive event.

The parade moves down Clifton Street where there are very few spectators. The area to the right is Unity Flats and is the only predominantly Catholic area which the main parade passes. The army usually erects some large screens across a couple of side streets and security is heavier than in other parts of the parade. The parade moves onto Donegall Street and then right into Royal Avenue and Donegall Place, the commercial heart of Belfast. No. 6 District, having marched from the east of the city, waits at the junction of Donegall Street and Royal Avenue and joins the parade at its allotted position, and District No. 9, from the Shankill joins at the junction of Peter's Hill and Royal Avenue.

The centre of Belfast is packed with spectators and there is a sense in which the Institution is displaying itself to the City of Belfast by going through the centre (cf. Kertzer 1988: 120). All good vantage points are taken, with people standing on benches, on waste bins and lamp-posts, and on top of telephone kiosks. Red, white and blue are the predominant colours worn with patriotic hats, t-shirts, and umbrellas bearing the Union 'Jack' in abundance. The football shirts of Glasgow Rangers and local clubs, Linfield and Glentoran, are also commonplace. Each lodge gets applauded through and each is cheered, particularly if its band's rendition of popular parading tunes such as 'The Sash' are played with the utmost vigour. Already there will be groups of teenagers gathering with their blue plastic bags full of varieties of cheap alcohol. The pavement really gets clogged as the groups of youngsters, singing and dancing, follow particular bands. A few of the bands' supporters push prams and have young children with them.

The parade turns right at the City Hall and is joined by District No. 10 who have proceeded via the Ormeau Road. The parade turns down the west side of the City Hall past and stops at the Cenotaph for a wreath-laying ceremony. This ritual element was apparently only introduced in 1990. The colour party, County officers and the Millar Memorial Band go into the Cenotaph area and wreaths are laid by the County Grand Master, Deputy Grand Master and Secretary. As part of the ceremony, all flags except the Union flag are usually lowered. Similarly, when the parade proceeds all flags being carried by lodges and bandsmen alike should be lowered as they pass the area and eyes turn left towards the monument. In spite of the importance of war memorials, some bands seem so involved in the parade that they do not notice where they are and continue playing regardless.

The parade then heads on its way south towards middle-class Belfast. It goes down Bedford Street along the Dublin Road, past the Grand Lodge head office 'The House of Orange', through Shaftesbury Square, Bradbury Place and onto the Lisburn Road. Since William of Orange presumably also headed south out of the city on his journey to the Boyne the parade can be understood as retracing the steps of the Williamite army. The 1996 *Twelfth Programme* informs us that he came up Sandy Row and went onto the Malone Ridge, and there is a plaque on a wall at the bottom of the Lisburn Road to commemorate his journey.

OPPOSING DECORUM

Much of what I have so far discussed gives the Twelfth the appearance of a military event. Its participants wear forms of uniform, the suits and collarettes of Orangemen and the colourful uniforms of the bands. The bandsmen and some of the Orangemen effectively 'march', whilst most of the Orangemen 'walk' in columns with a formalised step. It is a broadly male-dominated arena, the event controlled by a hierarchy of officials marked by insignia. The columns of men are started and stopped with the shout of military-style commands and much of the musical accompaniment is overtly military. In addition they carry flags of obvious military significance and bannerettes that refer directly to battles fought in the First World War by the

36th Ulster Division. Some bands carry 'colours' which have been presented to them, the lodges carry banners showing the Boyne or the Somme. For many Orangemen the Twelfth should be a 'respectable' march – the event expresses an idea of 'Christian Soldiers', of Protestants proclaiming their faith in public. Ministers walk with lodges. Bibles are sometimes carried and many District bannerettes and some lodge banners show the crown above the open Bible, and religious and biblical scenes. Some lodges express their religious heritage by being named after local churches, pictured on the banner, declaring that they are 'Total Abstinence' or 'Temperance' lodges. Some of the bands will play hymns. The parade is comparable to the parades of former soldiers on Remembrance Sunday.

At the same time there is much about the Twelfth which appears to contradict all this. Together with the military, religious, parade, it is also car-nivalesque. As the day wears on alcohol becomes more and more evident, but even early on many of the young girls following the bands are drinking. On the occasions along the route when the parade comes to a halt to allow for refreshment, some of it will be in the form of beer. Around the junction of Sandy Row and the Lisburn Road huge crowds collect all day drinking, singing and dancing, encouraging the blood and thunder bands that pass, particularly the south Belfast bands. Many of the bands play up to it; they often have young lads up front, twirling batons high into the air and attempting to catch them again, dancing up the road, some of them doing cartwheels as they go. Particular bands pride themselves on their athleticism. After the front row of side drummers comes the big bass drum, the centrepiece of the band and it is likely to be one of these drummers from a blood and thunder band that catches the attention of a first-time viewer of the Twelfth. They are often large men who hit the drum with tremendous force, their vigour becoming greater when they are at a part of the parade where the crowds are largest and most excited. Occasionally the bass drummer will bang the drum so hard and so long that his hands will start bleeding; and such a drummer will not simply walk up the road, but will weave a pattern across the road, swaying both body and drum from side to side. He seems to dictate the mood of that part of the parade. Indeed, such are the exertions of a bass drummer that most bands have a spare member walking alongside waiting to take his turn. Bell has suggested that this behaviour, for many young lads, becomes a marker of masculinity at a time when high unemployment and low-skilled work have reduced the ability of males to assert themselves.

Those who have witnessed the finely-honed skills and risk-taking routines of the drum majors of the marching bands . . . can be in no doubt that the marching bands provide such a peer-group milieu for the parading of 'skill'. (Bell 1990: 105)

Sometimes all of the band weave or zig-zag up the road in time to the music, and the girls dressed in short skirts and skimpy tops will dance along the pavement. Zig-zagging with them may well be the lodge with the banner moving from side to side up the road.

'The Sash' is always the most popular tune, but the bands invariably break from the more 'traditional' Orange tunes into a popular song or a sectarian chant. At the start of one particular tune a band might shout out 'UDA' or 'YCV' or sing a rendition of 'The Billy Boys': 'we're up to our necks in Fenian blood, surrender or you'll die, 'cause we are the Billy, Billy, Boys'. A band may gain particular appreciation if it has mastered a tune that is out of the ordinary. I have heard one band give a rendition of Simon and Garfunkel's 'Bridge over Troubled Waters'.

The rise of the blood and thunder band was noted in the *Twelfth Programme* of 1977.

> The phenomenon of the Twelfth in recent years must surely be the blood and thunder bands and whether you like or dislike their music or deportment there is no denying they have become an ever-increasing breed in Ulster today.
>
> Noisy, arrogant and untuneful are terms used to describe these bands. The criticism often comes from members of the more orthodox of Ulster bands and from some Orangemen, who feel the raucous antics and unbridled enthusiasm of the young bandsmen lowers the tone of an Orange parade.
>
> But for many other Orangemen and loyalists there is nothing quite like the drumming, fluting, and toe-in style marching of the groups of 'Young Defenders' or 'True Blues', clad in multi-coloured woolen jerseys and bonnets.[2]

In 1977 Billy Kennedy claimed that this style of 'Billy Boy' band made up half the bands in the parade (*Twelfth Programme* 1977). That proportion is now much higher, perhaps 75 per cent, and, given the reduced number of Orangemen, the bands almost appear to dominate the event. Consequently, just as a hundred years ago the drumming parties caused frictions within the parades, the blood and thunder bands, although apparently popular with many of the spectators, have become an element within the ritual that Orange officials have found hard to control.

Concern about the role of these bands on the parading scene has been expressed frequently in the *Orange Standard*[3] but also, more worryingly for the Institution, by the RUC. The introduction of the *Conditions of Engagement*, discussed above, which all lodges need to get their bands to sign, came after major civil disturbances in Portadown during 1985 and 1986 at which the ability of the Institution to control events was severely questioned (Bryan *et al.* 1995). Clause 3 demands a uniformity of dress, 'reflecting the dignity and decorum of the Institution'. While some of the uniforms are smarter and more sterling than the suits worn by Orangemen, the return journey on the Twelfth can produce some original adaptations in the form of fancy dress. Clause 4 states that 'shouting in an unseemly manner for the emphasis of certain tunes is strictly forbidden'. Clause 5 demands that bands 'employ Regulation Step only while on parade' and that 'Double or Twin Drumming (i.e. two people beating on one bass drum simultaneously) dancing, or jig time step by any member of the band is prohibited'. While I have not seen the 'Twin Drumming', all the other behaviour mentioned is easily observable. Indeed, the dancing or 'jig time step' is not only part of the blood and thunder routine but is utilised by some of the lodges as they zig-zag up the road. This is despite rules laid out by the Belfast County Grand Lodge that 'Lodges and bands must carry their banners or flags on the 12th July, 1990 (as on all other occasions) in a dignified and steady manner', and that disciplinary action will be taken against any lodge or band violating this rule.

Clause 10 of the *Conditions of Engagement* attempts to control the types of flags carried by the bands. As discussed in the previous chapter this has again been a subject of some internal debate within the Institution. Clearly the carrying of the Union flag, the Northern Ireland flag, and Scottish flags is not at issue, however, there are other flags which are more problematic. It is common for blood and thunder bands to carry UVF flags during the Twelfth parade. The UVF of 1912 is clearly part of an Orange heritage and as such most Orangeman do not question the carrying of this flag. Nevertheless, given the activities of the UVF *circa* 1966 and the Orange Institution's stated opposition to loyalist paramilitary groups, some Orangemen are ill at ease with the presence of these flags. The bands seemed to start carrying these flags in the mid-1970s. I have never noted a lodge carrying such a flag and my understanding is that strictly speaking they should not be carried in the parade at all. Nevertheless, the *Rules of Engagement* state that flags 'carried by bands are approved at the discretion of Parade Marshals' and it would be likely to cause uproar if a Marshal asked for a UVF flag to be removed. There are other flags that more clearly flout the rules that have appeared on the Twelfth at Belfast. Whilst the carrying of Red Hand Commando or UDA/UFF flags is not nearly as common, there have been at least one or two examples each year in Belfast during the 1990s. Whilst these more blatant violations of the *Conditions of Engagement* are relatively uncommon, nevertheless, everyone understands the nature of these symbolic displays. It is not as if the lodge hiring the band lets it happen as an oversight. Either the lodges and parade organisers are unwilling or unable to act on such infringements.

The parade stops at a number of points to allow participants to rest and take refreshments and perhaps have a smoke. One of the stranger rules that the Belfast County has is that participants are not allowed to smoke in the ranks before the Fire Station at Cadogan Park on the Lisburn Road. The rest also provides time for individuals to relieve themselves wherever they can find a 'convenient' spot. The image of Orangemen and bandsmen 'pissing' up against a wall or in someone's garden is often used by sections of the press and by those that dislike the parades to criticise the events.

The Lisburn Road, and Balmoral Avenue, into which the parade turns, are middle-class areas and, although in some areas the crowds will be three or four deep, there is less of a rowdy atmosphere than nearer the centre of the city. But the youngsters following their bands maintain the party atmosphere all the way. The parade turns right into Malone Road and then left down towards Shaw's Bridge. Approaching Shaw's Bridge the road is wide with some grassy banks on either side being ideal for spectators from out of town to watch from. After crossing the bridge, the parade turns right and continues for half a mile along a narrow county road to the large field at Edenderry. At this point the parade tends to become a little chaotic. Overhanging trees and narrow lanes would make negotiating the route difficult at the best of times, but many of the lodges and bands have booked their lunches at hotels or church halls around the Belfast area. Buses waiting to transport them line up on the main road where the parade turns in. All lodges and bands are supposed to go into the field before leaving to go to their bus, even though some can be seen leaving the parade at Shaw's Bridge. So whilst the parade and the bands' supporters are still heading up the lane, many who have reached the field are busy rushing back to Shaw's Bridge.

THE FIELD

The Twelfth parades at all venues in Northern Ireland end up at a Field. Since 1972, except in 1999, the Belfast County Grand Lodge have used the field at Edenderry, over 5 miles from their Clifton Street hall, which was specially purchased for this purpose. Each of the Districts marches out to their allotted spot on the Field, marked by a signpost. In one corner of the field is a raised, covered, platform from which the service will be held and speeches will be made. Tired marchers, if they are not leaving for their lunch, sit down in groups to a picnic or buy a burger from the range of catering stalls around the Field. But as well as stalls selling food, there are ones displaying a range of Orange and loyalist products: King William tea towels and Orange marmalade, tapes made by the bands, and pictures of Charles and Di dressed in Glasgow Rangers shirts. A couple of the stalls also sell paramilitary magazines and t-shirts.

Many of the bands stay in the Field, their uniforms making it a colourful sight. Now is the time that their supporters can sit with them. If the weather is good, people lie back and take in the sun. Those who strip off their bandsmen's uniform often have a band t-shirt underneath or, even more commonly, a Glasgow Rangers football shirt. So common are Rangers shirts, it feels as though all the bandsmen take off their variety of uniforms to reveal a common uniform underneath. The drinks are passed around, as teenagers lie in each other's arms. One friend described the Field to me as 'hickey city' since so many girls and bandsmen seem to come out with love bites on their necks. Younger band members take it in turn to have a go banging the big drum and the more enthusiastic flute players sit and practise their skills. This often continues despite the fact that the County Grand Lodge is trying to hold a service and politicians are giving speeches at the platform. Clause 8 of the *Conditions of Engagement* demands that no drumming should take place during the public meeting, but I have never visited a Field where it has not been the case that at least one band was told to stop playing. Most band members seem oblivious to the meeting even taking place.

The Service of Thanksgiving usually starts at 2.15 p.m. with the public meeting taking place around 3.00 p.m. The service involves prayers, a scriptural reading and an address given by a chaplain in the Order, which incorporates the resolution on faith. Two hymns are sung, one of which is usually 'O God, our help in ages past' which is sometimes described by Orangemen as Ulster's anthem. A senior member of the County Grand Lodge chairs the public meeting. After some introductory remarks the Secretary of the County Grand Lodge reads some announcements, which include a letter that the County Grand Lodge writes to the Queen every year offering their loyalty. The reply, from the Queen's personal secretary, is a polite thanks for their continued loyalty. This is followed by the more overtly political element of the platform speeches. Three resolutions are read out individually by different members of the Institution, resolutions on faith, loyalty and state. The resolution on faith will already have been 'spoken to' in the service. At least one Unionist MP has spoken in the last few years with the exception of 1994. In 1992 the UUP MPs Martin Smyth and James Molyneaux spoke, in 1993 it was Smyth, in 1995 Smyth and DUP MP Reverend William McCrea and in 1996, the new leader of the Ulster Unionist Party, David Trimble. The speaker constructs a speech around each resolution. At the end of each speech there is a call for everyone in support of the resolution to say 'aye'. There is no opportunity for a 'nay'.

Despite the large number of people in the Field, very few listen to the platform speakers, most continuing to eat, drink, sleep, and wander around the stalls. There are at most a couple of hundred people, including researchers and journalists, listening to the speakers. The only moment when more people start to concentrate on the platform speakers is towards the end of meeting when awards are handed out to bands. The awards were introduced in 1977, one of the aims being to try to improve the standard of bands taking part.[4] Awards are now given in categories covering style, appearance and music such as 'Best Band', 'Most Improved Band', 'Best Accordion Band', 'Best Outside Band' and 'Best Drum Major'. As the results are read out some of the competitiveness between the bands can be judged from the cheering and a little jeering that might take place. After a vote of thanks for all those who have helped to organise the day, the National Anthem is sung. This usually catches the attention of those in earshot of the public address system, but leaves most people in the Field oblivious.

Normally, with the relatively small numbers of people listening, there is very little crowd participation. I have never witnessed the sort of heckling that took place at Field speeches from the mid-1960s to the mid-1970s, nevertheless, the occasional heckle does take place. Martin Smyth in particular has had a few problems over recent years. If a heckler is too persistent, a Marshal usually goes to deal with him. At the Twelfth Field in Pomeroy in

1998, Spirit of Drumcree leader Joel Patton, already upset at the presence of a reformed IRA man in the Field, started to heckle the speaker, local Presbyterian minister and Armagh Orangeman, William Bingham, who, some days earlier, had recommended that the protest at Drumcree be stopped. The confrontation became physical and was captured by TV cameras, to be shown on the evening news programmes.

Orangemen offer a number of reasons for the poor attention paid to the proceedings. Quite obviously, the increased tendency of many lodges to travel to a hotel or church hall for lunch, rather than have a picnic at the Field, immediately reduces numbers. A couple of Orangemen have also suggested to me that in the past the Twelfth was the only time one got to hear one's MP speak. Now, of course, they are on television all the time. What is said in the speeches is highly predictable and they are, to a certain extent, aimed at the media. Press releases of the more important political speakers at the different venues are handed out in advance so they can make the editions of the *Belfast Telegraph*, Northern Ireland's evening newspaper. What is obvious is that, as far as most people in the parade are concerned, the service and platform speeches are simply not a part, let alone an important part, of the day and simply provide an opportunity to eat, drink and delay the moment of getting back to the parade.

THE RETURN HOME

At 4.00 p.m. in the afternoon the return parade begins to form up. From the apparent random chaos on the Field, the parade comes together surprisingly quickly. The order of the Districts in the parade remains the same and participants seem to know when they should be looking to fall in. That is not to say that all runs smoothly. Many are returning from lunch and trying to get to the Field, down the narrow road, as parts of the main body of the parade are trying to leave. Also, by now some have imbibed copious amounts of liquor and they make up a slightly confused if noticeably more relaxed element within the parade. Bandsmen and Orangemen hurry to join their lodge, that may have left the Field while they were busily relieving themselves. The odd band appears to be leaving the Field with fewer members than they had when they arrived, whether because they are late, drunk or otherwise involved. On one occasion I saw a lodge remonstrating with their band half way back to Belfast because the band was so short of numbers. This notwithstanding, by the time the parade reaches Shaw's Bridge and takes the main road back to Belfast most have found their place.

There are some noticeable differences in the return journey. There is a more carnivalesque atmosphere to the parade. Quite a few bands dress up in some way. This may involve face paint, or the wearing of masks or funny hats. One band must have been changing their uniform, since all the members cut the trousers to turn them into shorts. In 1994 another band wore sombreros which may have been related to the fact that Mexico had knocked the Republic of Ireland out of the recent World Cup. Arab headgear, rubber face masks and wigs are among some of the other additions. As the parade makes its way back there are even more exits from the rows of men to discreet, and not so discreet, points to relieve themselves. The deportment of bandsmen and Orangemen alike is not quite as military as in the outward journey. More of the bands and lodges zig-zag down the road and dance little jigs, whilst for a few the whole process becomes difficult and every so often an Orangeman staggers into the person in front of him. Yet many bandsmen do not drink. There are bands and lodges that remain smart and look as disciplined as when they started. Members of colour parties, and officials at the front of lodges, remain disciplined. If an Orangeman or a band go beyond the limits then they should have their sashes taken from them and be removed from the parade, or be told by a lodge Marshal to behave themselves. I have never actually seen anyone reprimanded during a parade.

The parade returns along the Malone Road, turns right into Balmoral Avenue and onto the Lisburn Road. The crowd has barely thinned and as the parade makes its way down the Lisburn Road there may well be more spectators than on the outward journey. There are at least two occasions when the parade again stops to give everyone time for a break. As the parade nears Sandy Row, at the end of the Lisburn Road, the atmosphere becomes even more relaxed. From the junction of Tate's Avenue down to the point where Sandy Row meets the Lisburn Road there are a lot of people drinking and the spectators are more animated; but the liveliest events take place at the top of Sandy Row. Crowds push in onto the road and squeeze the parade. Bands save their best for these spectators. Invariably there are a number of women, sometimes termed 'Orange Lils', dressed in red, white and blue clothes waving Union flags. As the integrity of the parade breaks down some of the women encroach into the middle of the road and encourage the bands to play louder or embrace an Orangeman that they know (and a few they do not). Baton twirlers will vie to see who can throw their baton highest or perform the most gymnastic routines. And almost every band that comes past plays one tune above all others – 'The Sash'. The biggest reception is saved for Sandy Row No. 5 District. A huge cheer goes up as the District bannerette appears down the road. As the parade continues along the Dublin Road, Sandy Row District turn off into Bruce Street, Hope Street, and onto Sandy Row. The District parade then proceeds up Sandy Row to the Hall, which is back near the junction with the Lisburn Road down which some of the parade may still be proceeding. The noise of the bands echoes off the walls of the buildings, creating a cacophony in the area.

At Shaftesbury Square, Ballynafeigh District No. 10 have in the past peeled off to head down Donegall Pass and onto the Ormeau Road back up to their District hall. However, in recent years they have accepted an alternative route back that takes them through the Botanic and University areas of Belfast, joining the Ormeau Road at the Embankment and then crossing the bridge. The rest of the parade moves into the city centre again back along Donegall Place and Royal Avenue. Shankill No. 9 District turn right up Peters Hill onto the Shankill. Districts 1, 2, 3, 4, and 7/8 return up Donegall Street to Clifton Street. Meanwhile Ballymacarrett No. 6 District turn off Donegall Place into Castle Place and High Street to proceed over Queen Elizabeth Bridge, down Middlepath Street onto the Newtownards Road turning right into Templemore Avenue.

The reception Ballymacarrett District get in east Belfast matches the reception Sandy Row got as they returned home. As they pass on the other side of the road from the nationalist Short Strand area a few Catholic kids watching at a distance, and there is some taunting between them and some of the teenagers following the bands. Orange Marshals stand keeping their eye on the behaviour of those in the parade. In Templemore Avenue the crowds gather to welcome the parade home; the local Gertrude Star Flute Band getting a particularly big welcome. The final act of the District feeder parade is for the colour party and officials to stand along the side of the road and receive the parade as it marches past. Then, as at the end of all parades, the National Anthem is played, all flags being lowered except the Union flag, and the parade breaks up. Even at this point a few bands and lodges might parade back towards their areas. Most of the bands finish up a side street and play the National Anthem before they break ranks. By the time they have finished the parade back in east Belfast, they will have marched at least 12 miles.

Belfast can be an eerie place immediately after the Twelfth. Most pubs in the centre of town remain closed, the streets are covered in litter, and the RUC withdraw some of the large numbers of officers from areas of con-frontation such as the lower Ormeau and the Short Strand. Some of the residents of those areas are only now allowed out of the streets onto the main road. There is often some tension in areas with a large Catholic community. Stone-throwing or taunting is not uncommon between rival groups, but, in the main, the centre of the city remains quiet.

THE THIRTEENTH AT SCARVA

For many loyalists the Twelfth is not the end of the commemorations. On 13 July, or 14 July if the Twelfth or Thirteenth falls on a Sunday, a large parade is held by the Black Institution in Scarva, a small village in County Down, where King William is supposed to have rested on his journey down to the Boyne. Members of the loyal orders flock from all over Northern Ireland and the very small village becomes so packed that it is hard to move. This parade ends up at Scarvagh House, a country house at one end of the village where a 'Sham Fight' takes place between King Billy and King James. This Sham Fight seems to date back into the first half of the nineteenth century, although it is only around the time of the First World War that the parade appears to have become a Black parade rather than an Orange parade. As with the Twelfth, the parade at Scarva has its feeder parades in other towns. In Belfast there will be Black parades from all the District lodges to different points in the town. Formerly, the parades were to a station, to get on a train to Scarva, but in recent years the parades have gone to particular areas where buses are parked. These parades are smaller than the Twelfth Orange parades and take place around 8.00 a.m.

The parade at Scarva makes an interesting comparison with the Twelfth at Belfast. It has many more of the attributes of a country parade. There are fewer blood and thunder bands and more kilty, accordion and silver bands. One bandsman from a blood and thunder band in Newry once complained to me that the parade was full of squealing cats, a reference to the bagpipes. Also, since the route is so narrow it is almost impossible for supporters to walk alongside the bands and most make their way straight down to the Field. The banners of the Black Institution display religious imagery, predominantly scenes from the Old Testament (Buckley 1985; Jarman 1995, 1997a). Members of the Black wear black collarettes and also an apron similar to that used in Freemasonry, with many of the symbols displayed also reminiscent of those of the Masons. On the whole, more smart, dark suits are worn by the Blackmen and the whole event has a relaxed but 'respectable' atmosphere to it. The spectators often appear to be in their Sunday best. There may be a few Glasgow Rangers shirts around, but not as many as in a Belfast parade. The parade route length is probably not much more than a mile, but by the time one has pushed one's way though the crowds, it feels longer. It goes through some large gates into the grounds of a moderately sized country house.

The scene at the Field at the rear of the house could probably best be described as a large church fete. The central part of the Field is a mass of people and around the outside is a selection of food stalls, stalls selling cheap patriotic gifts, and church stalls selling tea and sandwiches. In 1994 and 1995 there was also one alternative platform at the far end where a preacher gives sermons on salvation. The main platform is at the top of a hill, and is set up at the rear of the house overlooking the fields. A row of chairs is placed behind the microphone so the senior Sir Knights of the Black Institution can sit during the platform speeches. Most of the central part of the Field is taken up with spectators eating and wandering from stall to stall.

The parade comes in at the top of the Field, goes between the platform and the house, and then down into the Field before breaking up. Different elements of the parade head for different parts of the Field. Bands leave piles of instruments while they go off to look around the Field. Up at the main Field the Sham Fight takes place. It is not impressive. Four riders on horseback and about eight foot soldiers enter the Field dressed in seventeenth-century costume. William, astride a white horse, one other rider and four soldiers are dressed in red uniforms, James and his men in green. Each side is carrying a flag. They split up and approach each other in the middle of the Field where everyone is sitting. Picnickers hurry out of the way whilst others hurry from other parts of the Field to get a view. The 'kings' dismount and there is a small engagement with swords. Then the foot soldiers carrying shotguns fire buckshot at the opposing flags. After a minute or so the two 'armies' part and move up towards the platform where they engage again, both flags beginning to become peppered with holes. Again the 'armies' proceed further up the hill and shots are again fired as they engage. At either this engagement or a further engagement the green flag is eventually shot from its pole, making King Billy inevitably the winner. The crowd cheers and everyone goes back to whatever they were doing. The whole performance lasts no more than about 5 minutes.

The platform formalities again involve a religious service, followed by the three resolutions, of faith, loyalty and state. Thanks are given to the Buller family for the use of Scarvagh House. After the singing of the National Anthem, the parade begins to prepare for the short return journey. Blackmen from Belfast return to the city and complete another small parade to their respective Orange District hall.

The events at Scarva, however, also show some of the contradictions found at the Twelfth. In a neighbouring field, discreetly hidden by trees, is a large marquee containing a bar. Blackmen and bandsmen with their female following wander down to the bar, out of sight of the main event. Whilst elderly men support a pint of beer, teenagers are found sitting in groups or with a partner rolling about in the grass. Just as with the Twelfth on the previous day, the Thirteenth is as much about drinking as it is about Protestant temperance and as much about teenage sexuality as it is about loyalty to the throne.

POWER AND RESISTANCE, CONTINUITY AND DISCONTINUITY

In describing the marching season and the Twelfth I have highlighted the divergent interests that are revealed in the variety of parades and within the parades themselves. The Eleventh night, the Boyne commemorations in Belfast, and the Thirteenth at Scarva are complex rituals involving large numbers of people. I have suggested that within the events there is room for creativity and I have examined some of the changes that have taken place in the Twelfth and the attempts to limit those changes. Each event is unique. Yet whilst highlighting the uniqueness, the elements of continuity must not be ignored. Alternative perspectives on the events might focus on the ritual commemoration as social memory (Connerton 1989: 41–71). That embodied in the form of the event, in bodily movements such as marching, is a re-enactment of the past. Jarman has argued that the Twelfth in Belfast is a 'performative re-enactment' and that for a day 'the Orangemen constitute themselves as a replica army and the parade mimics the departure to and return from war' (1995: 150–1). Quite clearly the parades take place within a cultural sphere which in itself imposes limitations. Continuity is explicitly present on this level. It is also possible to read a direct historical narrative: the landing of William in Carrickfergus, re-enacted in mid-June, the march of the Orangemen on the Twelfth, south out of Belfast in the same direction that William took on his way to the Boyne, and the Sham Fight at Scarva, where William was supposed to have rested on his way to the battle. But I have heard very little evidence of such a discourse. The events at Carrickfergus, in Belfast and at Scarva are never described as being linked and interpreted in such a way. The Belfast Twelfth is not seen as being any more authentic than other Twelfth parades in Northern Ireland just because it could be linked geographically to the journey of the Williamite army in 1690. To do so would appear to give the Belfast Twelfth a priority over the other Twelfth venues that would run contrary to the general development of Orangeism. Indeed, some country Orangemen treat the Belfast parades with distaste. The Belfast parades are seen as a little rough and lacking in the decorum that would be found in a country Twelfth parade.

My approach has been to examine the more conscious and overt political pressures exerted on the Twelfth that have influenced the form, content and interpretation of the parade. The rituals are clearly a political resource because of the sense of continuity, a sense of continuity reasserted in the claim of 'tradition'. But to remain politically influential they must be able to adapt to changes in the political arena. The 'traditional' events provide an arena for the powerful and for the less powerful. The more obvious relationship between Catholic and Protestant ethnic groups, which is normally highlighted when discussing Orange parades, is only part of what is taking place. Within the events themselves are relations of power built on social class, geography, religious denomination and political differences. The public transcript of 'respectable' Orangeism is under constant threat from elements within the events that not only feel antipathy towards the Catholic community, or Irish nationalism or the police, but also towards the purveyors of 'respectable' Orangeism. In Belfast, as in many other areas, the Orange Order have been unable to direct events in such a way that they conform to their public explanations of what is taking place. The 'traditional' parade has been a resource for different elements of the Protestant community to express their understandings of a violent local political world. In the chapter that follows I look at how recent shifts in political power have influenced the parades and how the claim of 'tradition' is used to maintain the legitimacy of the event.

10 'TRADITION', CONTROL AND RESISTANCE

> O God, our help in ages past,
> Our hope for years to come
> Be thou our guard while troubles last,
> And our eternal home.
>
> ('O God, our help in ages past' – Ulster's national anthem?)

The dominant discourse used to legitimise the parades is that of 'tradition'. Despite the recognition that the events have altered considerably in living memory, and despite the quite apparent political utilisation of the events, the idea that 'traditional' parades express for Protestants a continuity with the past is present in the way people discuss the events, the way people write about the events, the speeches from the platform, and is evident in much of the discourse that emanates from those who report the events. In this chapter I will explore the way the event and the discourses that surround the Twelfth have been formed and controlled since the 1970s. I assess the ramifications for the Twelfth and the Orange Institution of the conflict since the 1960s and the introduction of direct rule from Westminster. In particular, I analyse the way in which the changing relationship between the state and the Protestant community has been reflected in the proliferation of blood and thunder bands, and the consequent attempts by the Orange Institution to keep control of the parades despite these changes.

In examining the development of the Twelfth and other parades in the north of Ireland the ritual occasions are revealed as being utilised by a variety of different interest groups at different periods of time. From 1795 to the 1870s Orangeism and its ritual expressions were predominantly a lower-class phenomenon which was both utilised and abandoned by the state at different times depending upon prevailing political conditions. Since the 1870s Orangeism and the commemoration of the Williamite campaign have become a focus of Protestant identity. Orangeism was taken up by the bourgeois classes in Ireland and attained a hegemonic position. Orangeism became 'respectable' and the ritual and symbolic manifestations of the Twelfth developed accordingly. I have already alluded to the changes that have taken place in the Twelfth in Belfast: its growth in size and prominence, the development of the Belfast Orange lodge structure connected to political and economic patronage, the increasing use of parades by politicians, the consequent development of banner images, the highlighting of the more 'respectable' and military bearing of the events, widespread coverage by the local press, and the growth in the variety and quality of musical accompaniment. These processes, I have argued, reached their zenith with the creation of Northern Ireland. The Twelfth became a ritual of state patronised by nearly all unionist politicians in Northern Ireland. As part of the ideology of the state, 'respectable' Orangeism, powerfully embedded within the structure of the state, was broadly paternalistic. Consequently, it became less overtly threatening than the Orangeism of the previous century and on a few occasions the state was prepared to intervene against the more sectarian manifestations of Orangeism. This, however, was from a position of strength and presupposed that expressions of Irish nationalism were kept strictly under control. The conduct of the Twelfth, and of 'respectable' Orangeism, was based upon a position of power.

I have also indicated that throughout these developments there have been divisions within Orangeism. While these divisions are significant at the level of religious denomination, they are fundamental at the level of social class. Crucial to understanding these frictions is the relationship between the British state and Orangeism, and the developing relationship between the British and Irish states, the developing ethnic identities within those states and most particularly the class relationships within the state of Northern Ireland (Bryan 1998b). The position of power that the Orange Institution has held since its formation has significantly changed at a number of points. The ideology of Orangeism has reflected those changes and the Twelfth parades play an important role in those dynamic relationships. From the mid-1960s onwards the very existence of the northern quasi-state was at stake. In 1972 the British state introduced direct rule. The political relationship of the Orange Institution and the state fundamentally changed. That is not to say that the Institution became powerless – far from it – but in relation to the state, and the forces of the state, it existed in a new environment. One of the consequences of these changes is that expressions of working-class loyalism, particularly in the form of the blood and thunder bands, became more assertive and have clearly developed a subculture of resistance to the forces of the state, specifically the RUC (Bell 1990: 97–141). This has had ramifications for 'respectable' Orangeism since it has increased the likelihood of Orange parades being utilised to confront the police, and therefore amplified the class frictions within the Institution.

For example, by 1972 the communal situation had worsened and, significantly, the defence of communities was now being claimed by a variety of paramilitary groups. Certain urban social spaces had become 'No Go' areas for the state security forces, a situation depicted by the authorities as 'a breakdown in law and order'. There were serious doubts about whether the annual Drumcree church parade in Portadown could go ahead. In late June the UDA had erected barriers in estates close to Portadown and tension in the Obins Street 'Tunnel' area was very high, there having been disturbances in preceding months. Eventually bulldozers cleared away barriers that had been put up in Obins Street on the Sunday morning and CS gas was used to disperse rioters. When the disturbances had subsided a contingent of Orangemen started their parade. They were led by a group of at least fifty UDA men who proceeded to stand either side of the road up to the Tunnel and who promised police they would go on through if one shot was fired. Not surprisingly, this show of strength and the apparent threat of 3,000 available UDA men, led to both the Official and Provisional wings of the IRA threatening to stop Twelfth parades going down Obins Street, warning the UDA that they would not be allowed to repeat such actions. Whilst the parades on 12 July and 13 July passed peacefully, three men were shot dead in Portadown on the morning of the Twelfth and later that month there was a bomb in Woodhouse Street (Provisional IRA), a bomb in a local Catholic church (loyalist paramilitary), and a gun battle in the Obins Street area involving, it would seem, members of the IRA, UDA and, subsequently, members of the security forces, to 'clear out IRA nests'.[1] Importantly it was 'community forces' such as the UDA that acted to protect the parade, the British state could only be relied on when the 'enemy' had been engaged. Many nationalists view such events as confirming an alliance between the state, Orangeism and loyalist paramilitaries. However, in retrospect, the development of community-based 'defence' organisations probably reveal the start of a breakdown of the network of power that existed between the forces of the state and the Protestant community. By the mid-1980s this was to bring sections of the Protestant community into conflict with the police over parades in Portadown.

The Twelfth was no longer an expression of the state and, under this new situation, those involved in the parades were forced to become more proactive in defence of their position. An ethnographic analysis of the parades reveals many of these tensions. Many of the more senior Orangemen came under criticism at platform speeches, particularly up until the mid-1970s (Bryan *et al.* 1995: 20). Symbolic displays within the parades developed, utilising the iconography of loyalist paramilitary groups. Bands took up names such as 'Defenders', 'Volunteer Force', 'Citizen Volunteers', and 'Young Loyalists' which they displayed on uniforms and on the drums. Flags reflecting allegiance to the UVF were introduced by blood and thunder bands. An Orangeman suggested to me that there were more Northern Ireland flags used than Union flags, and in the late 1980s there were even 'Independent Ulster' flags, which represented the thinking of a small section of loyalism, particularly within the UDA, in a few Apprentice Boys parades. Many of the new blood and thunder bands started to develop their own band parades. While most of the band parades took place along uncontentious routes within loyalist areas, these new events meant an increase in the number of parades and a lengthening of the marching season. A town such as Portadown not only had Orange, Black and Apprentice Boys parades at the 'traditional' points in the year, but also had three band parades plus some parades by the bands returning from band parades in surrounding towns. The whole environment within which the annual cycle of parades was taking place was changing in terms of the number of parades, the period of the year in which they took place, the content of parades, and the relationship of parades to the police and to the Catholic community. This appears to have been recognised by the RUC in the early 1980s with a 1984 'Force Order', which directs police policy, discussing 'an upsurge in the number of bands whose members are predisposed to overt and unruly displays of sectarian bitterness'.[2] John Hermon, the then Chief Constable, later reflected the changing attitude to parades in his autobiography.

By mid-May 1985, the Force [the RUC] was fully prepared to address the smoldering problem of loyalist parades. Over almost a century, these had been given a special position in Northern Ireland and appeared to have acquired a sort of temporal sanctity. Participants believed they could march wherever and whenever they chose. Their marches epitomised the right to civil and religious liberty, as long as the religion in question was Protestantism. . . . I was not alone in believing that the superior attitude of the loyalists, in respect to their marches, had to be changed. (Hermon 1997: 171–2)

If this was the prevailing attitude of an increasing number of senior police officers, and it coincided with more concerted opposition to loyalist parades by nationalists, then it is not surprising that the relationship between the RUC and elements of the parades was to become strained.

In 1985 it was public knowledge that the British government under Thatcher and the Irish government under Fitzgerald were having detailed discussions about their relationship with Northern Ireland. The insecurity this produced within unionism became apparent in the summer of 1985 when there were major disturbances in Portadown over Orange, Black and band parades. The Anglo-Irish agreement was signed in November and the protest from the unionist parties became intertwined with the parades issue resulting in further riots in the summer of 1986 (Cochrane 1997: 122–83). During the disturbances at an Apprentice Boys parade in Portadown at Easter one man was killed when hit by a baton round fired by the RUC. While in the nationalist community the police were still perceived as in the main protecting loyalist parades, the relationship between the police and loyalists was strained and certainly many people in the bands and Orange Order felt that the police were against them. Numerous stories circulated at the time of Irish government officials being present in Portadown, of Irish policemen being drafted into the RUC and of Catholic policemen being drafted in to the Mobile Support Units (MSUs) that deal with civil disturbances. All these stories implied that the police had become an out-group, no longer part of the Protestant community. Orangemen symbolically threw money at the feet of policemen, and a large number of police homes were attacked. It was widely perceived by unionists that Dublin was dictating the policy on parades (Bryan *et al.* 1995).

CONTROL

At the height of these confrontations the complexity of the events and diffuse nature of authority within the Orange Institution became evident. Particularly among the District, County and Grand Lodge officials and within the UUP there was great concern over the confrontations with the RUC and the utilisation of the parades by paramilitary elements. There was not only a sense in which they were unable to control some of what was taking place, but also a concern that other groups were trying to gain political legitimisation from the confrontations. As senior Orangemen and UUP politicians called for restraint, others could be seen as greater 'defenders' of Protestantism. The physical and ideological control of the parade was contested within the unionist community. A number of political figures followed strategies to maximise their political capital. It is interesting, for example, to examine the part that Alan Wright played in the 1985/86 Portadown controversy over the right to march through the nationalist Tunnel area of the town. For a short time Alan Wright, who had had no notable political profile previously, came to represent hard-line opinion within the Orange Institution. In 1985 his position was limited in that he had a role derived from his membership of the Portadown No. 1 District. However, by 1986 his political profile had grown as he acted as spokesman for the Ulster Clubs (Cochrane 1997: 134–7). This appeared to bring him into conflict with the Orange Institution when, prior to the Twelfth of July parade, he called for all Ulster Club members to come to Portadown for the day. District Master Harold Gracey immediately issued a statement pointing out that Wright was not speaking as a District representative. The same sort of dispute took place between Ian Paisley and Martin Smyth. Although Paisley has no official role within the Orange Institution, he nevertheless played a prominent role in the debate and during the Twelfth in 1985 turned up to offer support. When, on the Twelfth of 1986, Paisley described Portadown as a dispute about 'obedience and submission to Dublin', Martin Smyth reminded members of the Institution that only he, and not Paisley, dealt on behalf of the Orange Order. Paisley, Smith argued, could only appeal to 'non-Orangemen'. Similarly, Walter Williams, in his capacity as a member of the Grand Lodge, promised that the Institution would clamp down on outside elements. On the other hand, UDA leaders such as John McMichael were keen to give the impression that they were in control of events and that it was the UDA that could stem the violence. Indeed, at one point after Easter 1986, we find McMichael claiming that the UDA had advised the Apprentice Boys not to hold a proposed parade on 5 May. Both George Seawright, a well-known hard-line loyalist, and Peter Robinson, the DUP MP for east Belfast, made appearances at various times in Portadown and, whilst welcomed by some, were seen by others as outsiders (Bryan *et al.* 1995).

A similar struggle for control has taken place since 1995. Within the Orange Institution there developed a ginger group known as the Spirit of Drumcree which, on 14 November 1995, held a large meeting of Orangemen in the Ulster Hall, demanding that Martin Smyth resign, that the Institution should better reflect its members and that there should be no giving in on the right to parade. Martin Smyth's position was never seriously under threat given that he had a power base in the Grand Lodge, but the Grand Lodge did set up a commission with the aim of taking submissions from lodges on the reform of the Institution. The Spirit of Drumcree group was fronted by Joel Patton, an Orangeman from Tyrone. Over the years that followed he continually claimed to be the voice of 'grassroots' Orangeism and organised a number of protests, including on 9 and 10 December 1997, taking over the House of Orange building in Dublin Road, Belfast, and forcing a Grand Lodge meeting to be moved to the District lodge building on the Shankill. Patton criticised any move from local, District, County or Grand Lodges that appeared to him as appeasement over the parades issue (see for instance Kelly 1998: 41–4). His position was close to that of the DUP and he was also joined on many protests by a number of individuals whose profile had grown more prominent in their own areas during the parades disputes. He was trenchant in his critique of members of the Grand Lodge Education Committee, particularly the Reverend Brian Kennaway, who were actively promoting religious and cultural understandings of Orangeism over the political and recommending alternative strategies viewed as more conciliatory. Patton certainly voiced the views of a section of Orangeism, probably a more rural constituency, but actually was never able to repeat the large Ulster Hall meeting. There were a number of reasons for this. In 1997 Martin Smyth, who had been the focus of some of the criticism stood down as Grand Master, and was replaced by Robert Saulters from west Belfast and after that the Grand Lodge did take a relatively tough approach to the parades issue. But perhaps most importantly Patton's style, which often, in public, showed little respect for senior members of the Institution, would have upset many Orangemen. There were constant calls for Orangemen to settle their differences within lodge meetings. The final embarrassment seemed to come when Patton and his supporters heckled Reverend William Bingham and a confrontation took place with umbrellas at the Twelfth Field in Pomeroy in 1998. Later in the year Patton was suspended from the Institution and has since spoken of his disillusionment with the situation.

There have always been criticisms of senior members of the Orange Institution, particularly from Orangemen with fundamentalist views. From the mid-1960s onwards these Orangemen coalesced around Paisley. He has had some success in being perceived as being more 'Orange' than those in the Grand Lodge, without himself being a member of the Institution. This became even more acute in the early 1970s when the DUP became a real political force, with other politicians in the Orange Order such as the Reverend William McCrae using platforms to criticise moderate unionism. The role of loyalist paramilitary groups and some of the blood and thunder bands has also been important during the same period. Orange parades are at the focus of a complex network of political interests. Whilst they provide an opportunity for disparate unionist groups to walk in apparent unity, any exploration of the events or the discourses that accompany them soon reveals the parades as an arena for political opposition. Disputes over parades in Portadown have offered no more than the appearance of unity, and even that unity has been short lived. The control that the Grand Lodge and the Ulster Unionist Party wielded up until the mid-1960s was always questioned, but that control has been shattered by the enormous political changes which have since taken place.

DISCOURSES OF 'TRADITION' AND 'RESPECTABILITY'

The confrontations over parades in Portadown in 1985 and 1986 in part led to the introduction of the 1987 Public Order (Northern Ireland) Order. It significantly made no provisions that allowed 'traditional' parades any rights over and above other sorts of parades as had existed in the 1951 Act. Seven days notice had to be given for a parade and the powers given to police to impose conditions on the parades were increased. This was yet another reminder to unionists of their loss of power. They were no longer able to define rights to use the streets through the claim of 'tradition' (Jarman and Bryan 1998).

Despite 'the defence of civil and religious liberty' being a central tenet of Orangeism, it does not form a significant part of the discourse over the right to march. It is used more as a mantra. One possible reason for this is that taking a civil and religious liberty argument too far might have repercussions in terms of the nationalist right to march, which remained limited even after the introduction of direct rule (Jarman and Bryan 1998). The call for the right to use the 'Queen's highway' is not made through a discourse of human rights and the Orange Order have as yet made no significant move to use British or European courts to press for their right to parade. 'Tradition' and history remained a better source of legitimisation for Orangemen than some more general concept of civil rights. The more widespread reaction of Orangemen to the recent events within Northern Ireland has been a reasserting of 'tradition'. The late Harold McCusker's speech in the House of Commons at the start of the Portadown dispute in 1985 is typical.

When the men of North Armagh try to walk in Portadown it will be over a route they and their forefathers have traversed since 1796. They are not motivated out of a desire to break the law, but a sense of historic necessity to express, as they have always done, their legitimate pride in possession of their lands. They know instinctively that they only survive by their solidarity and determination.[3]

The use of history as a source for legitimisation can be seen by an examination of the speeches at the Field in Belfast from 1993 to 1996. Various common themes are linked together. The fundamental problem is perceived as the threat to the integrity of the Protestant, British, people of Ulster, a people loyal to the Protestant throne. The speeches construct Orangeism as the protector of Protestantism against the Catholic Church – Popery, and Jesuits, against Irish nationalism – the Social and Democratic Labour Party (SDLP) and Dublin government, against republicanism – Sinn Féin and the IRA, and against weak British governments – as evidenced in the signing of the Anglo-Irish Agreement and weak security policies. All of these issues are understood as battles fought throughout history, Luther, Calvin and Protestant martyrs, the Protestants massacred in Portadown in 1641, Cromwell's campaign in Ireland, the Siege of Derry, Enniskillen, the Boyne, Aughrim, the Diamond, Dolly's Brae, the UVF, the Somme, the formation of Northern Ireland, Stormont, the Second World War and Ireland's neutrality, the IRA campaign, the loss of the B-Specials, the loss of Stormont, the Anglo-Irish Agreement, the loss of the Ulster Defence Regiment which replaced the B-Specials, and the attack upon 'traditional' marching rights – and all are understood in terms of a Protestant community under threat and defending itself.

The service of remembrance and the speeches made to the three, or four, resolutions all reinforce this appeal to historical legitimacy.

We have also seen over the years that insidious campaign being carried on to take control of the heart of the city of Belfast and then the compulsory, underline compulsory, re-routing of and opposition to certain traditional Orange parades all indicate the evil campaign of Romanism not during the last 23 years but for generations, to move into Protestant areas – the Protestants move out and then the cry goes up of intimidation and persecution of these poor underprivileged Roman Catholics, who appear all too ready in many cases to be persecuted, to be insulted, and to be intimidated – they love it. But as Orangemen we are committed today as always to the Protestantism of Martin Luther . . . (Twelfth Platform 1993)

Our lives are under attack, our homes are under attack, our property, our commercial and industrial life, our faith and our freedom are under attack, our civil and religious liberty are being attacked, our British way of life is under threat. We are under attack from many quarters – from the SDLP, from Romanism, from republicanism, we have absorbed 23 years of misrepresentation, intimidation, outright attack, political manip-ulation and worst of all, let the message go out from this place today, inept government from British cabinets that lost their moral values, and have cut adrift from their spiritual moorings . . . (Twelfth Platform 1993)

Two hundred years on, history is repeating itself all over the province and again the attack of republicanism focuses again on Portadown as in 1795. We cannot ignore our history as some people would like us to do. We cannot forget the burning of Protestants in Loughgall, the driving of Protestants into the River Bann at Portadown, and followed by the ferocious attacks and atrocities since 1969 . . . (Twelfth Platform 1993)

We have read the history books, from 200 years ago the Roman Catholics forming into groups known as the Defenders, to get rid of the so called heretic dogs, better known by you and I as Protestant people. Well today is no different from 1795. There is a Pope on the throne, a Polish Pope who was around in the days of Hitler and the concentration camps of Auschwitz when they stood back and watched thousands go out to death without one word of condemnation . . . (Twelfth Platform 1995)

The Twelfth provides a ritual expression of this historical integrity. It not only commemorates the Boyne but, through the banners, through music, through the names of lodges and bands, through the appeals to history in the speeches, through dress codes, and through behaviour, it invokes and celebrates a perceived common Protestant past and a perceived common Protestant identity. The rituals on the Twelfth are formalised and repetitive, they appear unchanging (Larsen 1982b; Jarman 1995; Tonkin and Bryan 1996).

This discourse of 'tradition' is rarely questioned in the coverage of the parades by the media (Bryan 1998a). The two broadly unionist newspapers, the *Belfast News Letter*, which is more hard-line, and the *Belfast Telegraph*, which is generally more liberal, have both adopted a similar style of reporting of the events. The Twelfth is reported as a day when the Protestant community comes together as it has always done. Since the mid-1950s the detailed descriptions of the day and the speeches has given way to predominantly pictorial coverage. Typically in the 1970s these two newspapers produced a pull-out supplement showing a happy carnivalesque day, old men and young babies, women dancing in their union jack skirts, impressed overseas visitors, pretty girls from an accordion band seated in the Field, an Orangeman resting his feet, a group having a picnic, and occasionally a flute band.

Back in 1972 the *Belfast Telegraph* produced a 12-page supplement with pictures of Orangemen braving the rain, lambeg drums and plenty of smiling faces. Each page leads with a headline: 'Never mind if it rains', 'Lambegs catch the ear . . . and it's quite a sensation', 'A step through the tunnel', 'No-go is not an obstacle', 'The Somme remembered' and 'Thousands go on parade'. In 1978 we find: 'Impressive pageantry . . . and also in Portadown', 'A spectacular show. . . and its country style', 'Happy marchers . . . and the sun shines on' and 'An anniversary prelude . . . to a familiar sound'. In 1980: 'I'd walk a million miles', 'A day to enjoy and remember' and 1981: 'All the ceremony of the big day', 'Spectators show their own style' and 'A time to enjoy . . . for all ages'.

The *Belfast News Letter* provides us with similar themes, in a special pullout edition even if it uses fewer corny headlines. For instance, 1992 saw 'A piping hot extravaganza' and 'Night of flags and fun'. The local newspapers in unionist areas follow a similar style. Take for example *The Larne and East Antrim Times*: in 1980: 'Preserving 12th heritage, young and old share', 1981: 'A happy day for all', 'A smart turnout', 1982: 'Pageantry on parade',

'Brethren and bands relax', 1984: 'All decked out to celebrate', 1987: 'Glorious Twelfth'.

The main theme articulated in this pictorial form, and reinforced by the headlines, appears to be to show as little sign of division as possible. The over-whelming discourse is one of a community taking part in a 'traditional' occasion as they have through the generations. The 1972 the *Belfast Telegraph* did have a picture of marchers heading towards a roadblock under 'No-go is not an obstacle' and also pictures the controversial Tunnel area in Portadown although no protesters were in sight. We have people 'taking things in their stride', 'enjoying a well-earned rest' and 'doing it in style'. The *Belfast News Letter* gives us 'the spirit of the Twelfth'[4] and 'traditional tunes of the flutes'.[5] The *Ballymena Guardian* has the 'Family day out in Cullybackey' and the *Larne and East Antrim Times* also produces the same sort of material.

What is perhaps more significant is what is not shown. In all the supplements I have seen there is not one picture of anyone drinking alcohol or any suggestion that part of the fun might involve intoxication. Of even more interest, despite the recent proliferation of paramilitary symbols on flags, bannerettes, uniforms and drums carried by bandsmen, there are almost no pictures with even a hint of such regalia. I can find only three occasions when any such symbols appear anywhere in the pictures. This situation is particularly noticeable in Belfast where the blood and thunder bands, with their many references to the UVF, YCV, and even the Red Hand Commando, now dominate the parade. In 1996 the picture of a UFF colour party in a Twelfth parade in Randalstown reproduced in the *Newtownabbey Times* forced the Grand Lodge to suggest publicly that it would mount an investigation.[6] Major disturbances at parades, as there were in Portadown in 1985 and 1986, are kept to the 'news' section of the paper and not allowed to adulterate the 'traditional' community occasion reported in other parts of the paper. So marked is this separation that at times the heckling of a speaker is reported on the front page, but, in the special Twelfth supplement section, that same speech is reported as if nothing happened. In short, the image of the Twelfth produced by these newspapers is that of 'respectable' Orangeism.

This apparent division between the reporting of the events and the reporting of the 'news' surrounding the events is sustained in broadcasting. The first recorded programme of the Twelfth was made in 1952 and the Twelfth was shown on a TV newsreel the following year. The first live television broadcast from the Belfast parade occurred in 1958 and in 1961 a 'highlights' programme was shown in the evening. In 1964 even the Irish Republic's broadcasting company, RTE, covered the Twelfth, and in 1965 the BBC extended its coverage to venues outside Belfast. During the period up until the mid-1960s coverage appeared to be relatively unproblematic. With the civil unrest that engulfed Northern Ireland in 1969 being so closely connected to both civil rights and loyalist marches, Orange and Apprentice Boys parades started appearing in a new light on news and documentary programmes. Interestingly, it seems that the way the broadcasters dealt with the disturbances surrounding parades was not dissimilar to the way the *Belfast News Letter* and *Belfast Telegraph* dealt with them. Coverage and highlights of the parades were seen as separate from incidents that took place in and around the parades. The parades were seen live and on 'highlights' programmes, while the news showed incidents connected to the parades. Nevertheless, despite the continued patronage given to the Twelfth by broadcasters, their relationship with the Orange Institution became more fraught. Senior members of the Institution were concerned about documentary and news coverage of Orangeism. In 1986 the BBC decided not to have live coverage. One can only guess at the actual reasons for this decision, but in 1985 there had been major disturbances surrounding parades in Portadown and this probably gave the BBC the excuse it had been looking for. This coverage was replaced with extensive midday news reports and an extensive highlights package shown in the late evening. A similar package was shown on Ulster Television. Whilst the news reports cover 'incidents' occurring where marches take routes through nationalist areas, the highlights package provides us with images, a commentary and interviews that in many ways replicate the aforementioned newspaper coverage.

A review of recent programmes reveals the overwhelming stress upon the historical nature of parades. This is not only done by the frequent use of the word 'tradition' – and it is used often – but also by the way the subject matter is framed. There are continual references to past events – the Battle of the Boyne, the Battle of the Diamond, the Battle of the Somme, two World Wars, etc. There are continual references to 'the generations' taking part, as commentators seem to go out of their way to find the youngest and oldest participants in the parade. As we are told by the BBC commentators during an interview with two members of the Banbridge District in 1993: 'there may be 60 odd years between them, but they joined the Order for the same reason – tradition'. Commentators give the potted histories of lodges, banners and bannerettes as well as stories of founding members of the Institution. There are also plenty of interviews with older members of the Orange Order, often ones who have their 'long service' medals. A sample of the commentary on the BBC programme reporting a Ballinderry parade should suffice.

The road to Ballinderry in County Antrim. At the head of the parade the officers from host District Ballinderry No. 3, accompanied by the Orange Order's Imperial Grand Master James Molyneaux.

At the front a bannerette older than any of the marchers. A gift from a local Church of Ireland rector to Ballinderry No. 148 in 1883.

Six other Districts joined the march. Derriaghy, Lisburn, Hillsborough, Aghalee, Glenavy, and Magheragal. At one and a half miles this was a mere stroll compared to the old days. It is recorded then on the 12th of July 1849 the lodges of the area marched via Glenavy and Crumlin to Antrim and back, a round trip of some 40 miles.

The history of the Orange Order here goes back a long way . . . [interview with the District Master who tells us how lodges used to meet by the light of the moon].

For one of today's marchers, a certain brother . . . from Ballinderry, it was a double celebration, his birthday. Born on the Twelfth 33 years ago his parents called him William. Among the youngest at the parade 2-year-old . . . from Lisburn, watching out for her father . . . of Flower Hill lodge.

At the Field the main speaker was James Molyneaux, who accused the Irish Foreign Minister, Dick Spring, of firing an Exocet at the prospects of new political talks, by suggesting joint authority for the province. And Mr Molyneaux predicted news of moves towards better local democracy [interview with Molyneaux].

It is interesting that despite the introduction of modern party politics into the programme, through an interview with the then leader of the Ulster Unionist Party, other political aspects of the parades are conspicuous by their absence. Amongst the shots of happy smiling faces and prominent unionist politicians there are almost no pictures of paramilitary symbols. In fact, there is a general concentration on the Orangemen rather than the bands and on the 'respectable' bands rather than the blood and thunder variety. Neither are there any shots of alcohol being consumed or of the consequent behaviour. This type of television coverage is therefore very similar to the newspaper coverage discussed earlier.

The discourse of tradition is departed from when older Orangemen suggest that things are not what they used to be. For example a District Master in Fermanagh, interviewed on the 1993 highlights programme, suggests that the county lodges better represent the Orange Order than the city parade, which he believed sometimes brought the organisation into disrepute. However, even this is in some senses a call for a return to the past, to the way it used to be. The overwhelming image conveyed is one of 'respectability', continuity and historical stability.

When the line of respectability is crossed, when the BBC broadcasts an alternative reading of the Twelfth, the Orange Institution immediately reacts. On the morning of the Twelfth in 1994 BBC local radio transmitted an interview with some young lads in the Donegall Pass area who apparently said that the Twelfth was about getting drunk, having a good time and throwing stones at the 'taigs' (abusive slang to describe a Catholic). At the Twelfth speeches senior Orangemen gave their reaction.

I was shocked this morning as I listened to the early news, to hear what the BBC were sending out as regards our demonstration today as they approached young band members asking those young inexperienced boys, what does the Twelfth mean to you? And the reply, a time to get drunk, a time to celebrate, a time to attack the taigs. That's what they said. That may be the voice of pagan Protestantism, but it's not the voice of Orangeism. The voice of Orangeism is here to proclaim the truth of the reality of the living Christ and if the BBC want to hear what we stand for and what we are about, let them come with us to the central cross and find in Christ the Way, the Truth and the Life. (Twelfth Platform 1994)

A second Orangeman followed this theme:

I very much welcome and reiterate the remarks of our County Grand Chaplain in his sermon and address when he referred to the news bulletin this morning on Good

Morning Ulster, I was sitting in the studio and heard in the background this report coming from a young Protestant in Donegall Pass. It was sad as Brother Ryan has said, that this young man is misguided about what the Twelfth of July is all about. I trust that young man will reflect today on what he did say, I trust that he will come within the body of the colours that we wear and learn what Orangeism is all about and learn what Protestantism is all about and it is deplorable that the radio station concerned actually used that report and I trust that people will realise that what was said by that young man does not reflect the views of the Orange Institution or the Protestant people in this Province. (Twelfth Platform 1994)

Meanwhile, in the Field, youngsters were getting drunk and practising their sectarian tunes.

Given the 'ongoing' peace process in 1995, the BBC agreed to show the Twelfth live again. This threw up some interesting problems because without the editor's cutting room it is less easy to control an image. The BBC commentator mentioned both the problems with part of the parade on the Ormeau Road and the demonstration, at the front of the parade, by the fringe loyalist parties demanding the release of political prisoners. Nevertheless, the commentary, using Orangeman Clifford Smyth as co-host, was replete with historical references. The recent developments in the bands were mentioned, but the paramilitary insignia, when shown on camera, were completely ignored. When one recently dead paramilitary member was shown on a bannerette, Clifford Smyth failed to mention who it was, and simply described the lodge as having a 'militant nature'. Any discussion of the UVF or YCV took place in terms of their 1912 existence and not their contemporary manifestation. As such, although it was forced to reveal some of the more temporal aspects of the parade, the coverage nevertheless continually reverted to the historical model.

In 1996 the BBC was truly faced with a problem. On 7 July the Drumcree church parade in Portadown had been stopped by the police from following its 'traditional' route through the predominantly nationalist area of the Garvaghy Road. There followed four days of major disturbances in loyalist areas in Northern Ireland, with millions of pounds worth of damage being caused, and a Catholic taxi driver shot dead in Lurgan. Then, on Friday 11 July, the police forced a way through nationalist protesters attempting to block the route, triggering major disturbances in nationalist areas. On the day of the Twelfth a massive police and army operation over a twenty-four-hour period kept nationalist residents of the lower Ormeau Road hemmed into their streets to allow Ballynafeigh District to come down to meet the main parade. The BBC was obviously forced to abandon its original plans for coverage and integrate both their mid-morning live coverage and the evening highlights programme into a more news-style programme. This produced letters of complaint in unionist papers. Even so the sanitised live commentary, with Clifford Smyth as co-host again, was mocked in the nationalist *Irish News*.

The whole thrust of the coverage by the unionist newspapers, and some of the coverage by BBC and UTV, sustained the model of 'respectable' Orangeism as part of the local heritage keeping the community together. It almost completely ignored contemporary changes in the events, it tries to de-politicise what is taking place – even when covering political speeches – it ignores the drinking, it ignores the sectarianism, it ignores the conflict. Even as the burnt-out cars on road blocks smoulder, the discourse of 'tradition' and 'respectability' is maintained.

POLITICAL FRACTURE AND THE REASSERTING OF 'TRADITION'

I have attempted to detail the way the parades have been utilised by different interest groups. In particular I have tried to indicate how what I have called 'respectable' Orangeism has attempted to maintain the position that it attained from the end of the nineteenth century onwards. The Twelfth became a focus for unionist politicians to legitimate their position as leaders of the Protestant community by calling upon a particular understanding of the past that placed Orangeism as defender of that unified Protestant community against the Roman Catholic Church. To achieve that political legitimisation there was an ongoing attempt by politicians, and by senior Orangemen, to control the ritual occasions, and the discourse and meanings implicated in the rituals. Up to the mid-1960s, this control, while never complete and challenged from both the political left within unionism and from more fundamentalist Protestant positions, was relatively unproblematic given the relatively secure nature of the state. However, as the Orange and unionist elite failed, unable to deliver through economic and political patronage, so 'respectable' Orange hegemony came under pressure. It was not 'Orange' enough for the DUP and some of the loyalist paramilitary groups, which felt the need for a more pro-active opposition to a strength-ened nationalist community and to republican violence. On the other hand, Orangeism became less palatable for the British state, now more directly involved in an unstable and expensive part of the Union.

The Twelfth of July began to reflect new lines of political fracture, new relationships with the state, and particularly resistance to the forces of the state. No longer was it primarily a state ritual. No longer were the rights of Orangemen to parade the streets unquestioned. No longer was the police force prepared to defend the 'right to march' without question. From the mid-1960s on, the Twelfth began to reflect a more militant form of sectarianism developing in fractured working-class urban areas. By the 1970s the Twelfth in Belfast and other large towns expressed the insecurities in Protestant working-class areas brought about by an increasingly violent campaign waged by the Provisional IRA and disenchantment with the role of successive British governments. Intriguingly, the only period when the Twelfth regained some of its former confidence, according to press reports, was between 1977 and 1980. This coincided with the 'Ulsterisation' of the security situation involving a greater stress on the local police force and the UDR. Further, Roy Mason, the Labour Secretary of State for Northern Ireland, was widely viewed as being 'tough on terrorism', and there was a reduction in general paramilitary activity (Bruce 1992: 135–6). But after the Hunger Strikes the rise of Sinn Féin in elections brought new political pressures to bear. The British state, in order to undermine the support for the republican movement, looked to constitutional nationalism and towards deals with Dublin. For these relationships to work the RUC would have to make greater strides in policing all communities equitably. Given that the loyal orders dominated the sphere of public ritual displays, holding parades even in some towns with large Catholic majorities, and given the more militant nature of some of those displays, clashes between the RUC and loyalists using sensitive parading routes became inevitable. 'Respectable' Orangeism was caught between its support for the state and rule of law and growing disenchantment within the ranks of the Institution with the actions of that state. It had had little reason not to support the RUC in the past and yet militant loyalism, in the form of DUP fundamentalism and the paramilitaries, started to play a larger role within parades organised by the Orange Institution, as well as in newly developing parades, therefore increasing the possibility of the state intervening in the right to march. Attempts by the Institution, such as the introduction of *The Terms of Engagement* to control some of the new elements, were at best half-hearted. Moderation appeared to many Orangemen to win nothing. 'Respectable' Orangeism, the Orangeism of the 1950s, was in retreat. 'Respectable' Orangeism was no longer hegemonic. In 1992 militant elements within Orangeism were highlighted in the reaction of those in the Ballynafeigh mini-Twelfth parade as they waved five fingers at a handful of protesters who were outside the bookmakers on the Ormeau Road where five people had been shot dead by the UFF.

Towards the end of 1994, first the IRA, then loyalist paramilitary groups, announced cease-fires. For many Orangemen, the euphoria accompanying an apparent end to the Troubles was tempered by suspicions that they would be sold out. The peace process did not increase their security. It was revealed that the British government had been secretly negotiating with members of Sinn Féin in the lead-up to the cease-fires. Suddenly everyone appeared to be courting Gerry Adams, President of Sinn Féin. Residents on the lower Ormeau, and on the Garvaghy Road felt more confident about publicly opposing parades (Jarman and Bryan 1996). More parades were re-routed from the lower part of the Ormeau and the disputes began to become world news. On Sunday 9 July 1995 the RUC decided to block the Drumcree church parade from returning into Portadown along the Garvaghy Road. The first 'Siege of Drumcree' had begun. Two days later a parade went ahead, and on the Twelfth the police hemmed in protesters on the lower Ormeau to allow No. 10 District through. All the political fracture-lines, which I have discussed, became clear. Within the Orange Institution, Grand Master Martin Smyth was accused of weakness as he failed to appear at Drumcree, and Paisley appeared to take command of the situation whilst militants in the crowd attacked the police. The fracture between Orangeism and the state was revealed as policemen were threatened and abused, and, of course, the animosity between the Catholic community and Orangeism appeared as wide as ever as both accused the other of naked sectarianism and of not respecting the other's identity. The disputes were not reflecting the enmities of 1690, but the dynamic politics of 1995. Months after his dramatic appearance at Drumcree, Trimble became leader of the Ulster Unionist Party.

After the events of the summer of 1995 the Institution tried to state its case over parades by introducing a pamphlet called *The Order on Parade* (Montgomery and Whitten 1995). It set out to explain the reasons why the Institution organises parades. It described the celebratory nature of the events, the events as pageants, the events as a demonstration of strength, the parades as a testimony of religious belief and the events as 'a sense of tradition'.

This provides a sense of linking with past generations. There is a sense of confidence and pride in taking part in a ritual parade. It gives the impression of continuity through time. (Montgomery and Whitten 1995: 7)

The authors of the pamphlet, before linking the 'form' of contemporary Orange parades to the parades of the Irish Volunteers of the 1780s, quote my own words in arguing that ritual gives the 'impression of stasis, of lack of change, even timelessness; and thus a security of identity to those taking part' (Bryan *et al.* 1995: 10, quoted in Montgomery and Whitten 1995: 7). But they ignored completely our thesis that the parades were fundamentally dynamic events reflecting and acting upon the current political environment. They discussed the 'impression of continuity' and the 'impression of time-lessness' as if the word *impression* had not been used.

At the conclusion of *The Order on Parade* the authors do make some suggestions: they call for Orangemen to examine the use of flags and music in parades, they also call for a re-examination of the way 'the hangers on' that follow parades are controlled, and they suggest that more thought should be given to the appearance of paramilitary symbols in parades. 'The behaviour of brethren on parade is of paramount importance and it is on that behaviour that the eyes of the public and our media will concentrate' (Montgomery and Whitten 1995: 35). Appendix One of the document reproduced the *Conditions of Engagement* (1995: 36–7), Appendix Two reproduces a song entitled 'The Siege of Drumcree' (1995: 38):

> No more calls for compromise
> Or trying to appease.
> The Protestants of Ulster
> Have got up off their knees

THE SUMMER OF 1996

In the summer of 1996 the right to parade became the major issue in local politics. The RUC Chief Constable, Hugh Annesley, decided first to stop the Drumcree parade then, after four days of Orange parades, road blocks, and rioting he decided that the public order was best served by clearing away nationalist protesters and facilitating the Orange parade down the Garvaghy Road. This involved physically dragging people from the road and the use of plastic bullets to keep protesters back. It appeared to most nationalists that the state had caved in to Orange pressure. There were several days of rioting in nationalist areas with one man killed in Derry when hit by an army vehicle. The whole of Northern Ireland seemed to focus upon the right to parade. Although no agreement was reached the Secretary of State, Patrick Mayhew, announced a 'Review Body' with an academic, Dr Peter North, as chairperson. Under its terms of reference the *Independent Review of Parades and Marches* looked at the adequacy of the legal provisions covering parades, the power of the police and Secretary of State, the possible introduction of new machinery such as a tribunal for deciding on parade disputes and the possible introduction of a code of practice for public demonstrations. Its main recommendation was the setting up of an independent Parades Commission to make 'determinations' in cases where the right to parade was disputed.

The Orange Institution had also initiated an internal commission to take submissions from other Orangemen on the future of the organisation and the right to march. Prior to the setting up of the Parades Commission, David Trimble speaking at the Twelfth demonstration in Belfast, gave his opinion on the issue.

We will have to see whether we can find some arrangement that can get us out of the difficulty we're in. But it's important to bear in mind where the difficulty comes from because the difficulty is largely the work of the last decade and if anything it can be traced back to the public order legislation that followed the Anglo-Irish Agreement, because up until then we had enshrined in legislation the very clear distinction that must exist between traditional parades of a religious and cultural character and parades of a party political nature which are not traditional. And that distinction existed in the legislation. It wasn't a distinction as a preference given to Orangeism as against nationalism because it was a distinction that protected the traditional cultural and religious demonstrations of nationalism and Catholicism. It was a distinction drawn between what was traditional and related to particular cultures and what was party political. And that distinction existed in the legislation up until 1986 when the public order legislation was changed as a result of the Anglo-Irish Agreement. And the difficulties we have had stem from that. And we need to get back to a position that respects the established customs and practices of our country and protects also those traditional parades while still providing sufficient regulation to stop people who are out there coat trailing for party political advantage. That needs to be done. (David Trimble, 12 July 1996)

By the Autumn of 1996 all the political parties in Northern Ireland were preparing policy documents on the issue.

'TRADITION'

. . . effective political ritual evokes a complex cluster of traditional symbols and postures of appropriate moral leadership, but it orchestrates them to differentiate itself, this particular political authority, from what has gone before. Thus, ritual is built out of widely accepted blocks of tradition, generating a sense of cultural continuity even when the juxtaposition of these blocks defines a unique ritual ethos. (Bell 1992: 195)

The central form of legitimacy claimed through the Twelfth of July and other parades is that of 'tradition'. The claim of 'tradition' is an attempt to import a unity, a sense of stability, and a sense of timelessness to an ethnic identity. It attempts to draw a boundary around the Protestant community, not simply in the present, but through history, linking the perceived causes of the Protestant people, fought for at the Boyne, at the Diamond and at the Somme, with those of the present. The discourse that accompanies the parades rarely if ever questions the continuity of the events. The media reinforces a particular image of the ritual, helping it to work ideologically.

Yet I have tried to argue that this apparent continuity disguises the dynamic forces within the events. Each ritual occasion is unique. It is created, performed and utilised in the present. It exists within a field of relationships: of class, of denomination, of locality, of political party, of ethnicity and of age, which act to change it. The most significant of these relationships are those between the political elite in Northern Ireland and the working classes, and between the political elite and the state. By the time a particular form of the state effectively collapsed in 1972 the lines of political fracture, the lines of resistance, within the ritual events were already being re-drawn. The internal and external pressures changed. The 'traditional' ritual was being created in new conditions.

Tradition, of course, is not created once and then left to its own momentum. Tradition exists because it is constantly produced and reproduced, pruned for clear profile, and softened to absorb revitalising elements. (Bell 1992: 123)

In Belfast the 'traditional' Orange parade lost the lambeg drum, the silver bands, most of the accordion bands, the patronage of the middle classes and the legitimacy gained from the attendance of the state's political leaders. It gained the blood and thunder bands with their colourful uniforms, their paramilitary flags and their own particularly masculine marching displays. For many participants the 'traditional' Twelfth, which was once an expression of loyalty to the state, now provides an opportunity to express their opposition to the present form of the state.

11 RETURN TO DRUMCREE

On Sunday morning of 7 July 1997 the RUC and the British army conducted a major operation in Portadown to clear the Garvaghy Road of protesters. Hand-to-hand fighting took place through the night and into the morning. In the middle of the day the Orangemen of Portadown made their way down the road after their church service surrounded by journalists from all over the world and protected by army and police vehicles. Residents of the Garvaghy Road, unable to get to the church, held a Mass on the street. Rioting in the Garvaghy Road and other nationalist areas followed the end of the parade. For reasons that have been much speculated about since, the new Secretary of State for Northern Ireland, Mo Mowlam, and the new Chief Constable, Ronnie Flanagan, decided not to have a stand-off with Orangemen as had taken place in 1996. The previous day I, like many others, had believed that they would block the parade. However, a perceptive member of the Garvaghy Road Residents' Group suggested to me that they were probably in a win-win situation. Either the parade was stopped, or, beamed across the televisions of the world, local residents would be dragged, kicked and beaten by RUC men in paramilitary uniforms to allow Orangemen – the perceived aggressors – down a piece of road. That particular resident understood the longer political game, as did the IRA, which, on 19 July, after such aggression by the British state on Irish Catholics, announced a reinstatement of their 1994 cease-fire.

'Drumcree IV' in July 1998 may well prove to be a defining event for the Orange Institution. In April of 1998 the Public Processions (NI) Act had become law and the Parades Commission was empowered to make determinations on disputed parades (see Jarman 1999a). The Orange Order, in most areas, refused to talk to residents' groups, and, now they refused to talk to the Parades Commission. In making determinations the Parades Commission was bound to take account of conditions set out in section 8(6) of the Act:

(a) any public disorder or damage to property which may result from the procession;
(b) any disruption to the life of the community;
(c) any impact of the procession on relationships within the community;
(d) any failure to comply with the code of conduct (whether in relation to the procession in question or any previous procession); and
(e) the desirability of allowing a procession customarily held along a particular route to be held along that route.

Whilst the last criterion (e) had been put in to placate the Orange Institution, the Institution was not prepared even to make a case to the Parades Commission. As such, they were unlikely to get favourable decisions. In spite of a number of high profile efforts to negotiate between residents and Orangemen in Portadown, the two parties never met face to face, no resolution was found and the Parades Commission re-routed Portadown No. 1 District away from the Garvaghy Road.

On 5 July the parade left Drumcree church and met a large container placed by the army as a barrier across the road. In addition, miles of barbed wire were ringing the Garvaghy Road area. The Orange Order was facing the well-prepared forces of the state. The tactics of blocking roads had proved so counter-productive in 1996 that the Orange Order instead aimed to intensify the protests in Portadown. Nevertheless, there were disturbances in a number of other towns. Thousands of Orangemen and their supporters arrived at the field opposite Drumcree church. The crowd grew every night and diminished during the day but many camped in the field. The greatest fear for local residents and the RUC was that on 12 July Orangemen from all over Northern Ireland would descend on the fields at Drumcree.

Two elements made the dispute even more complex. First, three months previously the referendum on the Good Friday Agreement had produced 71 per cent of those who voted in Northern Ireland in favour, but amongst unionists there was probably only just over 50 per cent voting 'Yes' and unionist 'No' voters saw Drumcree as a point of mobilisation. Second, the breakaway element of the UVF known as the Loyalist Volunteer Force was strongest in Portadown. After the murder of their leader Billy 'King Rat' Wright the LVF had also moved to a cease-fire, but a number of other dissident loyalist groups were said to be in existence and active.[1] The restraining influences on loyalist groups in Belfast, based on a political analysis supporting the peace process, did not exist in Portadown where the Drumcree parade was a key opportunity to stand and fight. Early in the morning of 2 July ten Catholic churches around Northern Ireland took petrol bomb attacks and, in the days that followed, Orange halls were attacked in retaliation. Although the violence on the first two nights of the Drumcree stand-off was limited, it increased in the days that followed. Live on national television, young loyalists scaled the barriers and fought hand-to-hand battles with the RUC, fireworks were thrown at police lines over the barbed wire and then pipe bombs were used, seriously injuring a number of police officers. Each morning Orange spokesmen from the Grand Lodge desperately tried to distance themselves from the violence and focus on the issue but it was clear that they were unable or unwilling to control what was taking place. It was not easy to argue that the Orange Order was a respectable, law abiding, religious organisation. On the other hand, any sign of weakening by Grand Lodge was countered by Joel Patton and the Spirit of Drumcree Group claiming to speak for 'grassroots' Orangeism.

The result of this protest, once one has grasped the dynamics of the Orangeism, was inevitable. As soon as they had encouraged everyone to come to the protest confrontations were almost unavoidable. Each night parades by Orange districts from all of Northern Ireland were held down to police lines. Bands and lambeg drummers played in the field. Events remained relatively peaceful through bright summer evenings, but after about 10.00 p.m. things became more violent. On the nights of 8–11 July the violence at the field became progressively worse and shots were fired at the police. In my estimation the crowds started to get smaller at this point. As criticism came from Protestant church leaders, unionist politicians and the RUC, active support for what was taking place started to dissipate. The disparate nature of Orangeism meant that they could not maintain a protest. If members of the Orange Order wanted to keep the event peaceful they would have had to arrange low-profile protests and would be seen by many as weak. But in organising mass events they were allowing a range of interest groups, some within the Institution, others outside, to mobilise and utilise the protest. They were in the same dilemma as they had been throughout the Troubles.

On the evening of Saturday 11 July, in Ballymoney, County Antrim, a Drumcree protest provided the context in which a petrol bomb was thrown at a house with a Catholic family in it. Three young brothers Richard, Jason and Mark Quinn burnt to death. It was not an inevitable result of 'Drumcree IV' that children were going to die, but it was always inevitable that any strategy followed by senior Orangemen involving mass gatherings and sustained protests would end in violence, and support within unionism and within Orangeism would start to disappear. The Reverend William Bingham, an Orangeman who had been part of the County Armagh delegations negotiating with the government on the issue, made a public statement in his church that the Garvaghy Road was not worth a life and called for the protest to end. Ulster Unionist MP Ken Maginnis and Church of Ireland Primate Robin Eames, made similar appeals, and, crucially, First Minister designate David Trimble, the man who had come to lead the UUP partly because of his role at Drumcree, now called for the protest to end. Yet, whilst members of Portadown No. 1 District were not prepared to walk away and District Master Harold Gracey determined to stay, members of Grand Lodge appeared on TV clearly shaken. The Orange Order was divided and the Twelfth commemorations (held on Monday 13 July) did not become the day of reckoning that everyone had feared, rather it became an arena for all the differences to be aired both publicly at the platform speeches and privately to journalists and researchers alike.

The Drumcree protest has not ended at the time of writing. Harold Gracey and members of the Portadown District have been at the field right through to March 2000. There have been parades in the town every week for a year. Some have ended in violent confrontation and one policeman was killed by a blast bomb. Tension was high again for the Drumcree parade in 1999 but it was clear the Orange Order could not afford to mobilise as it had before. Senior members, committees and governing bodies in the Church of Ireland, the Presbyterian Church and the Methodist Church all produced damning criticism of the Orange Order. The synod of the Church of Ireland called for Orangemen not to be invited to Drumcree church, although they had no power to stop the select vestry at Drumcree church from giving the invitation, which they did. During 1999 David Trimble had face-to-face discussions with members of the Garvaghy Road Residents' Group but the Portadown Orangemen refused to involve themselves in anything but proximity talks. Consequently the parade was again re-routed by the Parades Commission and the security forces constructed even bigger barriers than before. On 4 July the Portadown No. 1 District came out of the church and headed down to police lines, they handed in a letter of protest to a waiting police officer, turned and headed back up the hill and dispersed. They were going to maintain their protest, but they were not going to allow a repeat of the mass gatherings of the previous years. The world's press only had an Orange church parade to report.

RITUAL AND POWER

Part of the cultural struggle is a struggle over the dominant symbolic paradigm, the struggle for hegemony. . . . It is the struggle for the privileged to protect their positions by fostering a particular view of people's self-interest. It is a process that involves defining people's identity for them. How else can people's strong devotion to such abstract entities as the nation or people's willingness to die for this unseen identity be explained? (Kertzer 1988: 175)

Ritual empowers, but only within limits; it enables domination and disguises domination but also only within limits. Ritual provides a space for resistance and negotiation. The parades in Northern Ireland take place within a complex set of relationships involving those with authority over the events attempting to exert control, those participating and watching (willingly or unwillingly), the wider political communities, and the forces of the state.

The mere existence of a plausible structure of expression of a grievance or of the mobilisation of a mass following might be sufficient to persuade people *with very different kinds of motivation* to gather behind its banner. (Anthony Cohen 1994: 148)

The interests that groups and significant individuals have in utilising parades varies and changes depending upon the particular political situation at the time. Whilst there are clear power differentials within these relationships, even the relatively powerless can use the parades as a resource to some degree.

I have tried to understand how a particular form of ritual action came to play a central role in the field of politics in the north of Ireland. I have argued that ritual action is a specific type or quality of action to which individuals commit themselves. I have tried not to make assumptions about why

Orangemen commit themselves to the parades, as personal commitments vary. The parades are complex events in which a diverse range of actors participate. The multi-vocality of symbols allows common allegiance to particular symbols without a common understanding of those symbols. Nevertheless, dominant meanings are attached to the parades by those with the power to impose meaning. These are meanings with which many participants might agree but which become dominant regardless of the mass of the participants. Most participants are not in a position to articulate their own motivations. The parades, to that extent, take on an existence over and above the motives of participants and can be appropriated by different interest groups in the labour of representation.

Over the last thirty years the Twelfth parades have exhibited obvious changes, such as the introduction of new symbols and new styles of band, reflecting the changing political positions of interest groups, and yet this has done little to disrupt the discourse of 'tradition'. There have been attempts by senior Orangemen to control these changes, such as the introduction of band contracts, but those attempts have, in the main, been ineffectual.

> Those in charge of the ritual may scold and insist on proper reordering, but if a growing number of ritual participants take the new direction, such officials may instead tacitly accept the spatial shift and even claim it as the 'real way' – allowing new agency by default. (Parkin 1992: 20)

I have found no evidence of widespread use of UVF flags prior to the 1970s. Yet they are now commonplace and defended by many Orangemen, even if senior Orangemen are not totally at ease with their presence. It has been part of the struggle 'respectable' Orangeism has undertaken, that it has had to deal with the changes taking place, particularly the antipathy of some in the parades towards the state, and yet argue that Orange parades continue to reflect the unity of Protestant people and their loyalty to the crown. As the relationship of many working-class loyalists with the state has become more uneasy it is not surprising that certain elements, those espousing 'respectable' Orangeism, have become ill at ease, abandoned the parades or developed discourses defending the legitimacy of the changes taking place and accepting them as the 'real way'. That is the nature of negotiations of power within the ritual. In the years since the mid-1960s, which have seen the demise of Stormont and a reduction in the willingness of the security forces to defend the perceived interests of the Protestant community, Orangeism has undergone great changes. These changes have, in the main, been driven by the working-class Protestant communities for whom Orangeism once acted as an institution of patronage.

The discourse of 'tradition' and the claim of continuity articulated by Orange and unionist politicians seem to have been used more frequently when participants felt that their power was being undermined or, as Bourdieu might put it, as orthodoxy was increasingly opposed by heterodoxy. It is now becoming particularly important for the senior Orangemen to utilise this discourse in an attempt to legitimate their position, which is being questioned both from outside and within the Protestant community. Orangeism is still important enough for Ian Paisley, from a position outside the Institution, to attempt to appropriate control of Orange parades by depicting himself as a greater defender of the rights of Orangemen than some of the leaders of the Institution. After all, those Orange leaders have been mostly UUP politicians and therefore competing with Paisley and the DUP for unionist votes. It has in part been Paisley's ability to depict himself as a sort of 'super-Orangeman' that has allowed him political success within unionism without actually being in the Institution. Even loyalist politicians, in parties such as the PUP who would be pursuing a broadly left-wing unionist agenda, find it difficult to criticise Orangeism, despite their antipathy towards the Institution because of the way they feel it betrayed working-class Protestants in the Stormont era. The Twelfth parade in Belfast in 1995 was still seen as the right occasion for the UDP and PUP to walk in front, with a banner demanding that UVF and UFF prisoners be released. Orangeism still remains important within the Protestant community. No unionist politician has yet managed to conduct a campaign on a unionist agenda that is critical of Orangeism, despite the enthusiasm that the British and Irish governments would have for such an approach.

Bell suggests that ritual is 'the way for people to experience a vision of community order that is personally empowering' (Bell 1992: 116). I think that this is an insightful way of understanding the Twelfth. The parades clearly provide a sense of belonging and identity. Individuals can place themselves within the wider Protestant community, even trace their relationship to the community's leaders. The parades not only embody the participants' belonging to the community but serve to remind leaders of their responsibilities. This explains why attempts to prohibit or undermine the rituals can create such violent reactions. And the same perspective provides an understanding of why politicians continue to find it such a useful, if complex and sometimes unwieldy, political resource. Drumcree had a powerful negative impact on the relationships between the Protestant and Catholic communities, it also further damaged the relationship of the Catholic community with the forces of the British state. But Drumcree was also significant for, and in many ways was driven by, the internal politics within unionism and Orangeism. Between Drumcree in 1995 and Drumcree in 1996 the Spirit of Drumcree group of Orangemen put pressure on mainstream 'respectable' Orangeism and on the Grand Master, Martin Smyth, in particular, to make greater efforts to defend the right to parade. Portadown, the Orange Citadel as it is sometimes called, was also the area where elements of the UVF were most keen to see an end to the loyalist ceasefire and where eventually the breakaway LVF was formed. The Ulster Unionist Party were concerned lest Paisley and the DUP were able to be seen as leading the battle in David Trimble's constituency. The Drumcree church parade became a political resource with which not everyone felt at ease but no-one could ignore. No unionist politician could possibly be seen not to defend the right to perform that particular ritual. For how then could he claim to be a defender of the Protestant people?

It is not easy to ascertain the motivations of past Twelfths, except from the perspectives of the powerful, who are more likely to influence the historical record. It is not impossible, however. We can try to reconstruct who was involved and their interests. The early commemorations from the Battle of the Boyne in 1690 to the formation of the Orange Institution in 1795 were encouraged in the first place by the Anglican elite in Dublin and then, after the 1870s, by the Volunteer movement, with its Protestant middle-class membership. Some in the Volunteer movement questioned the 'official' state understanding of the Boyne commemoration that had dominated the early rituals by using it to articulate a broader concept of the rights of citizens. In 1795 the Orange Order formed out of a particular set of class relationships in County Armagh, generating an alliance of lower-class Protestants and local landowners. Compared to the use of the Boyne commemorations by some members in the Volunteer movement, the membership of the Institution utilised the commemorations and the figure of William in a more conservative and sectarian way. Frank Wright (1996) has described these early parades as a form of localised communal deterrence. Under threat from the United Irishmen, the state effectively endorsed early Orangeism. As the Orange Institution spread and the Boyne commemorations on 12 July became occasions for regular sectarian civil disturbances, the state not only stopped its own Boyne commemorations but attempted to control, and eventually ban, the Twelfth parades. The increased political power of Catholics during and after O'Connell's campaign for emancipation in the 1820s introduced a new dynamic. 'Protestantism' became more than a religious category, developing into a wider ethnic identity linking place (Ulster rather than Ireland), politics (unionism), religion (an all-inclusive 'Protestantism' incorporating the Anglican and Dissenting Churches) and a version of history focusing upon William of Orange. From the 1870s onwards Orangeism, expressed through the Twelfth, developed as a form of economic patronage in Belfast and became 'respectable'. It maintained an uneasy alliance between Belfast's Protestant working classes and its Protestant bourgeoisie. Whilst this relationship was always disturbed by class friction, it was consistently strengthened by the threat of Home Rule and of domination from the Roman Catholic 'other'. The Twelfth became a major political event with politicians making speeches to the newly enfranchised Protestant workers. The British state found this political community problematic. Its sectarian foundations were anathema to many liberal English politicians yet, when the political power of Ulster unionists was needed in Parliament, English politicians would explicitly and implicitly support Orangeism and play the 'Orange card'.

When the six counties of Ulster were excluded from the final Home Rule provisions in 1920, the Twelfth effectively became the ritual that most fully symbolised the new state of Northern Ireland. Orangeism provided an ideological basis for the state in a sometimes uneasy hegemonic relationship between the Protestant working classes and an Orange and unionist elite.

> Ritualization can . . . take arbitrary or necessary common interests and ground them in an understanding of the hegemonic order; it can empower agents in limited and highly negotiated ways. (Bell 1992: 222)

The Twelfth empowered some politicians, but it also had its limitations for those using it as a political resource. When the interests of the state and the Protestant working classes did not coincide, the parades could become problematic for the Stormont political elite. Measures that could be understood to undermine the position of Protestants vis-à-vis Catholics always laid politicians open to accusations of disloyalty. The Twelfth was a source of legitimised power for a class elite, but the negotiated relationship between the class interests was ethnically based and the state of Northern Ireland was built on a partial exclusion of nearly a third of its population. Orangeism also attempted to hold together diverse Protestant religious groups, the more fundamentalist of which consistently argued that the Orange Institution was inadequate as a defender against the 'Popish hordes'. Eventually, in the 1960s the changing economic and political environment left the Orange Institution in an untenable position, and economic interests started to abandon Orangeism as a basis upon which the state was likely to work. The intensification of the civil rights campaign and subsequent development of the Provisional IRA put strains upon Northern Ireland that eventually forced the British state to intervene.

Whilst the British state shared some of the interests of unionists, and was always likely to sustain and protect the Twelfth as a policy of least resistance, it was never likely to protect the events at all costs. In the early 1970s, the Orange Institution made some adjustments to parade routes to make allowances for the new security situation, but as sectarian violence increased and republican control of 'No Go' areas demonstrated the impotence of the forces of the state, groups taking part in the parades became more pro-active in attempting to assert territorial control in Northern Ireland. Symbols of Britishness became more prominent within the parades but so too did a range of more locally based expressions of unionism and Protestantism such as the Northern Ireland flag, UVF flags and those of political groups such as Vanguard and the UDA. Fewer members of the middle classes involved themselves in the parades, the Institution lost members and there was a rise in the number of working-class blood and thunder bands developing their own constellation of loyal symbols, their own forms of dress and more overtly sectarian, aggressive and carnivalesque elements within the parades. Those more carnivalesque elements were in turn criticised by 'respectable' Orangemen and the relationship between those elements and the forces of the state was at best uneasy and often confrontational. New parades developed outside the control of the loyal orders, run by local bands and para-military groups, yet still utilising some of the symbolic patterns of Orangeism.

The RUC, still an overwhelmingly Protestant force, and protector of so many parades since the foundation of Northern Ireland, started to develop policies on parades that would have been unthinkable up to the 1970s. Jack Hermon, Chief Constable of the RUC from 1980 to 1989, made his distaste for blood and thunder bands known. In 1985 and 1986 parades were banned from the mainly Catholic area of Obins Street – the Tunnel – in Portadown. Coinciding with the signing of the Anglo-Irish Agreement the resulting disturbances seemed to demonstrate the level of distrust between the Protestant community and the British state.

This is not to say that the forces of the state had become a neutral force policing Protestant and Catholic alike and attacking the UVF and IRA with equal vigour. Clearly, the relationship between the state and the Protestant community was still very different to that between the police and the Catholic community, but through an examination of the changes taking place in the Twelfth and other parades, it becomes clear that through the 1970s and 1980s the relationship between the Protestant community and the British state changed. The ritual parades become a resource with which to express this changing relationship. This changed relationship became most evident at Drumcree with the apparent contradiction of Orangemen expressing loyalty to the Queen, and carrying the Union Jack flag, attacking the *Royal* Ulster Constabulary and the British army. The state no longer appears to share the same understanding of 'royalty' and 'loyalty' as some of its citizens. Different interests were expressed in a competition of physical, but particu-larly also of symbolic, dimensions. The continuities of form that undoubtedly exist through time cannot be assumed to reflect unchanging social rela-tionships. Rather, they reflect the ability of ritual and its symbolic patterns to be used and re-used within a variety of changing power relationships.

APPENDIX 1

The Number of Parades in Northern Ireland According to RUC Statistics

Year	Total	Loyalist	Republican	'Other'*
1997	3,314	2,582	230	502
1996	3,161	2,405	229	527
1995	3,500	2,581	302	617
1994	2,792	2,520	272	
1993	2,662	2,411	251	
1992	2,744	2,498	246	
1991	2,379	2,183	196	
1990	2,713	2,467	246	
1989	2,317	2,099	218	
1988	2,055	1,865	190	
1987	2,112	1,863	249	
1986	1,950	1,731	219	
1985	2,120	1,897	223	

Source: RUC Chief Constable's Reports 1986–98
* The category of 'other' has only been published since 1995

Note
Whilst there appears to be a significant rise in the number of parades categorised as loyalist it is unclear as to whether this is an actual rise in numbers or due to the methods used to collate the figures. Indeed, the definitions used for such categories are open to question (see Jarman and Bryan 1996 for a more detailed analysis).

APPENDIX 2

The 'Marching Season': Important Loyal Order Parading Dates

Date	Organisation	Venue	Parade type
Easter Monday	Apprentice Boys	Rotating venue	Social
Easter Tuesday	Belfast Junior Orange	Antrim/Down Seaside resort	Social
Late April	Orange Institution	Ulster Hall, Belfast	Church parade
May	Junior Orange, Armagh, Tyrone, Fermanagh	Seaside resort	Social
First Saturday in June	Apprentice Boys Belfast	Belfast	Social
Second Saturday in June	Orange Institution, South Antrim	Carrickfergus, Co. Antrim	Commemorative landing of William
	Orange Institution, Portadown District	Portadown, County Armagh	Mini-Twelfth
Third Saturday in June	Orange Institution, Belfast No. 4 District	North Belfast	Mini-Twelfth
Last Saturday in June	Orange Institution, Belfast No. 9 District	West Belfast, White Rock parade	Mini-Twelfth
Last Sunday in June	Orange Institution	Various venues	Church parades, Somme
1 July	Orange Institution, Belfast No. 6 District	East Belfast	Somme parade
	Orange Institution, Belfast No. 5 District	South Belfast	Somme parade
Saturday before the Twelfth	Scottish Orange Institution	Scotland	Boyne commemoration
	Orange Institution, County Donegal	Rossnowlagh, County Donegal	Boyne commemoration
Sunday before the Twelfth	Orange Institution	Various venues	Church Boyne parade
The Twelfth of July	Orange Institution	Nineteen venues in Northern Ireland	Boyne commemoration

Date	Organisation	Venue	Parade type
The Thirteenth of July	Black Institution, Armagh and Down	Scarva, County Down	Sham Fight
	Black Institution, Lurgan Preceptories	Bangor, County Down	Social
Saturday nearest 12 August	Apprentice Boys of Derry	City of Londonderry	Relief of Derry
	Black Institution	Fermanagh	Battle of Newtownbutler
Week prior to last Saturday of August	Black Institution	Various venues	Church parades
	Black Institution	Various local events	Social
Last Saturday of August	Black Institution	Six venues in Northern Ireland	Main parade
Last Sunday of October	Orange Institution	Various venues	Reformation Church parades
Saturday nearest to 18 December	Apprentice Boys	City of Londonderry	Closing the Gates – Burning of Lundy

NOTES

1 DRUMCREE: AN INTRODUCTION TO PARADE DISPUTES

1. *Fortnight*, No. 353, September 1996.

3 APPROPRIATING WILLIAM AND INVENTING THE TWELFTH

1. *Belfast News Letter* 6 July 1750.
2. *Belfast News Letter* 4 November 1785, 6 November 1789.
3. *Belfast News Letter* 30 June 1778.
4. *Belfast News Letter* 28 May 1796.
5. *Belfast News Letter* 11–15 July 1796.
6. *Belfast News Letter* 1 June 1824, *Northern Whig* 8 July 1824.
7. *Belfast News Letter* 6 July 1824, *Northern Whig* 8 July 1824.
8. *Belfast News Letter* 13 July 1824, 16 July 1824, 20 July 1824, *Northern Whig* 15 July 1824, 26 August 1824.
9. *Belfast News Letter* 25 March 1825.
10. *Belfast News Letter* 15 July 1825, 19 July 1825, 26 July 1825, *Northern Whig* 14 July 1825, 21 July 1825.
11. *Belfast News Letter* 7 July 1826, 11 July 1826, 14 July 1826, 22 July 1826, 20 July 1827, *Northern Whig* 19 July 1827.
12. *Northern Whig* 5 July 1825.
13. *Belfast News Letter* 15 July 1828, 18 July 1828.
14. *Belfast News Letter* 17 July 1829, 21 July 1829, 24 July 1828.
15. *Belfast News Letter* 25 July 1837, 17 July 1838, 2 July 1839, 12 July 1839, *Northern Whig* 1 July 1837, 13 July 1837.
16. *Northern Whig* 14 August 1845, 2 July 1846, 11 July 1846.
17. *Belfast News Letter* 3 July 1846.
18. *Belfast News Letter* 20 July 1849, *Northern Whig* 19 July 1849.
19. *Northern Whig* 6 July 1850.
20. *Belfast News Letter* 19 July 1852, 29 June 1853, 6 July 1853, 8 July 1853, 13 July 1853, 15 July 1853, 18 July 1853, 10 July 1854, 14 July 1854, 17 July 1854, 19 July 1854, 13 July 1855, 30 June 1856, *Northern Whig* 9 July 1851, 7 July 1853, 14 July 1855.
21. *Belfast News Letter* 19 July 1852, 6 July 1853, 8 July 1853, 13 July 1853, 15 July 1853, 18 July 1853, 2 July 1855, 13 July 1855, *Northern Whig* 7 July 1853, 14 July 1855.
22. *Sessional Papers* 1857–8 vol. xxvi: 251.
23. *Northern Whig* 3 July 1858.
24. *Belfast News Letter* 13 July 1858.

25. *Belfast News Letter* 13 July 1861, 15 July 1861, *Northern Whig* 13 July 1861, 15 July 1861.
26. *Belfast News Letter* 13 July 1864, 15 July 1864, 16 July 1864, *Northern Whig* 14 July 1863.
27. *Northern Whig* 8 July 1824.

4 PARADING 'RESPECTABLE' POLITICS

1.   *Belfast News Letter* 13 July 1867.
2.   *Belfast News Letter* 2 July 1868, 6 July 1868, 13 July 1868, 14 July 1868.
3.   *Belfast News Letter* 8 July 1872.
4.   *Belfast News Letter* 13 July 1872.
5.   *Belfast News Letter* 10 July 1873, 14 July 1873, *Northern Whig* 14 July 1874.
6.   *Belfast News Letter* 14 July 1873.
7.   *Belfast News Letter* 13 July 1881, 13 July 1882, 14 July 1884.
8.   *Belfast News Letter* 14 July 1884.
9.   *Belfast News Letter* 1 July 1881.
10. *Belfast News Letter* 10 July 1886.
11. *Belfast News Letter* 13 July 1900.
12. *Belfast News Letter* 13 July 1888, 13 July 1889, 13 July 1890, 13 July 1893.
13. *Belfast News Letter* 14 July 1884, 14 July 1891.
14. *Belfast News Letter* 3 July 1906.
15. *Belfast News Letter* 9 July 1888, 3 July 1897, *Irish Daily Independent* 13 July 1894.
16. *Belfast News Letter* 14 July 1896, 13 July 1897.
17. *Belfast News Letter* 12 July 1892, 13 July 1893.
18. *Belfast News Letter* 13 July 1895.
19. *Belfast News Letter* 13 July 1885, 21 July 1885, 12 August 1885.
20. *Belfast News Letter* 14 July 1902.
21. *Belfast News Letter* 14 July 1902.
22. *Belfast News Letter* 15 August 1902.
23. *Belfast News Letter* 19 August 1902.
24. *Belfast News Letter* 13 July 1903, 14 July 1903.
25. *Belfast News Letter* 13 July 1904.
26. *Belfast News Letter* 13 July 1906, 13 July 1907, 13 July 1908, 13 July 1909, 13 July 1910.
27. *Belfast News Letter* 13 July 1911.
28. *Belfast News Letter* 25 September 1911.
29. *Belfast News Letter* 28 October 1912, *Irish News* 30 October 1912.
30. *Belfast News Letter* 14 July 1913.
31. *Belfast News Letter* 14 July 1914.
32. *Belfast News Letter* 13 July 1914, 15 July 1914.
33. *Belfast News Letter* 14 July 1913.
34. *Belfast News Letter* 13 July 1917.
35. *Belfast News Letter* 2 July 1919, 9 July 1919, 12 July 1919, 14 July 1919.
36. *Belfast News Letter* 16 August 1905, 17 August 1908, 18 August 1908.
37. *Belfast News Letter* 16 August 1910, 17 August 1910, 18 August 1910, 20 August 1910.
38. *Belfast News Letter* 1 July 1912, 6 July 1912, 8 July 1912, 11 July 1912, 16 July 1912.
39. *Belfast News Letter* 11 August 1911, 13 August 1911, 15 August 1911, 16 August 1911.
40. *Belfast News Letter* 3 July 1918, 5 July 1918, 8 July 1918, 9 July 1918.

41. *Belfast News Letter* 13 August 1918, 14 August 1918, 16 August 1918, 18 August 1918, 19 August 1918.
42. *Belfast News Letter* 13 July 1920.
43. *Belfast News Letter* 13 July 1905, 13 July 1909, 13 July 1910.
44. *Belfast News Letter* 13 July 1909.
45. *Belfast News Letter* 13 July 1905.
46. *Belfast News Letter* 13 July 1906.

5 RITUALS OF STATE

1. *Belfast News Letter* 14 July 1953.
2. *Belfast News Letter* 8 July 1924.
3. *Belfast News Letter* 14 July 1926, 13 July 1927.
4. *Belfast News Letter* 14 July 1931.
5. *Belfast News Letter* 14 July 1937.
6. *Belfast News Letter* 13 July 1923, 6 July 1926, 13 July 1928, 12 July 1929, 12 July 1930, 12 July 1932.
7. *Belfast News Letter* 13 July 1922, 13 July 1925, 14 July 1930, 12 July 1932.
8. *Belfast News Letter* 13 July 1923.
9. *Belfast News Letter* 13 August 1931.
10. *Belfast News Letter* 15 August 1931, 17 August 1931, 18 August 1931, 19 August 1931, 31 August 1931.
11. *Belfast News Letter* 11 July 1932.
12. *Belfast News Letter* 12 July 1932.
13. *Belfast News Letter* 13 July 1932.
14. *Belfast News Letter* 14 July 1932.
15. *Belfast News Letter* 13 July 1933.
16. *Belfast News Letter* 4 July 1935.
17. *Belfast News Letter* 17 July 1935, 22 July 1935.
18. *Belfast News Letter* 24 July 1935.
19. *Belfast News Letter* 11 July 1935.
20. *Belfast News Letter* 2 July 1936.
21. *Belfast News Letter* 14 July 1936, 13 July 1939.
22. *Belfast News Letter* 11 July 1936.
23. *Belfast News Letter* 13 July 1938.
24. *Belfast News Letter* 4 July 1945, 13 July 1945, 14 July 1945, 11 July 1946, 12 July 1946, 13 July 1946, 12 July 1947, 12 July 1948.
25. *Belfast News Letter* 13 July 1948.
26. *Belfast News Letter* 13 July 1948.
27. *Belfast News Letter* 13 July 1952, 15 July 1952.
28. *Belfast News Letter* 6 July 1960.
29. *Belfast News Letter* 12 July 1952.
30. *Belfast News Letter* 13 July 1961.
31. *Belfast News Letter* 13 July 1948.
32. *Belfast News Letter* 13 July 1951.
33. *Belfast News Letter* 18 July 1959.
34. *Belfast News Letter* 13 July 1961.
35. *Belfast News Letter* 12 July 1949.
36. *Belfast News Letter* 14 July 1958.
37. *Northern Whig* 13 July 1956, *Belfast News Letter* 13 July 1963.
38. *Belfast News Letter* 11 July 1955.
39. *Belfast News Letter* 14 July 1953.
40. *Belfast News Letter* 12 July 1951.

41. *Belfast News Letter* 12 July 1956.
42. *Belfast News Letter* 3 July 1956.
43. *Belfast News Letter* 2 July 1957, 2 July 1960, 13 July 1962.
44. *Belfast News Letter* 12 July 1956.
45. *Belfast News Letter* 12 July 1960.
46. *Belfast News Letter* 13 July 1954.
47. *Belfast News Letter* 9 July 1958.
48. *Belfast News Letter* 14 July 1959.
49. *Belfast News Letter* 14 July 1959.
50. *Belfast News Letter* 13 July 1964.

6 'YOU CAN MARCH – CAN OTHERS?'

1. *Belfast News Letter* 13 July 1956.
2. *Belfast News Letter* 1 July 1966.
3. *Belfast News Letter* 9 July 1966.
4. *Belfast News Letter* 11 July 1966.
5. *Belfast News Letter* 13 July 1966.
6. *Belfast News Letter* 13 July 1966.
7. *Belfast News Letter* 29 August 1966.
8. *Belfast News Letter* 12 August 1966.
9. *Belfast Telegraph* 12 July 1966.
10. *Belfast News Letter* 13 July 1967.
11. *Belfast News Letter* 9 July 1968, 15 July 1968.
12. *Belfast News Letter* 30 June 1969.
13. *Belfast News Letter* 16 June 1969.
14. *Belfast News Letter* 13 June 1969, 14 June 1969, 16 June 1969.
15. *Belfast News Letter* 30 June 1969.
16. *Belfast News Letter* 4 July 1969, 5 July 1969, 7 July 1969.
17. *Belfast News Letter* 8 July 1969, 12 July 1969.
18. *Belfast News Letter* 12 July 1969, 14 July 1969.
19. *Belfast News Letter* 14 July 1969.
20. *Belfast News Letter* 14 July 1969.
21. *Belfast News Letter* 14 July 1969.
22. *Belfast News Letter* 14 July 1969.
23. *Belfast News Letter* 6 August 1969, 8 August 1969, 9 August 1969, 11 August 1969.
24. *Belfast News Letter* 12 August 1969, 13 August 1969, 14 August 1969, 15 August 1969.
25. *The Times* 14 August 1969.
26. *Belfast News Letter* 8 July 1970.
27. *Belfast News Letter* 9 June 1970, 15 June 1970, 22 June 1970, 26 June 1970.
28. *Belfast News Letter* 1 July 1970.
29. *Belfast News Letter* 14 July 1970.
30. *Belfast News Letter* 14 July 1970.
31. *Belfast News Letter* 14 July 1970.
32. *Belfast News Letter* 23 July 1970, 24 July 1970, 25 July 1970, 27 July 1970, 28 July 1970.
33. *Belfast News Letter* 29 July 1970, 30 July 1970, 31 July 1970, 4 August 1970, 5 August 1970, 6 August 1970, 8 August 1970, 10 August 1970, 12 August 1970, 13 August 1970.
34. *Belfast News Letter* 27 August 1970, 28 August 1970, 31 August 1970, 21 December 1970.
35. *Belfast News Letter* 14 April 1971.

36. *Belfast News Letter* 11 June 1971.
37. *Belfast News Letter* 14 June1971.
38. *Belfast News Letter* 16 June 1971, 17 June 1971, 18 June 1971, 19 June 1971, 21 June 1971.
39. *Belfast News Letter* 3 July 1971.
40. *Belfast News Letter* 10 July 1972, 13 July 1972, *Portadown Times* 14 July 1972, 21 July 1972, 28 July 1972.
41. *Belfast News Letter* 7 July 1969.
42. *Belfast News Letter* 30 June 1971.
43. *Belfast News Letter* 12 July 1971.
44. *Belfast News Letter* 1 July 1971.
45. *Belfast News Letter* 9 July 1969.

7 THE ORANGE AND OTHER LOYAL ORDERS

1. *Orange Standard* December 1995.

8 THE MARCHING SEASON

1. *Orange Standard* June 1982.
2. *Orange Standard* June 1977, July 1979, September 1981, May 1982, September 1985, December 1985, September 1986, November 1986, May 1987, September 1987, July 1988.
3. *Combat* November 1986, *Ulster* November 1986.
4. *Orange Standard* October 1987.
5. *Irish News* 11 July 1992.

9 THE TWELFTH

1. *The Twelfth Programme*, Belfast County Grand Lodge: 1967, 1970, 1971, 1985, 1986.
2. *The Twelfth Celebrations: The Queen's Silver Jubilee 1977*.
3. *Orange Standard* June 1977, July 1979, September 1981, May 1982, September 1985, December 1985, September 1986, November 1986, May 1987, September 1987, July 1988.
4. *The Twelfth Programme 1978*.

10 'TRADITION', CONTROL AND RESISTANCE

1. *Portadown Times* 14 July 1972, 21 July 1972, 28 July 1972.
2. *Belfast Telegraph* 4 July 1986.
3. *Portadown Times* 19 July 1985.
4. *Belfast News Letter* 13 July 1993.
5. *Belfast News Letter* 14 July 1992.
6. *Belfast Telegraph* 20 July 1996.

11 RETURN TO DRUMCREE

1. *Sunday Life* 5 July 1996.

BIBLIOGRAPHY

Ahern, E. 1981. *Chinese Ritual and Politics.* Cambridge: Cambridge University Press.
Anderson, Benedict. 1983. *Imagined Communities: Reflections on the Origin and Spread of Nationalism.* London: Verso.
Arthur, Paul and Keith Jeffery. 1988. *Northern Ireland since 1968.* Oxford: Blackwell.
Bakhtin, Mikhail. 1984. *Rabelais and His World.* Trans. Helene Iswolsky. Bloomington: Indiana University Press.
Bardon, Jonathan. 1982. *Belfast: An Illustrated History.* Belfast: Blackstaff Press.
—— 1992. *A History of Ulster.* Belfast: Blackstaff Press.
Beckett, J.C. 1979. *A Short History of Ireland.* London: Hutchinson and Co.
Bell, Catherine. 1992. *Ritual Theory, Ritual Practice.* Oxford: Oxford University Press.
Bell, Desmond. 1990. *Acts of Union.* London: Macmillan.
Bew, Paul and Henry Patterson. 1985. *The British State and the Ulster Crisis.* London: Verso.
Bew, Paul and Gordon Gillespie. 1993. *Northern Ireland: A Chronology of the Troubles 1968–1993.* Dublin: Gill and Macmillan.
Bew, Paul, Peter Gibbon and Henry Patterson. 1995. *Northern Ireland 1921–1994: Political Forces and Social Classes.* London: Serif.
Binns, C. 1979–80. 'The Changing Face of Power: Revolution and Accommodation in the Soviet Ceremonial System', *Man* (NS) 14: 585–606, (Part 2) 15: 170–87.
Bloch, Maurice. 1986. *From Blessing to Violence.* Cambridge: Cambridge University Press.
Boal, F.W. 1982. 'Segregation and Mixing, Space and Residence in Belfast', in F.W. Boal and J.N.H. Douglas (eds) *Integration and Division: Geographical Perspectives on the Northern Ireland Problem.* London: Academic Press.
Boissevain, Jeremy. 1992. *Revitalising European Rituals.* London: Routledge.
Boulton, D. 1973. *The UVF, 1966–73: An Anatomy of Loyalist Rebellion.* Dublin: Gill and Macmillan.
Bourdieu, Pierre. 1977. *Outline of a Theory of Practice.* Cambridge: Cambridge University Press.
—— 1985. *Distinction: A Social Critique of the Judgement of Taste.* Cambridge, MA: Harvard University Press.
—— 1990. *In Other Words.* Cambridge: Polity Press.
—— 1991. *Language and Symbolic Power.* Cambridge: Cambridge University Press.
Bowyer Bell, J. 1989. *The Secret Army: The IRA 1916–1979.* Co. Dublin: Poolbeg.
Boyce, George D. 1990. *Nineteenth-Century Ireland: The Search for Stability.* Dublin: Gill and Macmillan.
Boyd, Andrew. 1969. *Holy War in Belfast.* Tralee: Anvil Press.
Boyle, J.W. 1962–3. 'The Belfast Protestant Association and the Independent Orange Order, 1901–10', *Irish Historical Studies* 13: 117–52.
Brewer, John and Gareth Higgins. 1998. *Anti-Catholicism in Northern Ireland: The Mote and the Beam.* London; Macmillan.
Bruce, Steve. 1986. *God Save Ulster! The Religion and Politics of Paisleyism.* Oxford: Oxford University Press.

—— 1992. *The Red Hand: Protestant Paramilitaries in Northern Ireland.* Oxford: Oxford University Press.

Bryan, Dominic. 1994. 'Interpreting the Twelfth', *History Ireland* 2(2): 37–41.

—— 1995. 'Orangutango', *Fortnight* 341: 14–15.

—— 1998a. ' "Ireland's Very Own Jurassic Park": The Mass Media and the Discourse of "Tradition" on Orange Parades', in Tony Buckley (ed.) *Symbols in Northern Ireland.* Belfast: Institute of Irish Studies.

—— 1998b. ' "The Right to March": Parading a Loyal Protestant Identity in Northern Ireland', *International Journal on Minority and Group Rights* 4: 373–96.

—— 2000 'Drumcree and "The Right to March": Ritual and Politics in Northern Ireland', in T.G Fraser (ed.) *We'll Follow the Drum: The Irish Parading Tradition.* Basingstoke: Macmillan.

Bryan, Dominic, T.G. Fraser and Seamus Dunn. 1995. *Political Rituals: Loyalist Parades in Portadown.* Coleraine: Centre for the Study of Conflict.

Bryan, Dominic and Neil Jarman. 1996. *Parade and Protest: A Discussion of Parading Disputes in Northern Ireland.* Coleraine: Centre for the Study of Conflict.

—— 1997. 'Parading Culture, Protesting Triumphalism: Utilising Anthropology in Public Policy', in H. Donnan and Graham McFarlane (eds) *Culture and Policy in Northern Ireland: Anthropology in the Public Arena.* Belfast: Institute of Irish Studies.

—— 1999. *Independent Intervention: Monitoring the Police Parades and Public Order.* Belfast: Democratic Dialogue.

Bryan, Dominic and Elizabeth Tonkin. 1997. 'Political Ritual: Temporality and Tradition', in Asa Boholm (ed.) *Political Ritual.* Gothenburg: Advanced Studies in Social Anthropology.

Bryson, Lucy and Clem McCartney. 1994. *Clashing Symbols: A Report on the Use of Flags, Anthems and Other National Symbols in Northern Ireland.* Belfast: Institute for Irish Studies.

Buckland, Patrick. 1980. *James Craig.* Dublin: Gill and Macmillan.

—— 1981. *A History of Northern Ireland.* Dublin: Gill and Macmillan.

Buckley, Anthony. 1982. *A Gentle People: A Study of a Peaceful Community in Ulster.* Cultra: Ulster Folk Museum.

—— 1985. 'The Chosen Few: Biblical Texts in the Regalia of an Ulster Secret Society', *Folklife* 24: 5–24.

Buckley, Anthony and T.K. Anderson. 1988. *Brotherhoods in Ireland.* Cultra: Ulster Folk and Transport Museum.

Buckley, Anthony and Mary Kenney. 1995. *Negotiating Identity: Rhetoric, Metaphor and Social Drama in Northern Ireland.* Washington: Smithsonian Institute.

Budge, Ian and Cornelius O'Leary. 1973. *Belfast: Approach to the Crisis.* London: Macmillan.

Burke, Peter. 1978. *Popular Culture in Early Modern Europe.* Hants: Wildwood House.

Burton, Frank. 1978. *The Politics of Legitimacy: Struggles in a Belfast Community.* London: Routledge Kegan Paul.

Campbell, Flann. 1991. *The Dissenting Voice.* Belfast: Blackstaff Press.

Cannadine, David. 1983. 'The Context, Performance, and Meaning of Ritual: The British Monarchy and the "Invention of Tradition", c. 1820–1977', in Eric Hobsbawm and Terrence Ranger (eds) *The Invention of Tradition.* Cambridge: Cambridge University Press.

—— 1987. 'Introduction: Divine Rite of Kings', in David Cannadine and S. Price (eds) *Rituals of Royalty: Power and Ceremonial in Traditional Societies.* Cambridge: Cambridge University Press.

Cecil, Rosanne. 1993. 'The Marching Season in Northern Ireland: An Expression of Politico-Religious Identity', in Sharon MacDonald (ed.) *Inside European Identities.* Oxford: Berg.

Cleary, Rev. H.W. 1899. *The Orange Society.* London: Catholic Truth Society.

Cochrane, Fergal. 1997. *Unionist Politics and the Politics of Unionism since the Anglo-Irish Agreement.* Cork: Cork University Press.

Cohen, Abner. 1969. 'Political Anthropology: The Analysis of the Symbolism of Power Relations', *Man* (NS) 4(2): 215–35.

—— 1974. *Two-Dimensional Man: An Essay on the Anthropology and Symbolism in Complex Society*. London: Routledge and Kegan Paul.

—— 1979. 'Political Symbols', *Annual Review of Anthropology* 8: 87–113.

—— 1980. 'Drama and Politics in the Development of a London Carnival', *Man* (NS) 15: 65–87.

—— 1993. *Masquerade Politics: Explorations in the Structure of Urban Popular Movements*. Oxford: Berg.

Cohen, Anthony. 1982. *Belonging: Identity and Social Organisation in British Rural Cultures*. Manchester: Manchester University Press.

—— 1985. *The Symbolic Construction of Community*. London: Tavistock.

—— 1986. *Symbolising Boundaries: Identity and Diversity in British Cultures*. Manchester: Manchester University Press.

—— 1994. *Self-Consciousness: An Alternative Anthropology of Identity*. London: Routledge.

Connerton, Paul. 1989. *How Societies Remember*. Cambridge: Cambridge University Press.

Coulter, Colin. 1994. 'Class, Ethnicity and Political Identity in Northern Ireland', *Irish Journal of Sociology* 4: 1–26.

—— 1999. *Contemporary Northern Irish Society: An Introduction*. London: Pluto Press.

Cowan, Jane K. 1992. 'Japanese Ladies and Mexican Hats: Contested Symbols and the Politics of Tradition in a Northern Greek Carnival Celebration', in Jeremy Boissevain (ed.) *Revitalising European Rituals*. London: Routledge.

Crawford, Lindsay and R. Braithwaite. 1904. *Orangeism: Its History and Progress – A Plea for First Principles*. Independent Grand Lodge of Ireland.

DaMatta, Roberto. 1977. 'Constraint and Licence: A Preliminary Study of Two Brazilian National Rituals', in Sally Moore and Barbara G. Myerhoff (eds) *Secular Ritual*. Netherlands: Van Gorcum.

——1991. *Carnival, Rogues and Heroes: An Interpretation of the Brazilian Dilemma*. Trans. John Drury. Indiana: University of Notre Dame Press.

Dewar, M.W., J. Brown and S.E. Long. 1967. *Orangeism: A New Historical Appreciation*. Belfast: Grand Orange Lodge of Ireland.

Doherty, Paul and Michael Poole. 1995. *Ethnic Residential Segregation in Belfast*. Coleraine: Centre for the Study of Conflict.

Dooley, Brian. 1998. *Black and Green: The Fight for Civil Rights in Northern Ireland and Black America*. London: Pluto Press.

Dudley-Edwards, Ruth. 1999. *The Faithful Tribe: An Intimate Portrait of the Loyal Institutions*. London: Harper Collins.

Dunn, Seamus and Valerie Morgan. 1994. *Protestant Alienation in Northern Ireland: A Preliminary Survey*. Coleraine: Centre for the Study of Conflict.

Durkheim, Emile. 1915. *The Elementary Forms of Religious Life*. London: Allen and Unwin.

Farrell, Michael. 1980. *Northern Ireland: The Orange State*, 2nd edn. London: Pluto Press. (Original 1976.)

Gibbon, Peter. 1972. 'The Origins of the Orange Order and the United Irishmen', *Economy and Society* 1: 134–63.

—— 1975. *The Origins of Ulster Unionism*. Manchester: Manchester University Press.

Gillis, John. 1994. *Commemorations: The Politics of National Identity*. Princeton, NJ: Princeton University Press.

Goody, Jack. 1977. 'Against "Ritual": Loosely Structured Thoughts on a Loosely Defined Topic', in Sally Moore and Barbara G. Myerhoff (eds) *Secular Ritual*. Assen: Van Gorcum.

Gray, Tony. 1972. *The Orange Order*. London: Bodley Head.

Hadden, Tom and Anne Donnelly. 1997. *The Legal Control of Marches in Northern Ireland*. Belfast: Community Relations Council.

Haddick-Flynn, Kevin. 1999. *Orangeism: The Making of a Tradition*. Dublin: Wolfhound Press.

Hall, Stuart. 1977. 'Culture, the Media, and the "Ideological Effect"', in James Curran, Michael Gurevitch and Janet Woollacott (eds) *Mass Communications and Society*. London: Edward Arnold.

Hall, Stuart and Tony Jefferson (eds). 1976. *Resistance through Rituals: Youth Subcultures in Post-War Britain*. London: Hutchinson.

Hamilton, A.L. Moore and T. Trimble. 1995. *Policing a Divided Society: Issues and Perceptions in Northern Ireland*. Coleraine: Centre for the Study of Conflict.

Hanlon, K. 1994. *Community Relations in Ballynafeigh: A Study of Attitudes to Community Relations in a Mixed Area of Belfast*. Belfast: Ballynafeigh Community Development Association.

Harbinson, John F. 1973. *The Ulster Unionist Party, 1882–1973: Its Development and Organisation*. Belfast: Blackstaff Press.

Harris, Rosemary. 1972. *Prejudice and Tolerance in Ulster*. Manchester: Manchester University Press.

Harrison, Simon. 1995. 'Four Types of Symbolic Conflict', *Journal of the Royal Anthropological Institute* (NS) 1: 255–72.

Hepburn, A.C. 1990. 'The Belfast Riots of 1935', *Social History* 15: 75–96.

Hermon, John. 1997. *Holding the Line: An Autobiography*. Dublin: Gill and Macmillan.

Hill, Jacqueline. 1984. 'National Festivals, the State and "Protestant Ascendancy" in Ireland 1790–1829', *Irish Historical Studies* 24(93) May.

Hobsbawm, Eric. 1983. 'Introduction: Inventing Traditions', in Eric Hobsbawm and Terrence Ranger (eds) *The Invention of Tradition*. Cambridge: Cambridge University Press.

Holloway, David. 1994. 'Territorial Aspects of Cultural Identity: The Protestant Community of Donegall Pass, Belfast', *Causeway* 1(5): 9–12.

Humphrey, C. and J. Laidlaw. 1994. *The Archetypal Actions of Ritual: A Theory of Ritual Illustrated by the Jain Rite of Worship*. Oxford: Oxford University Press.

Jakubowska, Longina. 1990. 'Political Drama in Poland: The Use of National Symbols', *Anthropology Today* 6(4): 10–13.

Jarman, Neil. 1992. 'Troubled Images', *Critique of Anthropology* 12(2): 133–65.

—— 1993. 'Intersecting Belfast', in B. Bender (ed.) *Landscape Politics and Perspectives*. Oxford: Berg.

—— 1995. 'Parading Culture: Parades and Visual Displays in Northern Ireland'. Unpublished D.Phil. thesis, University College London.

—— 1997a. *Material Conflicts: Parades and Visual Displays in Northern Ireland*. Oxford: Berg.

—— (ed.). 1997b. *On the Edge: Community Perspectives on the Civil Disturbances in North Belfast, June–September 1996*. Belfast: Community Development Centre, North Belfast.

—— 1999a. 'Regulating Rights and Managing Public Order: Parade Disputes and the Peace Process, 1995–98', *Fordham International Law Journal* 22(4): 1415–39.

—— 1999b. *Displaying Faith: Orange, Green and Trade Union Banners in Northern Ireland*. Belfast: Institute of Irish Studies.

—— 2000. 'For God and Ulster: Blood and Thunder Bands and Loyalist Political Culture', in T.G. Fraser (ed.) *We'll Follow the Drum: The Irish Parading Tradition*. Basingstoke: Macmillan.

Jarman, Neil and Dominic Bryan. 1996. *Parades and Protest: A Discussion of Parading Disputes in Northern Ireland*. Coleraine: Centre for the Study of Conflict.

—— 1998. *From Riots to Rights: Nationalist Parades in the North of Ireland*. Coleraine: Centre for the Study of Conflict.

Jarman, Neil, Dominic Bryan, Natalie Caleyron and Ciro De Rosa. 1998. *Politics in Public: Freedom of Assembly and the Right to Protest – A Comparative Analysis*. Belfast: Democratic Dialogue.

Jenkins, Richard. 1983. *Lads, Citizens and Ordinary Kids: Working-Class Youth Life-Styles in Belfast*. London: Routledge and Kegan Paul.

—— 1997. *Rethinking Ethnicity: Arguments and Explorations*. London: Sage.

Jones, David, James S. Kane, Robert Wallace, Douglas Sloane and Brian Courtney. 1996. *The Orange Citadel: A History of Orangeism in Portadown*. Armagh: Portadown Cultural Heritage Committee.

Kelly, John D. and Martha Kaplan. 1990. 'History, Structure, and Ritual', *Annual Review of Anthropology* 19: 119–50.

Kelly, Grainne (ed.). 1998. *Mediation in Practice: A Report of the Art of Mediation Project*. Derry/Londonderry: INCORE.

Kertzer, David. 1988. *Ritual, Politics, and Power*. London: Yale University Press.

Kürti, L. 1990. 'People vs. the State: Political Rituals in Contemporary Hungary', *Anthropology Today* 6(2): 5–8.

Lane, Christel. 1981. *The Rites of Rulers: Ritual in Industrial Society – The Soviet Case*. Cambridge: Cambridge University Press.

Larsen, S.S. 1982a. 'The Two Sides of the House: Identity and Social Organisation in Kilbroney, Northern Ireland', in Anthony Cohen (ed.) *Belonging: Identity and Social Organisation in British Rural Cultures*. Manchester: Manchester University Press.

—— 1982b. 'The Glorious Twelfth: A Ritual Expression of a Collective Identity', in Anthony Cohen (ed.) *Belonging: Identity and Social Organisation in British Rural Cultures*. Manchester: Manchester University Press.

Leach, Edmund. 1976. *Culture and Communication: The Logic by which Symbols are Connected*. Cambridge: Cambridge University Press.

Lee, J.J. 1989. *Ireland 1912–1985: Politics and Society*. Cambridge: Cambridge University Press.

Lewis, Gilbert. 1980. *Day of the Shining Red: An Essay on Understanding Ritual*. Cambridge: Cambridge University Press.

Leyton, Elliott. 1974. 'Opposition and Integration in Ulster', *Man* (NS) 9(2): 185–92.

Loftus, Belinda. 1990. *Mirrors: William III and Mother Ireland*. Dundrum: Picture Press.

—— 1994. *Mirrors: Orange and Green*. Dundrum: Picture Press.

Lukes, Steven. 1975. 'Political Ritual and Social Integration', *Sociology* 9: 289–308.

McCann, Eamonn. 1974. *War and an Irish Town*. London: Penguin.

McClelland, Aiken. 1990. *William Johnston of Ballykilbeg*. Lurgan: Ulster Society (Publications) Limited.

McDowell, R.B. 1979. *Ireland in the Age of Imperialism and Revolution 1760–1801*. Oxford: Clarendon Press.

McFarlane, Graham. 1986. ' "It's not as Simple as That": The Expression of the Catholic and Protestant Boundary in Northern Irish Rural Communities', in Anthony Cohen (ed.) *Symbolising Boundaries: Identity and Diversity in British Cultures*. Manchester: Manchester University Press.

Mach, Zdzislaw. 1992. 'Continuity and Change in Political Ritual: May Day in Poland', in Jeremy Boissevain (ed.) *Revitalising European Rituals*. London: Routledge.

—— 1993. *Symbols, Conflict and Identity*. Albany: State University of New York Press.

Millar, David. 1978. *Queen's Rebels*. Dublin: Gill and Macmillan.

—— 1990. *Peep O'Day Boys and Defenders: Selected Documents on the County Armagh Disturbances 1784–96*. Belfast: Public Record Office of Northern Ireland.

Moloney, Ed and Andy Pollak. 1986. *Paisley*. Co. Dublin: Poolbeg.

Montgomery, Graham and Richard Whitten. 1995. *The Order on Parade*. Belfast: Grand Orange Lodge of Ireland.

Moore, Sally and Barbara Myerhoff. 1977. *Secular Ritual*. Assen: Van Gorcum.

Morgan, Austen. 1991. *Labour and Partition: The Belfast Working Class 1905–23*. London: Pluto Press.

Morgan, Valerie, Marie Smyth, Gillian Robinson and Grace Fraser. 1996. *Mixed Marriages in Northern Ireland*. Coleraine: Centre for the Study of Conflict.

Morley, David. 1980. 'Text, Readers, Subjects', in Stuart Hall, Dorothy Hobson, Andrew Lowe and Paul Willis (eds) *Culture, Media Language*. London: Hutchinson,

Murtagh, Harman. 1993. 'The Williamite War 1689–91', *History Ireland* 1(1): 39–42.

Myerhoff, Barbra. 1984. 'A Death in Due Time: Construction of Self and Culture in Ritual Drama', in John J. MacAloon (ed.) *Rite, Drama, Festival, Spectacle*. Philadelphia: ISHI.

Nelson, Sarah. 1984. *Ulster's Uncertain Defenders: Loyalists and the Northern Ireland Conflict*. Belfast: Appletree Press.

Ó Dochartaigh, Niall. 1997. *From Civil Rights to Armalites: Derry and the Birth of the Irish Troubles*. Cork: Cork University Press.

Officer, David. 1996. 'In Search of Order, Permanence and Stability: Building Stormont, 1921–32', in Richard English and Graham Walker (eds) *Unionism in Modern Ireland: New Perspectives on Politics and Culture*. London: Macmillan.

Parkin, David. 1992. 'Ritual and Spatial Direction and Bodily Division', in Daniel de Coppet (ed.) *Understanding Rituals*. London: Routledge.

Patterson, Henry. 1980. *Class Conflict and Sectarianism*. Belfast: Blackstaff Press.

Poppi, Cesare. 1992. 'The Political Economy of Tradition in the Ladin Carnival of the Val di Fassa', in Jeremy Boissevain (ed.) *Revitalising European Rituals*. London: Routledge.

Purdie, Bob. 1990. *Politics in the Street: The Origins of the Civil Rights Movement in Northern Ireland*. Belfast: Blackstaff Press.

Radcliffe-Brown, A.R. 1952. *Structure and Function in Primitive Society*. London: Cohen and West.

Rolston, Bill. 1991. *Politics and Painting: Murals and Conflict in Northern Ireland*. London: Associated University Press.

Roth, Klaus. 1990. 'Socialist Life-Cycle Rituals in Bulgaria', *Anthropology Today* 6(5): 8–10.

Ruane, Joseph and Jennifer Todd. 1996. *The Dynamics of Conflict in Northern Ireland: Power, Conflict and Emancipation*. Cambridge: Cambridge University Press.

Scott, James C. 1990. *Domination and the Art of Resistance: Hidden Transcripts*. New Haven, CT: Yale University Press.

Scullion, F. 1981. 'History and Origin of the Lambeg Drum', *Ulster Folk Life* 27: 19–38.

Senior, Hereward. 1966. *Orangeism in Ireland and Britain 1795–1836*. London: Routledge and Kegan Paul.

Sibbert, R.M. 1914/15. *Orangeism in Ireland and Throughout the Empire*, vols I and II. Belfast: Henderson and Co.

—— 1938. Vol. II reprinted and extended (unnamed). Belfast: Henderson and Co.

Simms, J.G. 1974. 'Remembering 1690', *Studies – Irish Quarterly Review* 63 (autumn): 231–42.

Smyth, Jim. 1995. 'The Men of No Popery: The Origins of the Orange Order', *History Ireland* 3(3): 48–53.

Stewart, A.T.Q. 1981. *Edward Carson*. Dublin: Gill and Macmillan.

—— 1989. *The Narrow Ground*, 2nd edn. London: Faber and Faber.

Sugden, John and Alan Bairner. 1986. 'Northern Ireland: Sport in a Divided Society', in Allison Lincoln (ed.) *The Politics of Sport*. Manchester: Manchester University Press.

Tambiah, Stanley Jeyaraja. 1985. *Culture, Thought and Social Action*. Cambridge, MA: Harvard University Press.

Tonkin, Elizabeth and Dominic Bryan. 1996. 'Political Ritual: Temporality and Tradition', in Asa Boholm (ed.) *Political Ritual*. Gothenburg: Advanced Studies in Social Anthropology.

Turner, Victor. 1967. *Forest of Symbols*. Ithaca, NY: Cornell University Press.

—— 1968. *The Drums of Affliction*. Oxford: Oxford University Press.

—— 1969. *The Ritual Process: Structure and Anti-Structure*. Chicago: Aldine Publishing.

Walker, Brian. 1989. *Ulster Politics: The Formative Years 1868–86*. Belfast: Institute of Irish Studies.

—— 1991. '1641, 1689, 1690, and All That: The Unionist Sense of History', *Irish Review* 12 (spring/summer).

——1996. *Dancing to History's Tune: History, Myth and Politics in Ireland*. Belfast: Institute for Irish Studies.

Weber, M. 1968. *Economy and Society*. Edited by G. Roth and C. Wittich. Berkeley: University of California Press.

Weitzer, Ronald. 1995. *Policing under Fire: Ethnic Conflict and Police–Community Relations in Northern Ireland*. Albany: State University of New York Press.

Whyte, John. 1990. *Interpreting Northern Ireland*. Oxford: Clarendon Press.

Willis, Paul. 1977. *Learning to Labour: How Working-Class Kids Get Working-Class Jobs*. London: Saxon House.

Wright, Frank. 1972. 'Protestant Ideology and Politics in Ulster', *European Journal of Sociology* 14: 213–80.

—— 1987. *Northern Ireland: A Comparative Analysis*. Dublin: Gill and Macmillan.

—— 1990. 'Communal Deterrence and the Threat of Violence in the North of Ireland in the Nineteenth Century', in John Darby, Nick Dodge and A.C. Hepburn (eds) *Political Violence: Ireland in a Comparative Perspective*. Belfast: Appletree Press.

—— 1996. *Two Lands, One Soil*. Dublin: Gill and Macmillan.

Wright, Susan. 1992. ' "Heritage" and Critical History in the Reinvention of Mining Festivals in North-East England', in Jeremy Boissevain (ed.) *Revitalising European Ritual*. London: Routledge.

OTHER DOCUMENTS

Constitution, Laws and Ordinances of the Loyal Institution of Ireland. Grand Orange Lodge of Ireland, 1967.

House of Commons Select Committee, *Report from the Select Committee Appointed to Inquire into the Nature, Character, Extent and Tendency of Orange Lodges, Associations or Societies in Ireland*. Sessional Papers 1835, vols 15, 16, 17.

Official Brochure of the Tercentenary Celebrations of the Apprentice Boys of Derry Association. Apprentice Boys of Derry, 1989.

Pat Finucane Centre. 1997. *For God and Ulster: An Alternative Guide to the Loyal Orders*. Derry: Pat Finucane Centre.

Public Order (Northern Ireland) Order 1987, Statutory Instrument 1987 No. 463, Northern Ireland Office.

Public Processions (Northern Ireland) Act, 1998.

Report (1857–58) from Commissioners of Enquiry into the Origin and Character of the Riots in Belfast in July–September 1857. Sessional papers 1857–8 , vol. 26.

Steadfast for Faith and Freedom: 200 Years of Orangeism. Grand Orange Lodge of Ireland, 1995.

The Twelfth Programme (1966–96) Belfast: Belfast County Grand Orange Lodge.

History of the Royal Arch Purple Order. (n.d.) 'The Research Group'.

Wilson, Mark (ed.). 1995. *The Future of the Orange Order*. Report of a conference organised by the Irish Universities Shield of Refuge LOL 369.

INDEX

Compiled by Julita Clancy

197